Voting in America

Voting in America

How America Votes: Law, Process, and Voter Participation

Volume 1

Edited by
Morgan E. Felchner

Foreword by
Senator Kay Bailey Hutchison

Praeger Perspectives

Westport, Connecticut
London

Library of Congress Cataloging-in-Publication Data

Voting in America / edited by Morgan E. Felchner ; foreword by Kay Bailey Hutchison.
v. cm. — (Praeger perspectives)
Includes bibliographical references and index.
Contents: v. 1. How America votes : law, process, and voter participation — v. 2. What influences the American voter : interest groups, issues, and the media — v. 3. American voting systems in flux : debacles, dangers, and brave new designs.
ISBN: 978-0-275-99804-2 (set : alk. paper)
ISBN: 978-0-275-99806-6 (v. 1 : alk. paper)
ISBN: 978-0-275-99808-0 (v. 2 : alk. paper)
ISBN: 978-0-275-99810-3 (v. 3 : alk. paper)
1. Voting—United States. 2. Elections—United States. 3. United States—Politics and government.
I. Felchner, Morgan E., 1981-
JK1976.V69 2008
324.60973—dc22 2008004555

British Library Cataloguing in Publication Data is available.

Library of Congress Catalog Card Number: 2008004555
ISBN: 978-0-275-99804-2 (set)
ISBN: 978-0-275-99806-6 (vol. 1)
ISBN: 978-0-275-99808-0 (vol. 2)
ISBN: 978-0-275-99810-3 (vol. 3)

First published in 2008

Praeger Publishers, 88 Post Road West, Westport, CT 06881
An imprint of Greenwood Publishing Group, Inc.
www.praeger.com

Printed in the United States of America

The paper used in this book complies with the Permanent Paper Standard issued by the National Information Standards Organization (Z39.48-1984).

10 9 8 7 6 5 4 3 2 1

Contents

FOREWORD

Senator Kay Bailey Hutchison

On September 18, 1787, at the close of the Constitutional Convention in Philadelphia, Benjamin Franklin, one of America's greatest and wisest statesmen, walked into the streets. According to legend, a group of citizens gathered around him and asked him what sort of government the delegates had created. Franklin's answer: "A republic. If you can keep it."

The Founding Fathers created a republic because they genuinely believed, in the words of James Madison, "the people are the only legitimate fountain of power," and the government must be accountable to the people. The Founders devised specific instruments—which are enshrined in the Constitution—to ensure that high level of accountability.

One of the most important instruments is the right to vote. In the early years of our republic, the right to vote was restricted to a small, select group of people—predominantly, white males who owned property—but over a period of many generations—not to mention many fierce struggles—that right was extended across the barriers of race, sex, and class. This is one of America's important and enduring accomplishments.

However, the right to vote is not the only instrument the Founders created to ensure the survival and success of America. The early leaders valued democracy, but they also recognized that democracy, when taken to an extreme, can be detrimental—and in some cases, even suicidal—to a country's development.

"In republics," according to Madison, "the great danger is that the majority may not sufficiently respect the rights of the minority." In order to prevent what others have called "the tyranny of the majority," the Founders chose to secure freedom for the tiniest minority of them all: the individual. The Constitution ensures an individual's right to speak and worship freely, own private property, and receive a fair trial, among other things.

Consider a typical day in America: a woman attends a church service in Dallas, a young entrepreneur starts building his own company in Silicon Valley, a college student in Boston speaks passionately about a political issue, and a Chicago lawyer works to ensure fair compensation for his clients in an eminent domain case. These freedoms—which are written into the Constitution and can easily be taken for granted—have preserved the life, conscience, and integrity of the individual for over two centuries.

Freedom has also been the catalyst for America's dynamic economy. As Albert Einstein once said, "Everything that is really great and inspiring is created by the individual who can labor in freedom"—which probably explains why Einstein immigrated to America. The roots of today's Information Age economy, with all of its productive gadgets and gizmos, can be traced to the genius of the Founders, and the government they devised.

This point has been made by many economists, including Alan Greenspan, the former Chairman of the Federal Reserve Board. In a 2004 speech, Mr. Greenspan said: "When asked abroad why the United States has become the most prosperous large economy in the world, I respond, with only mild exaggeration, that our forefathers wrote a constitution and set in motion a system of laws that protects individual rights, especially the right to own property." Those rights have been extremely rare throughout human history, and they are still quite rare in many parts of the world today.

Nevertheless, we should be encouraged that in the past three decades or so, many countries have chosen to grant more freedom to their citizens. In 1976, Freedom House, a nonprofit organization, rated 26 percent of the world's nations as "free," 31 percent as "partly free," and 43 percent as "not free." In 2006, those figures were 47 percent, 30 percent, and 23 percent, respectively. In other words, the number of "free" countries has almost doubled, while the number of "not free" countries has been sliced nearly in half. Altogether, this expansion of freedom is truly remarkable.

However, there is reason for some concern about the future of freedom. In recent years, in places as diverse as Russia, Venezuela, and the Palestinian Territory, we have seen free elections lead to more, not less, authoritarianism, along with a reversal of civil liberties. In the Middle East, in particular, the simple act of voting has not always led to an increase in peace and government accountability.

There are many reasons for this development, but one of the most important reasons is the increasing confusion about the relationship between voting and freedom. The right to vote is a significant advance in the cause of freedom; indeed, the image of thousands of people waiting patiently in line to cast their ballots—whether it's in America, Iraq, or any other country—is still one of the most enduring and inspiring images of the modern era. But the right to vote—despite everything we've psychologically attached to it—is merely a tool to ensure that the government protects the other freedoms we cherish: free speech, freedom of religion, property rights, and so on. What makes America great is not voting per se, but *freedom.* And a freely elected government that robs its citizens of freedom—like, say, Nazi Germany—is not a democracy at all.

In his widely praised 2003 book, *The Future of Freedom: Illiberal Democracy at Home and Abroad,* Fareed Zakaria warns about the dangers of what he calls "illiberal democracy"—a new situation in which developing countries are trapped in a stage that combines democratic and illiberal elements, with often hazardous results. As Mr. Zakaria points out: "Democracy without constitutional liberalism is not simply inadequate, but dangerous, bringing with it the erosion of liberty, the abuse of power, ethnic divisions, and even war."

This doesn't mean that America should stop advocating for democracy. Rather, it simply means that America should strive to "consolidate democracy where it has taken root and to encourage the gradual development of constitutional liberalism across the globe," according to Zakaria.

One of the best ways to encourage constitutional liberalism is to protect and promote America's complicated system of checks and balances. The separation of powers between the legislative, executive, and judicial branches is sometimes vilified by political advocates who want to "do something," and are then horrified when their agenda is suffocated by the U.S. Senate, the Supreme Court, or an obscure federal agency. But while that frustration is certainly understandable, it must be muted by an appreciation of the Founding Fathers, who created a system that tames the public's passions and ensures not just democratic, but *deliberative* government—in other words, a republic.

At a time when it seems the world is becoming *more* supportive of the idea of democracy while showing *less* understanding of what democracy actually means, we need educated and active citizens to preserve the republic that our Founders created, and that has been a beacon of liberty for over 200 years. We are those citizens.

Regardless of what profession you choose to enter, I encourage you to stay involved in the political process. As former president Dwight Eisenhower said, "Politics ought to be the part-time profession of every citizen who would protect the rights and privileges of free people." Our republic doesn't run on automatic pilot; if we want to "keep it," we must know how to "keep it." And we must have the courage to act on that knowledge.

Voting is the first step in a democracy. You can't have a democracy without the right to vote, but the right to vote does not guarantee democracy.

This valuable series will help you understand and master the voting process in America. By absorbing its lessons, you will be better equipped to understand the evolution of our system of government with the foundation laid by the geniuses who devised it.

PREFACE

Morgan E. Felchner

In an election year, it seems as though the only thing on the country's agenda is politics. Everyone from the candidates to the media focus nearly all of their energy on election-related tasks. Citizens across the country fall into the fold too, tuning in to debates and watching cable news channels to gather information on candidates. All of this attention indicates the level of importance elections hold in American life. Citizens see many examples throughout history of elections determining who would guide the country through turbulent times and events such as war, stagflation, and depression. Especially in uncertain times, the stakes are high in U.S. elections and Americans recognize the importance of voting.

Given the current tumultuous political environment, it is helpful to examine the nuances of voting to understand how the election process in the United States has changed over time. First, we must look at the legal foundations and historical trends associated with voting. To do this effectively, we must examine past election laws, including the disenfranchisement that kept large groups from the polls.

Next, we must look at the demographics of voter participation. Who votes and why? It is only once we know who votes that we can analyze voting patterns. Then we must determine what causes voters to behave the way they do. In this time of constant media coverage, what drives voters to the polls? What interest groups are cutting through the clutter and impacting voters? Voters dread election years because their mailboxes fill up with literature from candidates and interest groups and the phone rings off the hook with pleas for support. Understanding the motivation for these calls and flyers will help to truly illuminate the workings of elections.

Finally, to fully understand elections in the United States, experts must tackle one of the most controversial issues of recent elections: voting machines. The stakes are high in U.S. elections; eliminating controversy by ensuring that voting machines will accurately track votes is key. The importance of elections is clear and understanding the details of the voting process is imperative. Although the specific issues might change, elections will always be subject to controversy. Learning the details now will provide a solid base for all future election debates.

Toward that end, *Voting in America* is organized into three volumes that address every aspect of voting. Volume 1 (*How America Votes: Law, Process, and Voter Participation*) looks back at the underbelly of politics in the United States, identifying when different groups got the right to vote and covering the basics of U.S. elections. It examines the laws associated with voting and how elections are conducted in the United States. Then Volume 1 shifts away from the laws associated with voting to the people who cast ballots. Not everyone in the eligible population chooses to go to the polls on Election Day. This volume analyzes both the laws that regulate elections and how these laws and outside factors get voters to the polls, or keep them away.

Volume 2 (*What Influences the American Voter: Interest Groups, Issues, and the Media*) addresses the fact that not every person who is eligible actually votes and looks only at those who do. What motivates people to vote varies widely, but certain issues tend to turn out more voters than others. And the political parties exploit such issues in an effort to turn out only their supporters. Volume 2 details these issues and other influences on voters.

Volume 3 (*American Voting Systems in Flux: Debacles, Dangers, and Brave New Designs*) addresses problems with the voting system and looks to the future of voting in the United States. Voting will always come with more than its share of controversy, and these new technologies and developments could serve to either silence the critics or fuel the fire.

I am grateful to all of the chapter authors. My goal was to assemble an authoritative look at voting in the United States and provide easy-to-follow readings on the most complicated topics, including election law. Without the participation of the experts who contributed the chapters that follow, this would not have been possible.

VOLUME 1: HOW AMERICA VOTES: LAW, PROCESS, AND VOTER PARTICIPATION

The intricacies of the voting process in the United States have a large impact on the results of elections. Everything from how people vote, to the type of elections they vote in, to the laws governing elections profoundly alter the results, both positively and negatively. Beginning with the birth of the country, laws governing who can cast a ballot have influenced elections and prompted significant debate. To address this, in Part 1 of this volume I have assembled a group of chapters that address the laws that have regulated the voting process throughout history.

Part 1 opens with "Decoding the Electoral College: The History and Controversy," a look at how the United States selects its president. Several chapters addressing the right to vote follow, including "Old Enough to Vote: Voting Age in the United States," "Women in Politics: From Fighting for Suffrage to Fighting for Votes," and "African Americans and the Right to Vote: A Look at the Voting Rights Act Then and Now." The next set of chapters covers current laws, including such contributions as "Absentee Voting in the Twenty-first Century" and "Casting Votes by Mail: Will Other States Follow Oregon's Lead?" Finally, Part 1 examines the different types of elections with "The Rise of Ballot Initiatives" and the all-important issue of money in politics with "Navigating the Maze of Election Law Changes: Campaign Finance Laws and the United States Constitution."

Part 2 turns to the impact of these laws, and looks at who votes and who doesn't and why. Voter turnout is addressed more generally in "Trends in Voter Participation," "Voter Participation in the United States versus Other Democracies," and "Why We Vote: Civic Duty and Voter Apathy." The next topic is specific voting groups, with readings such as "The Urban/Rural Divide: Understanding Voter Participation by Location," "The Elusive Young Voter: How to Break into the Group," and "The Typecast Voters: Security Moms, Seniors, and the Young."

VOLUME 2: WHAT INFLUENCES THE AMERICAN VOTER: INTEREST GROUPS, ISSUES, AND THE MEDIA

American voters are independent beings; they vote according to their own feelings and principles. Political campaigns attempt to decode these principles and reach a voter through various types of communication and ensure that he or she casts a ballot for their candidate. These campaigns surely influence voter behavior; they are intended to. Television commercials, direct-mail pieces, and phone calls are all focused pleas to voters, but there are also less direct and less partisan influences on voters. Issues, regardless of whether a candidate makes use of them or not, influence voters. Special-interest groups, which are decidedly partisan, in most cases influence voters. And the media, which is supposedly nonpartisan and an outside observer, also influences voters. The media, although frequently harpooned for being too liberal, serves as a filter for many voters. All of these influences directly impact elections.

Certain voters are influenced more strongly by selected groups or issues, and these voters are often considered a "sure thing" by campaign strategists. These people will definitely be going to the polls, and pollsters find that they can predict with near certainty how they will vote. Volume 2 first addresses the "sure thing" voters in Part 1. Included are such titles as "Women as the Swing Vote," "Blacks and the Democratic Party," "The Democratic Party and Unions: The Partnership Continues," and "The Republican Party and the Religious: Courting Evangelicals as the Way to Victory."

Part 2 turns to the influences and addresses the "big voting groups." These are the special-interest groups whose sole purpose is to influence voters and election outcomes. These groups often issue endorsements that can have a significant impact on a race. Part 2 begins with "Substantial Endorsements and Influential Report Cards: The Impact of Interest Groups on Voting in America." Unions and religious leaders can also have a major influence on members or followers. "Evangelical Voters and Leaders and Their Impact on Elections" and "Unions and GOTV" examine these important voting blocs.

Part 3 looks at the issues that get voters to the polls. Certain issues influence voters, and others motivate them to get out and vote. They are not always one and the same. The chapters look at several "hot button" issues that influence voters every election, in articles such as "Immigration in 2006 and Beyond," "*Roe v. Wade* Politics: Abortion and Voting in the United States," "Gay Marriage: How State Amendments and Passionate Voters Are Influencing Elections," "The Politics of Hope, Health, and Morality: Stem Cell Research as a Reason for Voting," and "The Politics of Fear: Terrorism and National Security in Post–9/11 Elections." In addition to these contentious issues, economics always plays an important role, as do healthcare and local issues. These topics are investigated in "The Economics of Voting: Pocketbook Issues in U.S. Elections," "Keeping the Country Healthy: Healthcare as a Campaign Issue," and "All Politics Isn't Local, It's Personal: Local Issue Trends in Politics."

Finally, Part 4 looks at the role of the media in politics. Whether it is old media, like newspapers and network television, or new media, such as blogs, the influence is apparent. First, the traditional media outlets are discussed in "Buying Time: Twenty-first-Century Campaigns and Political Advertising" and "The Old Guard: Mainstream Journalism Outlets' Impact on Elections." Next the focus turns to the new media that are impacting elections today, with "The New Guard: Entertainment Talk Shows and the Not-So-Fake News," "What Changed It All: Online Media in Elections," and "The Social Web: Social Networking and Online Activism in U.S. Politics."

VOLUME 3: AMERICAN VOTING SYSTEMS IN FLUX: DEBACLES, DANGERS, AND BRAVE NEW DESIGNS

"Hanging chads," "dimpled chads," and "pregnant chads" are new phrases that have entered our voting vocabulary because of punch card voting machines. These machines, outlawed by the Help America Vote Act, are no longer in use but the debate over how people cast their votes is far from over. Selections in this volume address where the problems started and some possible solutions. Part 1 looks at where the problems began: the presidential elections of 2000 and 2004. It opens with "The First Major Sign of Trouble: Florida in 2000" and examines specific problems with the voting system in the United States. It ends with "The Solution: Help America Vote Act and Voting Now."

Part 2 turns to issues involving online voting and voter registration. First, voter registration is tackled in "The Future of Voter Registration." Coverage then turns to the possibility of online voting in the United States with "Falling Behind: The Future of Online Voting in the United States," and "Voting Online around the World."

Finally, Part 3 examines electronic voting, the companies that sell the voting machines, and the most recent debate over voter-verified paper audit trails. Included are such titles as "Owning the Vote: A Look at Diebold, ES&S, and the Rest of the Voting Industry," and "The Paper versus Electronic Debate: The Trouble with Electronic Voting Machines and Paper Audits."

Acknowledgments

Voting is a learned behavior; statistics show that if you vote in two elections in a row, you are likely to be a voter for the rest of your life. Whereas most voters cast ballots mainly in federal elections, I go to the polls nearly every chance I get. Participating in democracy is one of our most important roles as citizens. But I'm not a voter by accident; throughout my childhood I accompanied my parents to the polls. I stood in line with them, and in some cases I was allowed to cast my own ballot—for Mickey Mouse or Donald Duck—but it got me excited about going to the polls every two years. Without the leadership and encouragement of parents, children don't learn the importance of voting. Luckily, my parents encouraged voting and discussed political issues at home so that we would understand the process and its importance. It is largely because of this that I am a voter, and not only a voter but an observer with a keen interest in the process. Thank you, Mom and Dad, for teaching me to be a voter, teaching me to be curious, and encouraging me to follow my dreams.

Thank you to all of my contributors; without your expertise this series could never have come to fruition. Your knowledge helped shape what this series has become: the most comprehensive look at voting ever assembled. Your writing is provocative, informative, and explanatory. It has made this just what a political series on one of the most important issues facing Americans today should be. My thanks also go to Praeger and my editors, Hilary Claggett and Elizabeth Potenza. Thank you for your wisdom and for guiding me through this process.

Thank you to my entire family (both the Felchners and the Naiks). Your excitement, love, and encouragement throughout this process made this project a joy. Mom, Dad, Adam, and Erin, thank you for pushing me throughout my life to be the best I can be and for showing me that we can all truly accomplish our dreams.

Finally, thank you Raj. Your patience, love, encouragement, ideas, and support really made this set of volumes possible. Without you, this set would be a shell of what it is.

Introduction: The History and Tradition of U.S. Voters

How Laws and External Factors Impact Turnout

Morgan E. Felchner

THE HISTORY OF VOTING IN AMERICA

In the 2000 presidential election just 537 votes separated George W. Bush and Al Gore after the first counting in Florida, the state that ended up determining the next president. This small margin illustrates not only the importance of counting votes correctly but also the importance of voting. If just 537 people had stayed home or gone to the polls and been turned away, the outcome of the election may have been different. Every vote counts, and voter registration groups highlight that point in order to encourage citizens to register and get to the polls. Special-interest groups go to community meetings, stand outside grocery stores or in university meeting places, and send e-mail, all with the goal of getting people to exercise their right to vote. Today, when nearly all adults are eligible to vote, these voter registration drives conducted by special-interest groups are the centerpiece of elections.

In the early 1900s and even into recent times special-interest groups served a different purpose: getting people the right to vote. Throughout history election laws have changed numerous times, but the most important changes and the ones that have impacted the country and its elections the most deal with extending the right to vote to all citizens. For many years laws prohibited certain groups from casting a ballot. Both women and African Americans were at one time turned away from the polls. Civil rights groups and women's rights groups fought for years to have these groups included in the electoral process. This fight and the resulting amendments to the Constitution make up the sordid history of voting in the United States.

Originally, only white men who were property owners or who paid a poll tax were eligible to vote. In addition, states were allowed to dictate their own rules and many added religious restrictions that governed who could vote. All in all, the rules left only 6 percent of the adult male population eligible to vote.[1] By 1850 the religious and property requirements were abolished, but still only white men were allowed to vote. This was the first step toward near universal suffrage, but it would be a long time before other races and women were granted the right to vote.

After the Civil War and the 1865 passage of the Thirteenth Amendment, which outlawed slavery, and the Fourteenth Amendment, granting citizenship to all people born or naturalized in the United States, the groundwork was laid for granting suffrage legally to all races. The first step was the Fifteenth Amendment, which states, "The right of citizens of the United States to vote shall not be denied or abridged by the United States or by any state on account of race, color or previous condition of servitude." Although it was a good beginning, the Fifteenth Amendment left room for states to enforce poll taxes, literacy tests, "good character" tests, and grandfather clauses.[2] The right to vote was not granted uniformly across races, and many Southern states created new barriers to keep African Americans from voting. One of these barriers was literacy requirements and tests. Literacy tests were subjective and enforced unfairly; a white voter who couldn't read was allowed to pass through while a black voter with a Ph.D. failed the test. In addition to the literacy requirements, several states implemented grandfather clauses that allowed anyone who had voted prior to 1866, or anyone who was a descendent of someone who had voted prior to 1866, to vote without restriction. This meant that nearly all African Americans were left out of the process or were subjected to many more requirements, like the literacy and property ownership rules.

It took another amendment to the constitution and the Voting Rights Act of 1965 to fully grant all races the right to vote. In 1964 the Twenty-fourth Amendment abolished the poll tax. That meant states were no longer able to discriminate based on voters' economic status. At the time of the amendment only five Southern states still had a poll tax.[3] This removed what seemed to be the last barrier to voting for African Americans, but the actual participation among African Americans was a different story. Because of the years of barriers, most African Americans in the South had never registered to vote. The Voting Rights Act of 1965 eliminated the literacy tests that had been in place in many Southern states and encouraged people of all races to register to vote.

Race wasn't the only barrier to voting; gender also interfered with citizens' right to vote. In 1776 Abigail Adams asked the Continental Congress to support women's rights and her husband, President John Adams, vowed to end the "despotism of the petticoat." Although women's rights were on the mind of Adams before the Constitution was even adopted, it would be a long time before women achieved equal status with men in the eyes of the law. Those opposed to granting women the right to vote argued that women were weak-minded and lacked the ability and temperament necessary to reason through the voting process.[4] As with African Americans, states dictated for themselves whether women were eligible to vote. Initially women were eligible, but between 1777 and 1807 all of the states that had allowed women to vote rescinded the law. From that point until 1920, when women were again granted the right to vote, a vibrant women's rights movement fought for equal treatment.

In 1872 Susan B. Anthony and fifteen other women in Rochester, New York, registered to vote and cast ballots for the presidential election. The law was very clear that women were not allowed to vote, but these sixteen women voted out of protest and were subsequently arrested for voting without a legal basis to do so. This example of civil disobedience set off a number of other marches and protests by women across the country. Although Anthony was a champion for women's rights throughout her life, she would not live to see women granted the right to vote. The Nineteenth Amendment, ratified in 1920, declared "the right of citizens of the United States to vote shall not be denied or abridged by the United States or by any state on account of sex." This was a huge victory for the women's suffrage movement.

The final major change in voting rights was the lowering of the voting age in the United States. Prior to the enactment of the Twenty-sixth Amendment, the voting age was 21. The first calls for reducing the voting age sprang up during World War II, but it wasn't until the next time the legal voting age was called into question, during the Vietnam War, that the protests made a difference. During the war in Vietnam the draft forced young men of all ages into the military. Men as young as 18 risked their lives for the country but could not cast a ballot. Students across the country decried the injustice of their inability to vote, and in 1971 Congress agreed, passing a bill that would amend the Constitution to reduce the voting age to 18.

Today, although many believe the major barriers to voting have been overcome, not all citizens over age 18 are eligible to vote. Each state still determines the laws for its elections, and depending on the state some felons are ineligible to vote as are some mentally disabled people. Despite the restrictions, the voting-eligible population in the United States for the 2006 elections was approximately 207,336,873.[5] In 2004 over 122 million votes for president were cast, so although turnout does not come close to 100 percent of those eligible, the United States has come a long way from the 6 percent of adult men that once constituted the voting-eligible population.

VOTER TURNOUT IN U.S. ELECTIONS

Although laws dictate who can cast a ballot in the United States, outside factors also play a role in determining who actually does. Turnout in U.S. elections is low compared with many other democracies, but recent trends show that the country could be headed toward a more involved electorate.

In 2004 many factors came together to create an ideal voter turnout scenario: a borderline popular president, a continuing war in Iraq, and a more sophisticated voter mobilization effort than had ever been witnessed before. All of this combined to boost voter turnout to a higher level than in any election since 1968, reversing a downward trend in voter participation. Turnout reached 60 percent in the hotly contested election, a level 5.9 percent higher than in 2000.[6] Over 122 million Americans cast a ballot in the presidential election; this was nearly 17 million more than had voted in 2000.[7] Certain segments of the population turned out in higher numbers than ever before. Votes cast by 18- to 24-year-olds increased 11 percent in 2004.[8] In addition to young voters, non-Hispanic whites and blacks also increased their turnout. The 2004 election saw 67 percent of non-Hispanic whites (a 5 percent increase) and 60 percent of blacks (a 3 percent increase) casting their votes. Asian and Hispanic turnout saw no change in relation to the 2000 election; 44 percent of Asians and 47 percent for Hispanics cast ballots.[9] Turnout in individual states varied but was up in every state across the country. Minnesota had the highest overall turnout, with 78 percent (an 8.4 percent increase over 2000). Vermont had the smallest increase, with 64.9 percent turning out (a 0.8 percent increase).[10]

So what caused this bump in participation in 2004 after years of declining turnout? Although voter turnout has fluctuated throughout history, there are several factors that traditionally contribute to higher turnout; in 2004, those factors combined with a few specific issues resulted in record-breaking voter turnout.

A CLOSE RACE

In the days leading up to Election Day in 2004, one thing was certain: it was going to be a close race. With the war in Iraq raging on and Democrats attempting to unite in an effort to bring down Bush, no one could call the race. During the summer Bush's approval ratings were not giving his campaign much comfort. His rating in July was 47 percent, and history shows that an incumbent needs to have an approval rating of at least 46 percent to win the election.[11] Bush's rating was a little too close for comfort, but even before July the campaign knew it was going to be a tough battle. The challenger, U.S. Senator John Kerry (D-MA) was campaigning hard on the issues of terrorism and the war in Iraq, and polls showed the two were neck and neck. From summer to Election Day, polls showed that the gap was within the margin of error.[12]

Voters across the country (but especially in swing states) could not escape coverage of the election and were inundated with television commercials, direct-mail pieces, and constant news reports. All of this coverage meant voters were aware of the campaigns and likely recognized the potential for a really close race. The media coverage of the election along with the tightness of the race probably played a large part in increasing turnout. Historically, closer races draw more voters, even in non-presidential contests. The 2004 presidential race is only one of nine races since 1868 where the winning candidate received less than 51.5 percent of the two-party vote, and it was the fourth closest race since 1868.[13] It was also the narrowest margin of victory for an incumbent president ever.[14] The closeness of the race led to more media coverage and more interest from the general public, producing the highest turnout since the enactment of the Twenty-sixth Amendment, giving citizens age 18 to 20 the right to vote.[15]

In swing states, such as Minnesota, turnout was higher than in non-swing states. Several factors contributed to this; the closeness of the race had an impact, but more important is the fact that in a state or area deemed a "battleground" by the campaigns (meaning the area has the potential to go for either candidate), there is more media coverage and more mobilization efforts in the days and weeks approaching the election. In battleground states in 2004 turnout was up 8.3 percent, whereas in non-battleground states the increase was 4.7 percent.[16]

In addition to battleground status, close races at all levels increase turnout. In South Dakota, Senate Minority Leader Tom Daschle found himself in a dogfight against now-Senator John Thune. Voters received communications from campaigns many times a day, and both campaigns employed sophisticated voter mobilization strategies on Election Day. This highly competitive race produced the highest increase in turnout over the 2000 election (a 10.8 percent increase).[17]

LONG MEMORIES

The presidential election of 2000 left a bitter taste in many voters' mouths, as both sides felt they were cheated (Democrats more so than Republicans). The controversy in Florida, where literally every vote mattered, may have given voters across the country the sense that their vote really could make the difference in a close race. This sentiment, which is often not felt by voters, could have pushed more of them to the polls in 2004. No one wanted to see another 2000, where the winner of the presidential election was unknown for over a month.

ISSUE-DRIVEN VOTERS

In addition to the closeness of the race and voters' sentiments about the importance of their votes, other factors led to the high turnout, including ballot initiatives and other races on the ballot. In 2004, eleven states had a question on the ballot about banning gay marriage. These initiatives were highly publicized and are thought to have encouraged voters on both sides of the aisle to get to the polls. For Republicans, the initiatives are thought to have driven even voters who were unenthusiastic about Bush to the polls, simply to support the ballot measure to ban gay marriage. Not only did the campaigns themselves publicize the initiatives, so did the media. The media fueled speculation that the initiatives would increase turnout and publicized the impact of the campaigns heavily in the days leading up to the race. The campaigns on both sides of the initiatives were very sophisticated and worked to turn out as many extra voters as possible on Election Day. Controversial ballot initiatives are a common tactic for increasing turnout and generating buzz and interest in an election.

THE DOWNTURN

The 2006 elections had Republicans running for the hills because of bad news from Iraq, corruption scandals taking down the Party's elected officials, and strong Democratic party unity. Media coverage of the 2006 elections was again high and many races across the country were close. In a non-presidential year turnout expectations are much lower, as was the case with 2006. Traditionally, turnout averages just below 60 percent in a presidential year and below 40 percent in a non-presidential year.[18] In 2006, 37 percent of voting-age Americans turned out. Coming off of an election with record-breaking turnout, 37 percent is not particularly impressive, especially with Democratic candidates working to energize their party.

Data gathered prior to the election showed that a relatively large number of voters (compared with those who actually turned out) were interested in the election. According to a Pew Research Center poll, 51 percent of voters were engaged in the election, saying they thought "a lot" about it.[19] Many of those voters didn't make it to the polls on Election Day despite heavy mobilization efforts by Democrats, close races, and media coverage throughout the election cycle.

TURNOUT THROUGH HISTORY

In 2004 we know that factors specific to the race influenced turnout, but what influences turnout on a broader scale? Why was turnout in a steady decline prior to 2004?

The World War II generation, who saw voter turnout drop drastically during and immediately after the war only to rebound dramatically in the 1950s, viewed voting as a duty. Voting was something that contributed to the "American" identity and was seen as one's civic responsibility. In order to be a good citizen one had to exercise his or her right to vote and participate in democracy. Now this sense of civic duty has declined, and along with it so has voter turnout.

Many factors have contributed to the decline in voter turnout, including this lack of a sense of civic duty, but conventional wisdom also points to a disinterested public that is no longer engaged. Despite all of the media coverage, voters are paying less attention to elections. Although voters may watch Fox News or CNN, fewer and fewer Americans are watching presidential debates. In 1960, 60 percent of Americans tuned into the debates; in 2000, less than 30 percent did.[20] This decrease in interest in debates is likely caused by two factors. First, the variety now offered by television, with hundreds of cable channels, in 2000 gives voters more to chose from. Who is to say that in 1960 if voters could have switched to MTV they would still have watched the debates? Second, the increasing number of debates means that each debate holds less importance for individual voters, making them less likely to watch a significant number of them.

Although turnout was up in 2004, no one can accurately predict what will happen in 2008, when an equally competitive race will dominate headlines. However, it does seem that the public is paying more attention to the campaigns this cycle. Between September and October of 2007, 52 percent of voters said they were following the presidential election very or fairly closely. Twenty percent said they were following it very closely.[21] That level of interest could produce an active electorate for elections to come.

NOTES

1. Elizabeth Yang, "History of Voting in the United States," *Update on Law-Related Education* 20 (Fall 1996): 4–7.
2. Yang, "History of Voting."
3. Yang, "History of Voting."
4. Yang, "History of Voting."
5. United States Election Project, George Mason University, http://elections.gmu.edu/Voter_Turnout_2006.htm (accessed November 4, 2007).
6. Michael P. McDonald, "Up, Up and Away! Voter Participation in the 2004 Presidential Election," *The Forum* 2(4), article 4.
7. James E. Campbell, "The Presidential Election of 2004: The Fundamentals and the Campaign," *The Forum* 2(4), article 1.
8. CIRCLE, http://www.civicyouth.org/?page_id=241.
9. U.S. Census Bureau press release, http://www.census.gov/Press-Release/www/releases/archives/voting/004986.html.
10. McDonald, "Up, Up and Away!"
11. Campbell, "Presidential Election of 2004."

12. McDonald, "Up, Up and Away!"

13. Campbell, "Presidential Election of 2004."

14. McDonald, "Up, Up and Away!"

15. McDonald, "Up, Up and Away!"

16. McDonald, "Up, Up and Away!"

17. McDonald, "Up, Up and Away!"

18. United States Election Project.

19. Pew Research Center for the People and Press, *November Turnout May Be High* (October 11, 2006).

20. http://hnn.us/articles/1104.html.

21. Pew Research Center for the People and the Press, *Modest Interest in 2008 Campaign News* (October 23, 2007).

Part 1

How America Votes

1

Decoding the Electoral College

The History and Controversy of Selecting the President

Robert W. Bennett

DISSONANCE BETWEEN REALITY AND PERCEPTION

The selection of a president is probably the signature event of American democracy, but most Americans understand very little about the process. For all appearances popular elections for president and vice president are conducted every four years in early November, on Election Day. These elections are integrated with those for federal congressional offices and typically for state and local positions as well. At these elections voters are asked to cast their ballots for one of the pairs of candidates advanced by the political parties to fill the offices of president and vice president of the United States. Although the media typically report nationwide vote totals for the various pairs of candidates, attentive observers understand that the cumulative popular vote across the nation is not decisive. Instead, the count for each state determines which pair of candidates is awarded that state's electoral votes. The number of electoral votes varies from state to state, and it seems clear that a state's population determines the precise number. In most elections there are only two pairs of candidates that garner the electoral votes of respective states, and it is assumed that the one with the larger total captures the two offices. The winning pair is then sworn into office in January of the following year.

This picture, however, shrouds the complexity of the election process. It is in fact candidates for the office of elector for whom votes are cast on Election Day. Each state is entitled to a number of electors—and electoral votes—equivalent to its representation in the House of Representatives and the Senate. This number is related to the state's population, but the relationship is not all that close for the less populous states, because each state is entitled to two senators regardless of population. Moreover, the form of the ballot varies across and even within states, and in many places the names of electors do not appear on the ballot; indeed, there is often no mention of the office at all. But even when votes are cast for the presidential and vice presidential candidates of the respective political parties, state law dictates that those votes are "really" votes for electors.

Slates of electors are advanced by state political parties, and the electors are usually assumed to be committed to the national candidates of those parties. State statutes govern the formation of the slates, with most delegating broad authority to the state parties. Some parties use primary elections, and others nominate electors through conventions, central committees, or some mixture of designation mechanisms. The selection process clearly emphasizes party loyalty, but other considerations—such as celebrity status or geographic, ethnic, or gender balance—may enter the slate formation process. Although states can allow votes for electors from different slates, that approach has withered over the years in favor of the winner-take-all approach. The entire slate with the most votes becomes the state's representatives in what is known as the Electoral College. Currently, only two states diverge from this pattern. Maine and Nebraska select all but two of their electors through popular voting in individual congressional districts, with the other two electors determined by the statewide vote.

To win the presidency or the vice presidency a candidate must obtain a "majority of the whole number of Electors appointed."[1] Despite the use of the term "Electoral College," electors around the nation never meet as a body. Each state's contingent (and the delegation from the District of Columbia, as provided for by the Constitution's Twenty-third Amendment) gathers and votes separately some forty-one days after the November election. The date for these gatherings is set by Congress and is constitutionally required to be "the same throughout the United States."[2] The electoral votes do not become official, moreover, until a counting session at a joint meeting of the newly installed House and Senate in early January. At that session, presided over by the outgoing vice president (in his capacity as presiding officer of the Senate), electoral votes can be challenged on a variety of grounds. If, because of these challenges or for other reasons, no candidate receives the required majority, the selection process is relegated to "backup" procedures in the House of Representatives for the president, and in the Senate for the vice president.[3]

Development of the Dissonance

The dissonance between the formalities and the seeming reality of the presidential selection process is the product of an original concept that has not stood the test of time. The framers of the U.S. Constitution were decidedly ambivalent about the general populace controlling governmental processes. The "people" were regularly depicted as the repository of sovereignty for the new nation, but they were also treated warily, because they were seen by more than a few of the framers as insufficiently disinterested, as too likely to succumb to fleeting passions and to the pursuit of self-interest. The design of the new government reflected this ambivalence. The House of Representatives was to be chosen by the "people of the several States," but the Congress was to be bicameral, with the Senate originally chosen not by popular election, but by state legislatures. Both houses would have to concur before a measure became "law."[4] The judicial branch was given some prominence in the constitutional design, but it was not to be popularly elected. This was also the case for the president, the repository of "executive power."

The Electoral College was conceived as an elite collection of individuals who would engage in genuine deliberation about who should be entrusted with the presidency. The "manner" of choosing the state's representation was left up to the state legislature.[5] Popular election was one possible approach, and some states opted for popular election of electors in the initial stages of the process. But reposing the choice of selection mechanism in the state legislatures was not intended as a device for instructing electors on how to vote. Actually, it was almost universally assumed that George Washington would be the first president in any event, so designation of the separate office of elector makes sense only if it was also assumed that after Washington's service, electors would exercise judgment and discretion in carrying out a momentous task. The disconnected—but simultaneous—meetings were likely required in part to help ensure genuine deliberation and informed choice by discouraging a state's electors from bargaining and coordinating with the other gatherings. Electors were also forbidden from holding any "office of trust or profit under the United States," further ensuring their independent judgment.[6]

Originally, the electors had no separate ballot for vice president; they instead had to cast two votes for two different people they deemed suitable for the presidency. If everything went smoothly, the total votes would be equal to twice the number of electors. The winner would be the person with the largest number of votes, if that represented a majority of the appointed electors, and the runner-up would become vice president. However, if no candidate obtained the required majority, the House backup procedure would be employed to choose a winner from among the five with the highest numbers of electoral votes. Some seemed to assume that the House procedure would be routinely practiced, for after the Washington era, the disconnected meetings might well yield votes scattered among many candidates. Indeed, another provision reflected some concern that electors might be parochial in their choices: they could not cast both of their votes for "inhabitants" of their own states.[7] In this original scheme the Senate backup procedure for vice president was to be implemented only in the seemingly unlikely event of a tie for runner-up in the electoral vote tally.

This concept was soon found wanting with the emergence of two formidable and antagonistic political parties, the Federalists and the Democrats. They dominated both national and state politics, and they advanced slates of candidates for president and vice president. Through the mediation of the parties, the state designation of electors—through whatever "manner" the legislature chose—was accompanied by a degree of assuredness that electors would vote for the party candidates. In this way, coordination among electors with similar party affiliations could be orchestrated well before all the electors met.

The rapid emergence of political parties seriously confounded things in 1800, just the fourth use of the electoral process. Washington had loomed so large in the first two presidential selections that the difficulties with the system remained shrouded until his retirement. In the first post-Washington election, that of 1796, although political parties advanced their candidates, coordination and party loyalty in elector voting had not yet taken firm hold. The result was a president and vice president of different parties: John Adams, the Federalist, and Thomas Jefferson, the Democrat. Both parties viewed this development as a failure of party discipline, and they tried harder the next time around. And they succeeded—only too well in the case of the Democrats.

Jefferson was understood to be the Democratic presidential candidate and Aaron Burr his vice presidential running mate. All the party's electors cast their votes for the two of them. Because the process did not differentiate between the two offices, the result was an Electoral College tie, with each candidate commanding the required majority. Burr did not step aside gracefully, and that sent the selection process to the House, where the Constitution provided—and still provides—that "the Representation from each state [is to have] . . . one Vote," and "a Majority of all the States shall be necessary to a Choice."[8] The Federalists initially supported Burr, but neither party controlled the required majority of state delegations. The situation resulted in a stalemate, which was broken in Jefferson's favor only on the thirty-sixth ballot.

Such difficulties led to the passage of the Twelfth Amendment in 1804, separating the Electoral College balloting for president and vice president, inserting an Electoral College majority requirement for the vice president, and designating the existing Senate backup procedure for the vice president if that majority was not attained. With only minor additional changes, however, the Twelfth Amendment left the process untouched. Most important, electors were still employed to choose the president and the vice president, and states were still allowed to designate the "manner" of their selection, even though in 1800 electors had acted as party functionaries rather than as independent decision makers. The Twelfth Amendment contained no hint of the role that political parties had come to play in the process.

At the time, states were still experimenting with a variety of approaches to the "manner" of choosing electors, including direct designation by the legislatures.

But soon thereafter, popular election carried the day and, with very few exceptions, has been employed in all the states since the 1830s. Some used elections within districts, but dominant political parties preferred winner-take-all elections, and almost all states have now embraced that approach. This led to the popular perception of state-by-state elections for president and vice president determining the electoral votes and, hence, the "election" outcome for the two offices.

Tensions in the Process

Winning While Losing the Nationwide Vote

Over the years, with the growing distance between formality and perception in terms of its workings, the Electoral College has become more controversial. The biggest controversy concerns the possibility of an Electoral College victory by a candidate who received fewer nationwide popular votes than his principal rival. Many object to this possibility on the grounds that a nationwide vote is the only truly "democratic" way to choose a president. Of course, because the electoral vote count is the one that matters, candidates do not campaign for the nationwide vote. However, the popular vote for presidential and vice presidential candidates is tabulated in each state, and the cumulative "results" are calculated and widely disseminated.

The 2000 election, like the one in 1888, saw different "winners" in the two counts. But there is some controversy about how to characterize several other elections. In 1824 Andrew Jackson received more popular votes than did the eventual winner, John Quincy Adams, but because not all states conducted popular elections at the time, there was no full tally of a nationwide popular vote. By 1876, in contrast, popular voting was universal, and the eventual Electoral College winner, the Republican Rutherford B. Hayes, garnered fewer votes in the popular counts that were eventually accepted than did his rival, the Democrat Samuel Tilden. This election, however, was fraught with other controversy, much of it traceable to widespread fraud and voter intimidation in a number of Southern states, where post–Civil War Reconstruction was still in force. As a result, no definitive assessment of what the popular vote total would have been, had the process been less tainted, is possible.

The final controversy concerns the 1960 election, where conventionally accepted totals showed the winning Democratic candidate, John Kennedy, with a little more than a 100,000-vote lead nationwide over the Republican Richard Nixon. The uncertainty arises because at the time Alabama allowed individual votes for electors, and the Democratic slate of electors in the state, which had been chosen through a primary election process, was split between those pledged to support Kennedy and those who ran as "uncommitted." All the Democratic electors won, and the Kennedy nationwide popular vote was calculated by ascribing to him an Alabama total equal to the largest number of votes obtained by any of the Democratic electors in the state. Any reasonable allocation of the total between Kennedy and "uncommitted," however, would have given Nixon a larger nationwide popular vote.

The Backup Procedures

Reverting to the backup procedures in the House and Senate has also troubled the process on occasion. By 1824 the Federalist Party had gone into steep decline, and the presidential election came down to an intra-party affair among the Democrats. Four candidates received electoral votes, but none garnered the required majority. The Twelfth Amendment provides that when recourse to the House is required, the choice for president will be decided among the three candidates with the highest number of electoral votes (not the top five, as in the original provisions). The House was able to choose John Quincy Adams on the first ballot, even though Andrew Jackson commanded 15 more electoral votes. Jackson did not take the rebuff lightly and remained suspicious that Adams had engaged in an unseemly deal with Henry Clay. Clay was the Speaker of the House, and he was also the candidate with the fourth highest electoral vote total. Excluded from the House procedure, Clay supported Adams and then became secretary of state in the new administration. Charges of an under-the-table bargain haunted the Adams presidency.

The only other actual use of the backup procedures was for the vice presidency in 1836. The Democrat Martin Van Buren captured the presidency with 170 out of the total 294 electoral votes. But his running mate, Richard M. Johnson, won only 147 electoral votes, 1 short of the required majority. The 23-vote difference between the presidential and vice presidential tallies was due to the defection of the Virginia electors—no doubt because Johnson was a controversial figure, having been married to a former slave. This brought the Senate backup procedure into play, and Johnson won handily.

Despite infrequent—and now long past—recourse to the backup procedures, the ongoing possibility cannot be dismissed. There are a variety of reasons why no candidate might obtain the required majority of appointed electors. We will return to the possibilities of elector disqualification and elector faithlessness—refusal to vote for a candidate to whom the elector was pledged—either of which might conceivably lead to an indecisive Electoral College count. Two other scenarios, however, seem more likely. The first scenario is one in which votes are split among three or more candidates, as happened in 1824. All the candidates that year came from the same political party, but more recent elections have seen third-party candidates who obtained electoral votes or who threatened to as the election approached. In 1948, for instance, Strom Thurmond won 39 electoral votes, and in 1968 George Wallace won 46. Perhaps even more suggestive is the third-party candidacy of Ross Perot in 1992 and 1996. He did not capture any electoral votes in either election, but that was because his rather sizable popular vote totals were spread more evenly across the country than were Thurmond's and Wallace's. In the run-up to the elections, the major-party candidates had been concerned that Perot would capture some electoral votes. In no election has a third-party candidacy prevented a decisive Electoral College tally, but the chances of an uncertain outcome obviously increase when votes are split among more than two candidates.

Finally, the Electoral College vote count might be indecisive even with all electors voting and only two candidates in the running. Currently there are 538 electors, equal to the combined size of the House (435) and the Senate (100) plus 3 electors allocated to the District of Columbia. This raises the prospect of an Electoral College tie. Apart from the "tie" in 1800, there has never been an Electoral College dead heat. But there have been elections that threatened or suggested the possibility of one. In 1876, with an odd total number of electors, the two candidates were eventually separated by only 1 electoral vote. And in 2000 the eventual margin of victory was 4 votes, excluding a "faithless" abstention by one elector who almost surely would have remained faithful to the Democrat Al Gore if her vote could have made a difference. Any number of plausible vote count reversals among the states would have led to a tie that year. As just one example, had Florida gone for Gore and Pennsylvania for the Republican George W. Bush—with the abstaining elector voting for Gore—there would have been an Electoral College tie. And even though other electoral vote counts have not been as close, there have been several elections in which conceivable reversals in a few states would have led to a tie.

Controversy about the backup procedures has focused on presidential selection in the House, and on the assignment of one vote to each state. This is said to be even more "undemocratic" than the Electoral College itself, because the states vary greatly in population. Vice presidential selection by the Senate is, of course, subject to the same criticism. The House process, however, is subject to a second objection. A substantial number of states have an even number of representatives, and a standoff in a delegation would result in the state being unable to cast a vote. This possibility looms particularly large if a state's delegation is evenly divided between the two major political parties. Because the Constitution requires an absolute majority of the state delegation for a choice, the House procedure holds the threat of a prolonged stalemate. That is just what happened in the 1800 election.

Faithless Electors

The recurrent phenomenon of faithless electoral votes has the potential to overturn the common perception that a state's popular balloting determines its electoral votes. As mentioned, there was a faithless abstention in 2000. There was also a faithless vote in Minnesota in 2004, though it may have been cast inadvertently in the state's secret electoral balloting. And over the years there have been other faithless votes—actual and threatened—going back by some accounts to 1796, when Samuel Miles cast his vote for the Democrat Thomas Jefferson, even though he had been a candidate for elector of the rival Federalists. But the concept of faithlessness is one that has gelled gradually. In 1836, for instance, the Virginia electors who refused to vote for Johnson for vice president may not have thought they were breaking any commitments.

This gradual change is not particularly surprising, given the evolution of the Electoral College from a body charged with debate, discussion, and the exercise of judgment, to a set of party functionaries, (almost always) casting purely formal votes for predetermined candidates. The original vision has certainly withered over time, and a number of state laws now discourage or even forbid elector faithlessness. But the possibility of independent voting by electors has never been formally disavowed on a national scale. In this setting the vast majority of votes are cast as committed votes, although occasional renegades refuse to be corralled. In the 1960 election Henry Irwin, an Oklahoma Republican elector, voted for Harry Byrd and Barry Goldwater in violation of a pledge he had taken under state law to vote for the party's candidates, Richard Nixon and Henry Cabot Lodge. And in the run-up to the 1968 election the novelist James Michener and others threatened to defect from their commitments to Hubert Humphrey, the Democratic presidential candidate, if the third-party candidacy of George Wallace threatened to give Wallace some leverage in the Electoral College balloting or in the House, if recourse to the backup procedure was required.

The tension over elector faithlessness is sometimes projected backward into campaign strategizing. When the 1976 election promised to be close, the Republicans, as they have since acknowledged, made plans to bargain for elector faithlessness. And similarly in the 2000 election drama, at different pre-election stages it appeared that each of the two major candidates might lose the popular vote but win—or, rather, initially seem to win—the Electoral College tally. Rumors abound of the two campaigns making contingent plans to urge electors to abandon their commitments. And in the joint meeting, challenges have sometimes been lodged against faithless votes. Those challenges have routinely been rejected—and the votes counted as cast—but it is important to note that those challenged votes never had the potential to change an election outcome.

Competing Slates of Elector

While the draftsmen of the constitutional provisions governing the Electoral College seem to have assumed that the choice of electors would be straightforward, that assumption has proved false. In fact, there have been competing slates of electors laying claim to victory on more than one occasion. In the traumatic election of 1876, the legitimacy of the electoral votes was contested in four states. Federal troops were still in the South, and, as we have seen, questionable voting on both sides of this close contest was very much in evidence. The result was the submission of rival sets of electoral votes in Florida, South Carolina, and Louisiana. There was also a dispute that year over a single elector in Oregon.

Samuel Tilden, the Democratic candidate, was an electoral vote shy of victory without counting any of the disputed votes. Tensions were high, and the joint meeting counting session seemed unlikely to resolve the disputes, because the two houses of Congress were controlled by different political parties. There was even talk of a renewed Civil War, and in that heated context legislation was passed providing for a special commission to evaluate the disputes. The commission's recommendations were to be binding unless rejected by both houses of Congress. It resolved all the disputes in favor of the Republican, Rutherford B. Hayes, and he became president with a single-vote Electoral College victory, the closest contest in the post–Twelfth Amendment era.

There were also rival slates before and after the 1876 election, but apart from 1876 only the 2000 election threatened to seat a president based on the resolution of rival claims. The dispute centered on Florida, and rival slates of electors never emerged there because of the intervention of the U.S. Supreme Court. Before that intervention, however, it seemed entirely possible that the Florida Supreme Court would designate one winner while the legislative and executive branches in Florida would insist on another. In the wake of the troubled 1876 election, Congress passed the Electoral Count Act, which, in the case of competing slates, presumptively favors the one certified by the state's governor. That might have resolved any Florida disputes, but not without stirring up a good deal of rancor. Indeed, even though the Supreme Court's intervention in the 2000 election remains controversial to this day, many defend the act on the grounds that it averted the potential of societal turmoil.

The problem of rival claims to the office of elector is affected by the short time frame for resolving claimed irregularities in the popular-vote tabulation. The forty days or so between Election Day and the meetings of electors is short enough, but further pressure is created by the Electoral Count Act's so-called safe harbor provision. This provision calls for state disputes to be resolved through procedures that are in place prior to the election, if the resolution is concluded "at least six days before" the elector meetings.[9] In the 1960 election Hawaii did not complete its recount within the safe harbor time frame; indeed, it finished the recount after the Electoral College meetings. The recount reversed the tentative result, but the competing slates had separately met and voted on the appointed day, and the joint meeting then accepted the votes of the recount winners. In the 2000 election controversy, in contrast, the Supreme Court interpreted Florida law to require the completion of any recount within the safe harbor time limits. Compliance with this requirement was impossible, and this provided the Court with justification for halting the state recount that was in progress.

Miscellaneous Problems

A miscellany of other Electoral College formalities has unsettled elections over the years. Despite separating the presidential and vice presidential balloting, the Twelfth Amendment retained the provision that an elector's 2 votes could not both be cast for inhabitants of the elector's state. Before the Florida dispute took center stage in the 2000 election, this "inhabitancy" limitation raised questions about whether Texas Republican electors could cast their presidential and vice presidential votes for George W. Bush and Dick Cheney, given that each had called the state home in the years preceding the election. The requirement that the meeting date for electors be the "same throughout the United States" raised questions in the 1856 election, when on account of a snowstorm the Wisconsin electors were unable to meet on the designated date. The constitutional insistence that an elector not hold an "office of trust or profit under the United States" was the basis for the 1876 Oregon dispute, as well as for a few other challenges to electoral votes over the years. And in 1872 the joint meeting actually rejected Arkansas electoral votes, ostensibly because the certificate submitted by the electors did not meet the statutorily required format.

Problems such as these seem trivial in today's context, but they are potentially potent because partisanship can rear its head in the joint counting session. The constitutional text gives no hint of the voting rules for this meeting, and a number of different approaches have been employed over the years. The Electoral Count Act does provide some guidance, but it raises interpretational problems of its own. Since the passage of that act in 1887, however, the disputes brought to the joint meeting have never threatened the outcome of an election, and for that reason they may not provide a true measure of the potential for Electoral College contentiousness.

THE MERITS AND PROSPECTS OF ELECTORAL COLLEGE REFORM

Contemporary discussion of the merits of the Electoral College takes the popular election of the electors for granted. And no one is seriously championing a return to the original notion of the body as one of discretion-laden choice. Although some commentators argue that elector discretion—"faithlessness" in the modern way of thinking about electors—cannot constitutionally be prohibited, a few defend the practice on its merits. If the faithlessness option is put aside, the contemporary Electoral College can be seen as a device for distributing input into presidential selection on a state-by-state basis. And as such, the Electoral College has both defenders and detractors.

With a nationwide popular vote as the most prominent alternative for electing a president, two major arguments are advanced in support of the modern version of the Electoral College. The first is that the Electoral College gives candidates an incentive to campaign across the nation instead of concentrating on certain sections of the country or on a few populous states, encouraging candidates to appeal to often neglected minorities across many states. The second argument is that the Electoral College makes the resolution of close elections more manageable by focusing on one or a few disputed counts in a small number of states. A nationwide vote, in contrast, might find contested counts in close elections all over the place. The second argument is cogent, but Electoral College critics have a powerful rejoinder to the claim of wholesome campaign incentives. Under the Electoral College system, the motivations of major-party candidates are in fact rather perverse. They concentrate their campaign resources—and promises—on the so-called swing states, where the political breakdown provides candidates with the incentive to campaign in order to have a realistic chance of influencing the overall electoral outcome. Politically lopsided states, in contrast, receive very little attention.

In addition, proponents of the Electoral College claim that a nationwide vote would raise a host of difficult questions. Currently states have some control over the qualifications for voting and, perhaps more important, over administration of the process. Would centralized control of voting be necessary in a nationwide vote, and if so, would that require separation of the different elections? Would sparsely populated and isolated states receive any campaign attention at all in a nationwide vote? Would American citizens residing abroad, or in overseas territories, be allowed to vote? Would a plurality of the vote suffice for victory, or would a runoff be required? In the face of these and other uncertainties, it is often argued that the Electoral College process has usually produced a decisive and reasonably smooth outcome, so that any imperfections should be viewed as tolerable.

It is also assumed that any move to a nationwide popular vote would require a constitutional amendment, which basically requires the assent of two-thirds of each house of Congress and three-fourths of the states. As difficult as this consensus is to attain on any matter, it would likely be especially difficult for elimination of the Electoral College system. It is difficult to parse the winners and losers resulting from such a change but resistance would probably arise in the least populous states, on account of their favorable electoral-votes-to-population ratio, and also in the most populous states, which benefit most from the winner-take-all factor. Resistance by only thirteen states would doom a constitutional amendment, and there are many more states where opposition would have some appeal.

Other proposals would retain the distribution of electoral votes by state but do away with winner-take-all elections. This would bring the Electoral College and popular-vote processes into closer alignment. Selection of electors by districts within states has ample historical precedent, and, as mentioned earlier, two states presently employ districting. Another possibility is for the states to award their electors in proportion to the popular vote in the state. Commentators have supported this proposal over the years, but it has never been adopted by any state. Colorado had a proportionality measure on the ballot in the 2004 election, but it went down in defeat. As the Colorado experience suggests, state-by-state adoption of proportionality—or of districting—would be hard to achieve because of the political incentives that led to winner-take-all in the first place. Either districting or proportionality could, of course, be accomplished by constitutional amendment, but any such amendment would likely be doomed by opposition both from large states, which, again, are advantaged by the winner-take-all approach, and from those who would settle for nothing less than a nationwide popular vote.

Some reform proposals focus more narrowly on unlikely but potentially dangerous possibilities. As mentioned, elector faithlessness has few contemporary defenders, which suggests that a constitutional amendment narrowly focused on that possibility might be attainable. Perhaps because elector faithlessness has never changed an election outcome, no nationwide effort against it has gained much political traction. In addition, any such amendment might be derailed by those using the occasion to press for a nationwide-vote amendment instead. For these reasons, a state-by-state effort to deal with elector faithlessness might have more chance of success. About half the states do have some statutes that forbid or discourage the practice, and proposals have been made for a uniform law forbidding the practice, which each state could adopt independently.

The House and Senate backup procedures also have few defenders. To change those procedures, however, would require a constitutional amendment, and that would, again, face daunting obstacles. It might be possible instead to deal with some of the factors that lead to the implementation of the backup procedures. A tie vote in the Electoral College could seemingly be prevented by increasing the size of the House of Representatives—and hence of the Electoral College—by one. This could be accomplished through federal legislation. Eliminating the possibility of third-party candidates forcing an election into the backup procedures would be a good deal more difficult. Even though states could take action to diminish this possibility, the role of minor parties in American democracy raises difficult issues that might be hard to disentangle from the Electoral College element of the puzzle.

The obstacles to Electoral College reform are many. Perhaps most important, there is no consensus on what needs reforming. Various proposals can thus stymie each other, particularly when a constitutional amendment is the chosen vehicle for reform. A second obstacle is the fact that the process often works reasonably well, which drains the sense of urgency of reform measures. And a third difficulty is the partisan bite associated with so many proposals for change. Actually, if one takes a long view, Electoral College peculiarities do not consistently favor one of the major parties over the other. But political actors tend to focus on the shorter term. For all of these reasons, real-world prospects for reform may depend on the presence of a shared sense of peril. Thus, the most propitious setting for reform might be in the wake of two problematic elections in a row, the first disadvantaging one of the two major political parties, and the next, four years later, disadvantaging the other.

NOTES

1. U.S. Const., Am. XII.
2. U.S. Const., Art. II, §1, cl. 4.
3. See U.S. Const., Am. XII.
4. See U.S. Const., Art. I, §2, cl. 1, §3, cl. 1, §7, cls. 2, 3.
5. U.S. Const., Art. II, §1, cl. 2.
6. U.S. Const., Art. II, §1, cl. 2.
7. U.S. Const., Art. II, §1, cl. 3.
8. Originally found in U.S. Const., Art. II §1, cl. 3, these provisions are now in the Twelfth Amendment.
9. 3 U.S.C. §1 et seq.

2

Old Enough to Vote

Voting Age in the United States

Karlo Barrios Marcelo and Mark Hugo Lopez

The Twenty-sixth Amendment to the U.S. Constitution extended suffrage rights to 18-, 19-, and 20-year-old citizens in federal, state, and local elections. Passed overwhelmingly in 1971 by the U.S. Congress in a favorable political and social climate, the amendment completed a campaign to lower the minimum voting age that began during World War II.

The Twenty-sixth Amendment first came into political consciousness in the 1940s. One of the reasons to enfranchise young people was the perceived unfairness of military conscription. While 18- to 20-year-olds could be drafted to serve in the military, fight in a war—World War II—and risk their lives for their country, they could not express their opinions through the ballot box. This remained the state of things during the Vietnam War as a new movement to extend voting rights to 18- to 20-year-olds began.

In the 1972 elections the eligibility of an additional 11 million 18- to 20-year-old citizens, or 8 percent of the population, introduced the possibility of swinging the outcomes of several federal and local elections. Turnout of these new voters in the 1972 presidential election was high, at 51 percent. The youth vote's impact is no less important today. Since the amendment's passage in 1971, political pundits and politicians have acknowledged both the potential and realized significance of the youth vote, generally understood to include those from 18 to about 29 years of age. In 2006, 12 million 18- to 20-year-olds, constituting 5 percent of the voting population, were eligible to vote because of the Twenty-sixth Amendment. In 2004, the last presidential election, the voter turnout rate for this population increased 14 percentage points over the 2000 figure, to 45 percent.[1]

THE ROAD TO RATIFICATION

The first formal attempt to enfranchise young people nationally occurred in 1970 with the Voting Rights Act (VRA) (see Table 2.1). After two wars—World War II and the Korean War—and political support from two presidential administrations—Eisenhower and Johnson—young people were still denied the right to vote, and still required to fight in wars as a civic duty. Beck and Jennings offer two important reasons, in addition to military service, for giving 18- to 20-year-olds the right to vote. First, they state that "by virtue of twelve years of education an individual must surely be prepared to vote; if not, it speaks ill of the nation's educational system."[2] In other words, postsecondary education is not compulsory, and so a high school degree is a marker not only of education, but also of citizenship. Second, Beck and Jennings posit that "eighteen-year-olds do indeed have enough experience to be able to exercise judgment, that they are as informed as most adults."[3]

Reasons aside, the story of the Twenty-sixth Amendment begins 100 years earlier. Prior to 1870, the Constitution granted states the ability to set voting rights. In 1867 the state of New York considered enfranchising young males ages 18 to 20, but the discussion had no traction.[4] In 1870 the Fifteenth Amendment enfranchised all male citizens 21 years or older, regardless of race or previous enslaved status. The Equal Rights (Nineteenth) Amendment extended the right to vote to all citizens, including women. Despite that enfranchising spirit and the popular support for lowering the minimum voting age, the Twenty-sixth Amendment could not have been conceived without the state of Oregon's strong defense of states' rights with its challenge to the VRA. In *Oregon v. Mitchell*, the state of Oregon argued that the VRA was unconstitutional because Congress has no authority over state elections. In a 5-4 decision, the Supreme Court sided with the state of Oregon. Although the Court ruled that the VRA was unconstitutional,

Table 2.1
The Road to Ratification: Timeline

1970	Voting Rights Act of 1970 (VRA) passes
December 21, 1970	*Oregon v. Mitchell* allows federal election age at 18, but not for states
March 10, 1971	Twenty-sixth Amendment passes the Senate (94-0)
March 23, 1971	Twenty-sixth Amendment passes the House of Representatives (400-19)
March 23, 1971	Minnesota is the first state to ratify amendment
June 30, 1971	Ohio becomes the thirty-eighth, and last, state to ratify
July 5, 1971	Twenty-sixth Amendment is officially certified
November 1972	Young people ages 18–20 vote for the first time

it provided guidance on how to extend voting rights to 18- to 20-year-olds. In writing the majority opinion, Justice Hugo Black stated that lowering the minimum voting age should come in the form of an amendment to the U.S. Constitution.[5]

Because of the Supreme Court's ruling, the voting age for federal elections was 18, but for state elections the voting age was set by the state. Owing to Black's strict interpretation, states were now saddled with a financial and administrative burden; two separate lists of registered voters would have to be maintained for state and federal elections. Not all states were affected equally by the decision. Prior to 1970, Kentucky and Georgia had already lowered the minimum voting age from 21 to 18 in state and local elections. Two other states, Alaska and Hawaii, had initially set lower age qualifications—20 and 19, respectively.

The architect of the Twenty-sixth Amendment was Senator Jennings Randolph (D-WV). Since the early 1940s, he had introduced the amendment, or something similar, many times. The Twenty-sixth Amendment, which he introduced in 1971, passed the House (400-19) and the Senate (94-0) with little opposition. Immediately after Congress passed the amendment, the state legislature of Minnesota ratified it, leading the way in a process that required ratification by thirty-eight states. Once Ohio became the thirty-eighth state to ratify it, the Twenty-sixth Amendment became part of the U.S. Constitution days later (see Table 2.1). The amendment was ratified in two months and seven days, the shortest ratification period of any amendment to date, and owed much to its groundswell of public support and to organizations such as Common Cause, which aided in the ratification process. In response to this historic moment, President Richard Nixon echoed a familiar refrain heard in World War II, the Korean War, and the Vietnam War:

> Some 11 million young men and women who have participated in the life of our nation through their work, their studies and their sacrifices for its defense now are to be fully included in the electoral process of our country.[6]

Not everyone shared Nixon's view. Even though 18- to 20-year-olds were given the right to vote, their ability to vote has been hampered since the amendment's passage. Even today, youth voting advocacy groups and lawmakers are working to remove voting barriers against young people.

REALIZING THE YOUTH VOTE THROUGH POLICY

Complications to realizing the youth vote materialized immediately. In 1972, the first election cycle following the passage of the Twenty-sixth Amendment, local governments, especially from college towns, challenged state governments over where young people could vote.[7] Many local election boards would not allow out-of-state students to register in their college towns. The fear among older, permanent residents of college towns centered on the potential of the youth vote to dramatically change the composition of local government and thereby local laws. These same residents did not want college students voting in college towns because young people, they argued, did not have a commitment to the town because they were not full-time residents. Common Cause worked on behalf of students, bringing lawsuits in many states to challenge state laws and local election board decisions designed to force college students to register where their parents lived.[8] Some states, like Massachusetts, sided with college students, arguing that enfranchising young people required equal treatment under the law.[9]

Registering to vote is sometimes more difficult than the act of voting itself.[10] Because of this, many recent federal and state laws have made registration and voting easier and more accessible. For instance, the National Voter Registration Act of 1993 (NVRA) enabled all citizens to register to vote at the same time they applied for or renewed their driver's licenses. Moreover, the NVRA or "Motor Voter" law allowed citizens to register by mail. From 1972 to 2004, the registration rate for presidential elections among 18- to 20-year-olds increased 5 percentage points, from 60 percent in 1972 to a record high of 65 percent in 2004 (see Table 2.2). Registration among 18- to 20-year-olds in midterm elections also increased, but by a margin of only 1 percentage point, from 39 percent in 1974 to 40 percent in 2006 (see Table 2.3).

The Help America Vote Act of 2002 (HAVA) further lowered barriers to voting by establishing a Help America Vote College Program, introducing young people to elections through the nonprofit National Student and Parent Mock Election, and making provisional ballots mandatory at all polling sites. Provisional ballots are especially important for young voters as many young people often change residence. Provisional ballots allow young voters who have not been

Table 2.2
Registration Rates in Presidential Election Years, 1972–2004

Presidential Election Years	Ages 18–20	Ages 21–24	Ages 25 and Older
1972	60%	62%	78%
1976	50%	58%	73%
1980	49%	57%	77%
1984	51%	59%	78%
1988	49%	56%	76%
1992	55%	63%	78%
1996	55%	63%	80%
2000	52%	65%	81%
2004	65%	69%	84%

Note: Tabulations from the *Current Population Survey*, November (Voting) Supplements, 1972–2004.

Table 2.3
Registration Rates in Midterm Election Years, 1974–2006

Midterm Election Year	Ages 18–20	Ages 21–24	Ages 25 and Older
1974	39%	48%	70%
1978	37%	48%	73%
1982	38%	51%	74%
1986	38%	51%	74%
1990	39%	49%	72%
1994	41%	51%	71%
1998	40%	57%	77%
2002	43%	58%	78%
2006	40%	51%	71%

Note: Tabulations from the *Current Population Survey*, November (Voting) Supplements, 1974–2006.

able to change their address or find their new polling precinct a chance to vote. HAVA also required colleges and universities to make voter registration forms available to students, often through university Web sites.

Along with federal policies, state policies have also been initiated to encourage voting. Currently, seven states have Election Day Registration (EDR) laws—Idaho, Maine, Minnesota, Montana, New Hampshire, Wisconsin, and Wyoming—and a number of other states have introduced legislation to embrace EDR. EDR is important because it allows citizens the right to vote on Election Day, even if their names are improperly removed from voter rolls or if they are not added to the voter rolls in time for the election. More important for young people, EDR applies to new voters as well.[11] Above all, states that offer EDR boast some of the highest youth voter turnout rates in the nation. Minnesota, for instance, leads all states in youth voter turnout, at 43 percent in 2006.[12] Furthermore, Fitzgerald found that "young people are substantially more likely to vote if they are able to register to vote on Election Day."[13]

Allowing young people to vote where they reside and introducing federal and state policies that lower barriers to voter registration and voting have shaped how young people vote. Peter Levine cues in on the importance of removing "legal and practical obstacles to voting" when he states, "The idea is to make voting easier, thereby raising youth turnout, thereby giving politicians more reason to mobilize young people."[14]

LOWERING THE VOTING AGE TO 16

Coast to coast, from Berkeley, California, to the state of Minnesota and the city of Baltimore, Maryland, many proposals have been made to lower the voting age to 16.[15] None to date have been passed. Many supporters of these proposals argue that young people ages 16 and 17 are old enough to work in the labor force and to pay taxes, yet they have no direct voice in the electoral process to change the laws and public policies that affect them. Organizations such as the National Youth Rights Association also argue that young people deserve to vote because, presently, education policy directly affects them and, looking forward, their retirement appears increasingly less secure.

These communities are not alone in their desire to lower the voting age. Proposals are in place in the United Kingdom, the European Union, and Austria to lower the voting age to 16. Countries, such as Brazil, Cuba, Nicaragua, and Germany have lowered the voting age to 16, although in Germany this is effective only for local elections; Iran's minimum voting age is lower still, at 15.

Although the national voting age in the United States is 18, certain localities have some experience with extending the right to vote to 17- and 16-year-olds. For example, many states allow citizens to vote in a primary election if they are 18 at the time of the general election. This was particularly important in Baltimore in 2003. In 1999 voters in Baltimore had approved a measure to move the mayoral election to November 2004 from November 2003. However, only state lawmakers can move the date of a primary; they adjourned in April 2003 without approving legislation to move the September 2003 primary election to September 2004. As a result, there was a 14-month window between the date of the primary and the date of the general election.

Because Maryland election law allows young citizens to register and vote in elections as long as they are 18 at the time of the general election, some 16-year-olds and all 17-year-olds in Baltimore were eligible to register to vote for the September 2003 primary. Unfortunately, this happenstance occurred at the end of the school year, allowing students only a few months to register to vote for the September 2003 primary. Despite this inconvenient timing, 35 percent of registered 16- and 17-year-olds voted in the 2003 primary, similar to the turnout for adult voters.[16]

REGISTRATION AND VOTING STATISTICS[17]

Generally, young people have lower voter registration and turnout rates than their adult counterparts. For example, in the 2004 presidential election, 58 percent of young people were registered to vote, and 47 percent of 18- to 24-year-olds voted. In contrast, among adults 25 years and older, 74 percent were registered and 67 percent voted. However, although young people have always registered and voted at lower rates than adults, there has been more volatility in their electoral participation relative to their adult counterparts.

This lower level of electoral participation among young people is likely the result of several factors. First, young people are often more affected by barriers to voting than their less transient adult counterparts. Second, young people must learn how to get involved in the electoral process. Although every state requires civic education as a graduation requirement, not all young people learn how to navigate the voting process.[18] Third, young people are less likely to be contacted by political and get-out-the-vote campaigns, though this appears to have been less of a problem in recent elections.

Voter Registration Rates Among 18- to 20-Year-Olds

Patterson notes, "Turnout is also reduced by registration requirements." It follows that getting young people registered to vote will, in turn, boost voter turnout. After 1972, there was reportedly a decline in the voter registration rate of 18- to 20-year-olds, followed by notable increases between 1992 and 2004. Since 1992, registration rates have remained above 50 percent, reaching a zenith of 65 percent in 2004. The peaks and valleys in the registration rate generally correspond to upward and downward voter turnout rates. In other words, when the registration rate rose from one election cycle to the next, a rise in voter turnout followed (the exception being 1992).[19]

Voter Turnout Rates Among 18- to 20-Year-Olds

In presidential elections from 1972 to 2004, 18- to 20-year-old citizens had lower voter turnout rates than those 21 to 24 years old (see Table 2.4). This gap was greatest, at 9 percentage points, in 2000. Since 1972, there has been a decline in the youth voter turnout rate, with notable breaks in 1992, 2004, and 2006. The 2004 and 2006 elections suggest a reversal of the declining voter turnout trend among young people. Turnout for the 2004 presidential election was the highest (45 percent) since 1972 (51 percent), the first election in which

Table 2.4
Voter Turnout Rates in Presidential Election Years, 1972–2004

Presidential Election Year	Ages 18–20	Ages 21–24	Ages 25 and Older
1972	51%	53%	68%
1976	40%	48%	65%
1980	39%	47%	68%
1984	40%	47%	69%
1988	36%	42%	66%
1992	44%	52%	70%
1996	34%	37%	62%
2000	31%	40%	63%
2004	45%	48%	66%

Note: Tabulations from the *Current Population Survey*, November (Voting) Supplements, 1972–2004.

Table 2.5
Voter Turnout Rates in Midterm Election Years, 1974–2006

Midterm Election Year	Ages 18–20	Ages 21–24	Ages 25 and Older
1974	22%	28%	52%
1978	21%	28%	54%
1982	21%	30%	57%
1986	20%	26%	54%
1990	21%	25%	53%
1994	18%	25%	52%
1998	15%	21%	49%
2002	17%	22%	50%
2006	19%	25%	51%

Note: Tabulations from the *Current Population Survey*, November (Voting) Supplements, 1974–2006.

18- to 20-year-olds were eligible to vote, and the 2006 youth voter turnout rate was 3 percentage points higher than in 2002 (see Table 2.5). Only with further evidence of a relatively high youth voter turnout rate in 2008 and beyond will we be able to conclude that there has indeed been a break in the declining youth voter turnout rate trend.

CONCLUSION

Extending enfranchisement to 18- to 20-year-olds recognized the contributions and sacrifices that these young people have made to the country. Federal and state policies have made voting easier. Despite this success, the proper implementation and interpretation of these laws call for the entrance of another actor—advocacy and nonprofit organizations. These organizations provide needed oversight of the federal and state governments, allowing for transparency in a democracy, as well as encouraging the youth vote.

More recently, organizations such as Smackdown Your Vote!, the Hip Hop Summit, U.S. PIRG, and Rock the Vote, as well as partisan get-out-the-vote efforts, have targeted young people. And they have much the same goal as the government—to register and educate voters. The efforts of these groups and others have been fruitful. In the last two election cycles, the youth turnout rate has increased. Still, the electoral participation of youth can be volatile and should not be taken for granted. Young people, perhaps more than other voter demographic groups, need support in the electoral process—from registering to vote to educating themselves about candidates—and initiatives to make the electoral process easier for young voters are of paramount importance.

Finally, the question of whether one is "old enough to vote" is not resolved. Some localities are considering allowing even younger people, those age 16 and 17, to vote. The arguments for doing so reflect the spirit of the Twenty-sixth Amendment, but focus on different issues. The common theme is that young people (ages 16 and 17) should be able to participate in a process that makes decisions about their lives. During the Vietnam War, the rallying cry for lowering the voting age sounded over the corporeal sacrifices that young people were making on behalf of the U.S. armed forces. Today issues of taxes, education policy, and social security are behind the rallying cry.

NOTES

Authors' Note: We thank Peter Levine and Deborah Both for comments on previous drafts of this document. All errors, in fact or interpretation, are our own. Address correspondence to Mark Hugo Lopez, CIRCLE, School of Public Policy, University of Maryland, 2101 Van Munching Hall, College Park, MD, 20742-1821. E-mail: *mhlopez@umd.edu.* Phone: 301-405-0183.

1. Although young people ages 18 to 20 represented a higher percentage of the population in 2006 than in 1972, their proportion of the eligible voting population was lower in 2006 than in 2002. This was most likely due to the fact that the baby boomer generation was so large, even in 2006.

2. See page 377 of Paul Allen Beck and M. Kent Jennings, "Lowering the Voting Age: The Case of the Reluctant Electorate," *Public Opinion Quarterly* 33(3) (1969): 370–379.

3. See pages 377–378 of Beck and Jennings, "Lowering the Voting Age."

4. See Jane Eisner, *Taking Back the Vote: Getting American Youth Involved in Our Democracy* (Boston: Beacon Press, 2004).

5. See Howard Ball and Phillip J. Cooper, *Of Power and Right: Hugo Black, William O. Douglas, and America's Constitutional Revolution* (New York: Oxford University Press, 1992).

6. R. W. Apple, Jr., "The States Ratify Full Vote at 18: Ohio Becomes 38th to Back the 26th Amendment," *New York Times,* July 1, 1971, p. 1.

7. R. W. Apple, Jr., "Youth Vote Likely to Aid Democrats: Parties Step up Recruiting," *New York Times,* May 10, 1971, p. 1.

8. R. W. Apple, Jr., "A New Problem for the Pros—'The Kid Factor':18-Year-Old Vote," *New York Times,* July 4, 1971, p. E3.

9. Bill Kovach, "Residence Choice Held Voter Right; Attorney General in Boston Rules Youths May Select Site Where They Vote," *New York Times,* July 22, 1971, p. 21. See also William Farrell, "Appeals Court Invalidates State Vote Residency Law: State Appeals Court Invalidates Law on 90-Day Voter Residency," *New York Times,* June 8, 1972, p. 1.

10. See Raymond E. Wolfinger and Steven J. Rosenstone, *Who Votes*? (New Haven, CT: Yale University Press, 1980).

11. This is especially important for young people, because although the National Voter Registration Act of 1993 (also known as "Motor Voter") allows young people to

register to vote at the same time that they apply for a driver's license, many young people are eligible to drive before the age of 18. Thus, a number of young people do not register to vote at this time because they are not of voting age.

12. See Mark H. Lopez, Karlo B. Marcelo, and Jared Sagoffs, "Quick Facts about Young Voters by State: The Midterm Election Year 2006" (June 2007). CIRCLE Fact Sheet (www.civicyouth.org).

13. See Mary Fitzgerald, "Working Paper 01: Easier Voting Methods Boost Youth Turnout" (February 2003). CIRCLE Working Paper (www.civicyouth.org).

14. See page 207 of Peter Levine, *The Future of Democracy: Developing the Next Generation of American Citizens* (Lebanon, NH: University Press of New England, 2007).

15. Other cities and states that have considered lowering the voting age to 16 or 17 include Anchorage, Alaska; Cambridge, Massachusetts; Iowa City, Iowa; Texas; and Arizona. Currently, the organization Vote at 16 is working to lower the voting age to 16 in Florida.

16. See Susan Vermeer, "Voting Age," *Citizenship Education* (May 2004). Educational Commission of the States (www.ecs.org).

17. For a full discussion of the different ways voter turnout can be calculated, see "The Youth Voter 2004: With a Historical Look at Youth Voting Patterns 1972–2004." CIRCLE Working Paper 35. All voter turnout estimates presented in this chapter are calculated for U.S. citizens only, according to the "Census Citizen Method" described in Working Paper 35 (www.civicyouth.org).

18. According to a 2002 CIRCLE survey of 15- to 25-year-olds, 16 percent of young people ages 18–25 said they found it difficult to figure out how to register to vote, and 15 percent found it difficult to cast a vote. Although these proportions are small, they are substantial. Keep in mind that this survey was conducted before the recent surge in youth voter outreach.

19. See Karlo Barrios Marcelo, "Registration among Young People" (September 2007). CIRCLE Fact Sheet (www.civicyouth.org).

3

Women in Politics

From Fighting for Suffrage to Fighting for Votes

Kellyanne Conway

When future president of the United States John Adams was en route to the Continental Congress in Philadelphia in 1776, his wife, future First Lady Abigail Adams, implored him to "remember the ladies" when drafting documents that would codify the newly formed United States' recognition and protection of individual rights and liberties and determine the nation's form of governance. Abigail Adams was prophetic beyond the reach of her times. Then, women were 144 years away from securing the constitutional right to vote. In every presidential election since 1964, women have composed a majority of the U.S. population and a majority of the electorate, granting them the power to choose the nation's presidents and officeholders at every level of government.

Although the phrase "gender gap" may be overused and little understood by the media, it is true that such a divide exists in American politics. Traditionally, women tend to lean toward Democrats and are more in tune with social issues, whereas men are often more inclined to vote Republican and focus on fiscal concerns. There are three primary reasons for this divide between the sexes:

1. Men and women view the role of government differently. For women, the government plays the role of safety net and security blanket. Big Brother and Uncle Sam are generally welcome participants in their lives. One reason for this is that women outlive men by an average of 8 years, causing them to rely on the government for supplements or 100 percent of their subsistence for a larger proportion of their lives.
2. Men and women get their news and information from fundamentally different sources. Women are, by double digits, more likely than men to say they watch cable

television news channels such as CNN or MSNBC. Men, on the other hand, are significantly more apt to say they read a newspaper every day.

3. A "compassion gap" exists between the sexes. Women expect compassion in politics, not just budget figures, statistics, and arm's-length decisions. They agree with men in placing individual freedom and self-designation above reliance on government, but they are more favorable toward and more likely to rely upon government and its programs than are men. For many women, compassion is like the Supreme Court's obscenity test: it is difficult to define tangibly in politics, but women "know it when they see it."

With the desire of politicians and their strategists to "capture" the women's vote often comes the misconception that women constitute a single voting bloc. In reality, women vary in political dispositions and inclinations. Politicians tend to view women monolithically, often at their own peril. Women are a diverse segment demographically, psychographically, and behaviorally, and therefore politically. For example, a much more fascinating and telling component of modern American politics than the gender gap—that is, the differences between male and female political attitudes—is the "intra-gender gap" that persists among women when examined according to race, parental status, age, "stage," religiosity, and church attendance. The multiple combinations of these factors are what compel a woman to vote and decide how to vote. This is not to say that women ignore what groups, organizations, or political parties have to say; but for the "average" woman, there are several influencing factors that help determine who and what is worthy of receiving her attention, trust, and ultimately, her support at the ballot box.

Among the intra-gender differentiators is age. We know—thanks to the Census Bureau—that women routinely demonstrate higher voting rates than men. Consider the most recent example as indicative. In 2004 60.1 percent of women voted, compared with only 56.3 percent of men. What is more fascinating, however, are the turnout gaps between women and men across the age spectrum. Older women are much more likely than younger women to show up at the polls, but older men are more likely than older women to vote and younger women are more likely than younger men to vote. For example, 69 percent of women age 65 to 74 voted, compared with 45 percent of women age 18 to 24. But nearly 73 percent of men age 65 to 74 voted and only 39 percent of men age 18 to 24 came to the polls on Election Day.[1]

In 2004 36 million American women were not registered to vote (32 percent of the total female population), including 45 percent of women age 18 to 24. Although the number of unregistered 18- to 24-year-old females was high, the majority of 18- to 24-year-old males (51.8 percent) were not registered to vote in 2004. According to the Bureau's most recent data (2004), nearly half (47 percent) of women of all ages who were not registered to vote said that their decision was by choice, stating they are "not interested in the election or interested in politics." In 2004 the number 1 reason why registered women did not vote was "illness/disability" (19 percent), followed by "too busy/scheduling conflict" (17 percent) and "not interested" (10 percent).

The youngest women eligible to vote—18- to 29-year-olds—are a particularly fascinating study. In March 2007, on behalf of Lifetime television, The Polling Company, Inc., conducted a survey of Generation Y women (age 18 to 29) regarding their interest and engagement in politics. Key findings include the following:

- *60-second politics:* Fifty-four percent of women age 18 to 29 said that voting was the best way to make a difference in American politics, versus donating money or time, talking with friends and family about candidates and issues, or running for office themselves.
- *A polite "No, thank you":* Seventy percent said that they were "not at all likely" to run for public office themselves.
- *Entrepreneurial goals:* The majority would rather hold the corner office than the Oval Office, with "owner of my own company" coming in as the top aspiration of young women (47 percent). Winning a Nobel Prize (14 percent), being president of a major corporation (10 percent), being a celebrity (7 percent), and being president of the United States (4 percent) paled in comparison.

Another series of differences to consider is the gender gap across the races. In general, younger and middle-aged minority women are consistently more likely to be registered to vote and to actually vote than their male counterparts.

- In the 2004 election 67.9 percent of African American women were registered to vote, whereas only 60 percent of their male counterparts were. In 2004 a greater proportion of African American women than African American men voted (59.8 percent vs. 51.8 percent). Women made up the majority of 18- to 64-year-old African American voters, but a greater proportion of African American men over the age of 65 voted than did African American women in the same age group.
- Nearly equal percentages of Asian American women and men were registered in 2004 (34.9 percent and 35.0 percent, respectively) and voted in 2004 (30.5 percent and 29.0 percent, respectively). A greater proportion of Asian American women age 18 to 44 voted than did Asian American men, but the reverse was true after voters hit 45 years of age.
- A greater proportion of Hispanic women than Hispanic men were registered to vote (37.5 percent vs. 31.3 percent) and voted in 2004 (30.9 percent vs. 25.2 percent). Women were more likely than men to vote in each age category enumerated by the Census Bureau except for those 75 and older.

One must consider the differences among the racial and ethnic populations of this country when thinking about their voting behavior, because marriage, chil-

Table 3.1
Demographic Profile of Four Population Groups

	Whites	Blacks	Hispanics	Asians
U.S. population (in millions)	243.8	40.2	44.3	14.9
Median age	38.9	31.3	27.2	35.1
Median household income	$49,453	$30,939	$36,278	$60,367
Combined 2010 spending power (projected)	$10 trillion	$1.02 trillion	$1.09 trillion	$579 billion
Persons in poverty	10%	26%	22%	12%
Children in poverty	14%	36%	29%	13%
Age 25+ with college degree	29%	17%	12%	49%
Households with children	29%	35%	49%	39%
Households led by single women	10%	30%	19%	9%
Age 15+ and never married	25%	43%	35%	28%

Source: U.S. Census Bureau, 2005 American Community Survey (except for spending power projection).

dren, level of education, and income influence political beliefs. For example, African American households tend to be matriarchal, Hispanic households are generally the youngest and contain the most children, and Asian households stand out as the most educated (see Table 3.1).

Women are much steadier in their voting preferences with respect to political party than are men. On the national stage, women's shifts in party preference for U.S. Congress have been much more limited year to year compared with their male counterparts, and they have been very pro-incumbent with respect to the presidency.

As Table 3.2 demonstrates, in the last quarter century three out of four presidents—including both Republicans and Democrats—have increased their share of the women's vote from their initial run to reelection.[2] President George H. W. Bush stands as the exception; his portion of the women's vote dropped 13 points between his election in 1988 and his defeat at the hands of Bill Clinton in 1992. This election was unique, however, as it was a three-candidate race.

Thinking about the 2008 election and the women's vote leads many to ponder the role gender plays in women's voting behaviors because Senator Hillary Clinton was the first serious female candidate for the nomination on a major

Table 3.2
Percentage of the Women's Vote Garnered by Presidential Candidates

Year	Candidates	% Women's Vote	Change
1980	Ronald Reagan (R)	46%	
	Jimmy Carter (D)	45%	
1984	Ronald Reagan (R)	56%	+10
	Walter Mondale (D)	44%	
1988	George H. W. Bush (R)	50%	
	Michael Dukakis (D)	49%	
1992	George H. W. Bush (R)	37%	−13
	Bill Clinton (D)	45%	
	Ross Perot (I)	17%	
1996	Bob Dole (R)	38%	
	Bill Clinton (D)	54%	+9
2000	George W. Bush (R)	43%	
	Al Gore (D)	54%	
2004	George W. Bush (R)	48%	+5
	John Kerry (D)	51%	

party ticket. However, the question in 2008 is not about *a* woman; it's about *that* woman. The majority of women say that gender will not be the only factor they will consider in 2008. Consider the responses to a nationwide survey of 600 women registered to vote in August 2007:

In thinking about next year's presidential election, which of the following statements best describes your own position?

40%	I would vote for Hillary Clinton as the first woman president in 2008.
30%	I would vote for a woman for president in 2008, but not for Hillary Clinton.
16%	I would not vote for a woman for president in 2008 but might in the future.
7%	I would not vote for a woman for president at all.
6%	Do not know (volunteered).
1%	Refused (volunteered).

Although almost one-quarter of women voters have reservations about electing any woman president—either now (16 percent) or in the future (7 percent)—a full 30 percent are ready and willing. They simply haven't found a compelling female candidate to support.

BEYOND THE HORSE RACE NUMBERS: A STUDY IN CULTURE

To move women politically requires understanding them culturally. So beyond breaking the single class of women into demographic categories to analyze and predict their political inclinations and voting behaviors, one should consider how these demographic categories overlap and form multiple combinations. For example, one might think about *stage* instead of *age*. One concept is the "Three Faces of Eve." This notion explains how three different 48-year-old women, who most might lump together into one category based on age and gender, are in fact three drastically different women. Consider the unique characteristics of three average 48-year-old women in the United States: one woman is a blue-collar grandmother; one is a college-educated, never-married, childless, tireless executive; and one is a mother of a kindergartener and is pregnant with her second child.

These distinctions are a direct product of women exercising their myriad choices and engaging in various life stages—or forgoing them altogether—based on their individual blueprints for a life plan. The delay—or refusal—of many women to undertake marriage and motherhood has dramatically impacted U.S. commerce and culture, and the political system has been slow to recognize this. Here are some eye-popping facts about women and families:

- The average age of first-time marriage hovers around 26, up from 24.8 only 10 years ago, and the age of first birth has shot up from 21.4 in 1970 to 25 in 2000.[3,4]
- In 2007 women comprised 54 percent of the unmarried population.
- Twenty-three states and the District of Columbia now claim "majority unmarried" households.
- Of all households, 50.3 percent are now headed by single men or single women.
- Thirty-seven percent of children born in 2005 came into nonmarital households.

Despite these delays, women are no longer waiting for "me" to become "we" to enter the Ownership Society. Consider these facts about single women and their purchasing power:

- Single women make up one of the largest groups of first-time homebuyers. In 2006 single women constituted 22 percent of all homebuyers, whereas single men made up 9 percent. In 1995 those numbers were 14 percent and 9 percent, respectively. In fact, 17 million single women owned homes in 2006, a number that is expected to grow to 30 million by 2010.[5]

- Women purchase approximately 65 percent of all luxury goods.
- By 2004 women were already outspending men on technology: $55 billion versus $41 billion.

These facts about "Unmarried America" might lead one to ask, What does this have to do with politics? The simple answer: everything. First, unmarried voters make up a significant portion of the electorate. In 2004 36 percent of voters were unmarried. Single women represent 25 percent of the electorate, and turnout of these women has increased: fifty-two percent of single women voted in 1996 and 2000, and this number increased to 59 percent in 2004. Single African American women were the most likely to vote (61 percent), compared with 60 percent of single white women and 45 percent of single Hispanic women.

Home ownership and entry into the investor class means that more women are itemizing their tax returns and becoming more financially sensitive and sophisticated; hence, more of them claim to be offended by what they perceive as a tax-and-spend system that finances a nanny state and wastes and mismanages money.

Although marriage tends to be an indicator of likelihood to vote (71 percent of married women voted in 2004 compared with 59 percent of single women), political organizations are beginning to recognize the impact this often overlooked and untapped demographic could have on the nation's economy and political system. Women's Voices, Women's Vote (WVWV), a nonprofit group designed to "[improve] unmarried women's participation in the electorate," is one liberal organization seeking to capture these young women's votes. WVWV ran get-out-the-vote (GOTV) programs in thirty-two separate congressional districts and two states. The program reportedly made contact with more than 2.1 million single women by using 2.8 million mailers, 1 million automated phone calls, and 695,898 live phone calls.

Their efforts led to the registration of more than 100,000 people. The group's mixed media campaign "generated 100 million media impressions," with a total value of $3 million. In the twelve states in which WVWV worked, 25 percent of new registrants said that a mailer they received from WVWV compelled them to register, and 28 percent of the target audience could recall a message from the organization.

Of the thirty-two targeted districts, twenty-six had incumbent Republicans, two had incumbent Democrats, and four were open seats previously held by Republicans. After the election, half of the incumbent Republicans lost, the two incumbent Democrats retained their seats, and all four of the seats previously held by Republicans went to Democrats. Of course, these shifts in power cannot be wholly attributed to WVWV; voters were certainly influenced by the larger anti-Bush, anti-GOP, anti–Iraq War mood that gripped the nation. Still, the results are compelling.

HOW WOMEN OBTAIN THEIR POLITICAL CUES

Women's to-do lists rarely contain items such as "Check the Republican/ Democratic Party's Talking Points to Debate My Coworker" or "Make Sure My Friend Is Registered to Vote," because women are more likely to absorb politics rather than actively pursue it.

Women care about the issues at hand and have strong opinions about them when asked, but they are not taking their cues from the front pages of national newspapers, nightly newscasts, or their congressperson's home page; they subconsciously live aspects of the political system every day. They most certainly supplement their personal experience with knowledge from media sources, but rarely, if ever, rely on them to set their agendas.

THINKING THEMATICALLY

When women are asked to name the biggest problem facing the nation, they rarely say "abortion" or "the environment," as conventional wisdom might suggest. Rather, women report that the war in Iraq, national security and terrorism, healthcare, and kitchen table economics are some of their greatest concerns.

It frequently seems candidates think that female voters focus on the "S.H.E." cluster of issues (social security, healthcare, and education), while men vote based on the "W.E." issues (war and the economy). Although some polls might affirm this gravitation, the issues also can bleed together into several *themes*.

The S.H.E. issues perennially rank as the most pressing day-to-day concerns of women in America. One caveat, however, is that women do not always view these issues as *political* matters so much as *cultural* or *familial* ones. They do not automatically deem the political process an acceptable means or the government an effective steward by which to accomplish these ends, and they often resist allowing the ugliness of politics to seep into and infect such consequential, close-to-home matters.

In addition, the W.E. issues have dominated the American political lexicon for more than five years now, and are assigned primacy among woman as well as men. As such, many women voters may feel they *can't* decide their vote based on more personal concerns because politicians are not giving these issues their due or offering understandable, let alone viable, solutions.

A 2006 postelection survey conducted by the firm The Polling Company, Inc./WomanTrend found that the situation in Iraq was the most important issue to women in deciding how to vote, the answer provided by 22 percent of women, an increase from 16 percent in 2004. Equal percentages of men and women named Iraq as the most influential issue, but men were more likely than women to say that the War on Terror was the most important issue (21 percent vs. 15 percent).

In deciding on whom to vote for in the election today, which of the following issues was most important to you?

Actual Women Voters on Election Night

2006	2004	
22%	16%	The situation in Iraq
15%	23%	The War on Terror
11%	17%	Morality/family values
11%	16%	Jobs/the economy
6%	7%	Healthcare/Medicare/Rx drugs
5%	3%	Taxes
5%	n/a	Abortion
4%	n/a	Immigration
2%	2%	The environment

The Polling Company, Inc., Postelection survey of 800 actual voters, 11/7/06.

When reaching out to women voters, candidates and parties must not pigeonhole them as being concerned only about "women's issues" or assume they are not just as focused on the fiscal issues as on the social ones. Broad themes are often more appropriate in communicating with women, and the two that top the list are *security* and *affordability*. Taken together, these themes form the twin pillars of women's voting calculus. Women do not see matters of security and affordability as Republicans or Democrats; rather, they see the multiple facets of the two complex concepts as citizens, employees, wives, mothers, daughters, and/or grandmothers.

Security

In terms of security, Americans mention Iraq and terrorism as two of their top concerns when asked to name the most important issue facing the country. However, taking a step back, we can see that Iraq and terrorism are just narrow components of a broader concern about security.

Someone who says Iraq is his or her main issue often leans toward Democratic candidates, but those who name terrorism as their primary concern tend to vote Republican. As the two most recent elections have demonstrated, it will be important to focus the conversation on the broader theme of terrorism. Republicans were victorious when the discussion emphasized terrorism in 2004. However, when the debate turned to Iraq in 2006, Democrats capitalized on voters' perceptions of failure.

Healthcare security: Women tend to be the Chief Healthcare Officers for their families. From writing checks for medical bills, to picking up the prescriptions, to taking their children and aging parents to the doctor, women are involved in every step of their families' healthcare decisions and needs.

Social security: Although men and women may not think any differently about planning for retirement, the six-year difference in life expectancy causes women to think more about this issue.

Personal security: For the first time in decades, there has been a double-digit increase in concern about crime, particularly from suburban women who having to deal with bored kids experimenting with drugs and household substances. In addition the increased awareness of Internet predators has many mothers (and fathers) on edge because of their children's vulnerability.

When it comes to crime, the difference between men and women is striking. Whereas men prefer a punishment-based response to crime, women favor a prevention-oriented approach. Men would like to see stronger sentencing guidelines, reduced access to parole, and an overall strengthening of the system. Women, on the other hand, want to see the school bus stop 30 feet closer so they can see their children head safely off to school or want to see after-hours security instituted in the company parking garage.

Women may not see what is happening on the national level as a direct threat to their own individual sphere, and often adopt the very opposite perspective: women will translate a lack of personal security (be it physical or economic) to their national perspective or political radar. This is not to say that women do not see terrorism as a general threat, but they find the threat to "I" or "me" much more distressing.

Affordability

The economy is a macro-level concern, often parsed by the experts in terms of the unemployment rate, the gross domestic product, the budget deficit, and the trade balance. When discussed in these terms, many women voters—and even some women candidates—obliquely defer to men as more capable of "doing the math." We revert back to our stereotypes of men as superior at all things numerical and women as having an edge in communication and feelings.

Although women hold only 15.7 percent of the corporate-officer positions in Fortune 500 companies, they make or control the majority of household financial decisions. In fact, they make or influence 80 percent of all purchasing decisions and by 2010 are expected to control more than 60 percent of the country's wealth.

Kitchen table economics: For regular citizens, "the economy" refers to one's own wallet, healthcare and housing costs, taxes, tuition, and job security—the "kitchen table" issues that real people confront. Perhaps a more appropriate term—one more in touch with everyday Americans, and one that people are increasingly nervous about—is "affordability."

Women are the financial managers and planners for themselves and their families. They not only know about the economic pressures and concerns gracing the front pages of the *Wall Street Journal* and the *New York Times*, but they experience them every month as they try to balance the family checkbook while planning for future expenses.

Affordability touches on everything from healthcare and prescription drugs to school tuition to retirement and, most recently, to housing values/costs. Primary concerns include the following:

- Health and healthcare: *Will I be able to afford healthcare and prescription drugs for myself and my family? How will I be able to care for my parents in their old age?*
- Education: *Will I be able to afford to send my children to college? How about private schools or tutoring?*
- Retirement: *Will social security be solvent when I retire? Do I need to delay my retirement to save more money? How will I pay for healthcare?*
- Home ownership: *Is it within my means to buy a home? Will housing costs prevent me from living where I choose?*
- Entrepreneurship: *Can I afford to start my own business? If I quit my current job to start a business, will I be able to provide my family with healthcare and put food on the table?*
- Employment and job security: *How secure am I in my current job? Can I afford my current lifestyle on what I am making?*
- Taxes: *Do tax rates pose a financial hardship for my family? Will I have enough left of my paycheck after taxes to afford the necessities?*

One of the primary ways in which women have increased their role in both the economy and in the ownership society is in the entrepreneurship/small business arena. Whereas pursuing a successful career and raising a family were once thought to be mutually exclusive goals, women are increasingly taking control of the small business world, transforming their hobbies into marketable products and services. They are bucking the traditional workplace and its inflexible requirements to start their own companies, providing themselves with more control over their schedules and more flexibility with their time. Consider the following facts about women-owned small businesses:

- In 2007 women-owned businesses (firms with 50 percent or more woman ownership) totaled 10.4 million, accounting for 41 percent of all privately held U.S. businesses. These entities generated $1.9 trillion in annual sales and employed more than 12.8 million women.
- 81 percent of women-owned firms have one employee. Women business owners contribute more than $3.6 trillion to the marketplace each year, and women account for more than 70 percent of consumer spending.
- Nearly one-half (49 percent) of all women age 18 to 59 would prefer to start their own business, while 40 percent would opt to stay in their current jobs.

Appealing to these women politically is essential, as they are reliable voters. However, reaching out to women business owners also has a trickle-down effect in many communities across the country, as they tend to be the leaders of women's organizations, active in community and philanthropic organizations in their towns, and well-known and respected voices in the media.

- In 2004 small business owners (SBOs) helped keep Republicans in the majority, favoring them by 14 points over Democrats (53 percent vs. 39 percent). Women SBOs were even more supportive of the GOP (60 percent vs. 34 percent).
- By 2006 many SBOs had become disillusioned with Republicans, picking GOP House candidates over Democrats by a paltry 2-point margin (50 percent vs. 48 percent) and actually preferred Democrats over the GOP for the Senate (50 percent vs. 44 percent).
- Although more women SBOs voted for the GOP in 2006 compared with voters overall, they did so by half the margin of 2004 in the House (52 percent vs. 46 percent) and showed even greater support for Democrats in the Senate (44 percent vs. 49 percent).
- When starting their own business, many women elevate the importance of healthcare as they do access to capital, clients, and employees. In 2006 11 percent of female small business owners placed healthcare above other factors (5 percentage points more than women in general).

Morality and Family Values

In a 2004 postelection survey, 59 percent of women said that the issue of traditional marriage was important in deciding who to elect president, compared with 55 percent of men. Women were also more likely than men—regardless of who received their vote—to say that a candidate's faith mattered. A full 75 percent of women who voted for President Bush said that the president's faith was of "high importance," compared with 64 percent of men who voted to reelect Bush. Meanwhile, 26 percent of women who voted for Senator John Kerry (D-MA) said his religious beliefs were of "high importance," compared with 20 percent of men who voted for him.

Looking at Abortion

In a 2006 postelection survey of actual voters on Election Day, a paltry 5 percent selected abortion as the top concern in their voter calculus.

In an August 2007 nationwide survey for the Susan B. Anthony List, 600 female registered voters confirmed that although abortion is still important to many women, the majority of women are far more focused on other concerns.

Would you be likely or unlikely to vote for a candidate for president of the United States who did not share your view on abortion, but did share your view on other issues, like the war in Iraq or fiscal issues?

59%	**Total Likely (Net)**
25%	Very likely
34%	Somewhat likely
35%	**Total Unlikely (Net)**
14%	Somewhat unlikely

21%	Very unlikely
5%	Don't know (volunteered)
1%	Refused (volunteered)

"Choice" is an enshrined American value, so when people are asked the over-simplified question "Are you pro-life or pro-choice?" inflated numbers gravitate toward the feel-good phraseology of choice. Yet when presented with *six* different positions, a gradation of viewpoints—the majority of them pro-life—emerges. In fact, an eye-popping 75 percent of women oppose abortion beyond the first three months of pregnancy.

Which of the following statements most closely describes your own position on the issue of abortion? (Note: rotated top to bottom and bottom to top.)

51%	**Total Pro-life (Net)**
12%	Abortions should be prohibited in all circumstances.
13%	Abortion should be legal only to save the life of the mother.
26%	Abortions should only be legal in cases of rape or incest or to save the life of the mother.
41%	**Total Pro-choice (Net)**
24%	Abortions should be legal for any reason, but not after the first three months of pregnancy.
8%	Abortions should be legal for any reason, but not after the first six months of pregnancy.
9%	Abortions should be allowed at any time during a woman's pregnancy and for any reason.
7%	Don't know/ refused (volunteered).

TALKING TO WOMEN (RATHER THAN AT THEM)

By knowing who and what influences women's political behavior, politicians can easily "woo and win" women voters. Candidates' rhetoric, however, must be able to pass the "five-*S* test" with American women:

- *Simplicity:* Drowning women (or men) voters in statistics or overwhelming them with complicated details is perhaps the fastest way to lose their support. Their eyes glaze over and their ears go shut and they simply do not get what you have to say. When people don't understand, they often opt for "no."
- *Specifics:* Speaking in generalities or pabulum or pledging generic "reform" is easy and can smack of insincerity. It is the how, why, and when that will truly engage women. Actual facts and figures trump opinions, but anecdotes and real-life examples remain important.

- *Security:* Voters, especially women, want to know that they, their families, and their livelihoods are safe. How will a candidate's election affect their ability to protect their children, buy a home, put food on the table, or retire when they want to?
- *Solvency:* The first things women often ask when presented with a proposal for change is, "How will it affect me?" and "Who's going to pay for it?" No matter how great a plan seems, families struggling to meet their tax burden and their everyday expenses might have trouble getting on board.
- *Solutions:* Typical Washington- and media-speak leads with a problem and ignores possible answers. When a problem is solved, the media rarely update Americans on the progress. Voters prefer a politician with answers. Giving the voters a positive, concrete roadmap compels them to listen and makes them believe something is being done about the problem.

CONCLUSION

In the most recent elections, "soccer" moms and "security" moms have been two of the most sought-after demographics. Although these women will continue to be key and reliable constituencies, there are some emerging groups—unmarried women, minority and young women, and women small business owners—that will play a greater role in influencing the outcome of an election. Understanding the demographic and cultural changes among women is much more useful in predicting and understanding their political behavior.

Women—and men—tend to operate in a "Ctrl + Alt + Del" world, where tasks and duties are bifurcated into distinct categories (Figure 3.1).

Figure 3.1
Ctrl + Alt + Del: Three Categories of Tasks and Duties

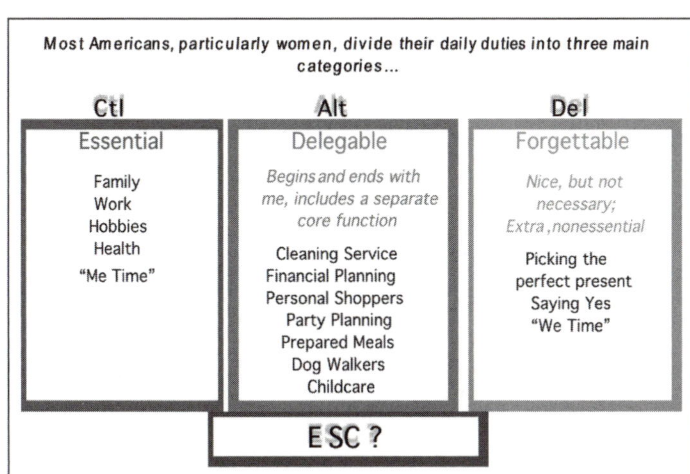

Understanding this system can aid a candidate's understanding of how to win and can increase an elected official's knowledge of how best to serve his or her constituents. But more important, understanding how politics does or does not fit into that scheme will lend the greatest insight into women voters and their ballot box decisions.

NOTES

1. U.S. Census Bureau.
2. Center for American Women and Politics, Eagleton Institute of Politics, Rutgers University, "The Gender Gap: Voting Choices in Presidential Elections."
3. U.S. Census Bureau.
4. Centers for Disease Control.
5. National Association of Realtors.

4

African Americans and the Right to Vote

A Look at the Voting Rights Act Then and Now

Marvin P. King, Jr.

Although a number of court cases challenged an unfair and undemocratic system, only the 1965 Voting Rights Act finally brought the full might of the federal government to the battle for equality in suffrage for American blacks. The Voting Rights Act of 1965 is responsible for a number of political changes throughout the United States, but especially in the South and especially for African Americans. African Americans now vote at a rate near that of whites, and the Act has allowed more African Americans to serve as elected public officials. Specifically, Section 2 and Section 5 greatly altered the political landscape for African Americans by requiring states to live up to the mandate of the Fifteenth Amendment and by allowing the federal government more power in ensuring that states did not stymie the voting rights of any citizens.

There are five distinct elements in understanding the relevance of the Voting Rights Act. First, it is necessary to consider African Americans and the vote prior to the Voting Rights Act of 1965. From the end of Reconstruction through 1965, large numbers of blacks throughout the South had little political voice. A combination of local and state laws and a federal government with a laissez-faire approach to voting rights allowed the political subjugation of American blacks. Resistance to change was at a level that is difficult for younger generations of Americans to appreciate.

Next is challenges to the denial of suffrage. Change did not come easily or quickly. Recalcitrant legislators in Congress and the states forced numerous court challenges preceding the Voting Rights Act. Because the Supreme Court often issues narrowly tailored decisions, activists challenging the status quo had to take the judicial route time and again.

Third is the Voting Rights Act. Only a book-length exposition on the subject can truly do the Act justice, but I briefly explain the most relevant criteria of the Act. These sections eliminate government-required impediments to the vote as well as rules that have the design of diluting the minority vote.

The next element is the effect of the Voting Rights Act on registration and voter turnout and on the number of blacks elected to public office. Finally, an examination of the myriad controversies and challenges to the Voting Rights Act is necessary to fully understand the issue. Key points include descriptive versus substantive representation and designing legislative districts in a manner that does not dilute voting strength of minority groups and does not use race as the sole criteria.

AFRICAN AMERICANS AND THE VOTE PRIOR TO THE VOTING RIGHTS ACT OF 1965

As originally written the U.S. Constitution is somewhat vague concerning the right to vote. Article II gives states the right to appoint electors who select the president and vice president. Because Article 1, Section 10 of the Constitution does not prohibit states from controlling voting, and the Tenth Amendment reserves to the states powers not delegated to the federal government, voting and all that it entails is generally the purview of the states.

Granting this traditional activity to the states has not been without consequence. Following the Civil War, the former Confederate states passed numerous Black Codes. The intent of these codes was to limit freedom of movement and restrict entry of blacks into the political arena. The North, led by the Radical Republicans, countered, requiring that to gain re-admittance into the Union, the Southern states must ratify the Fourteenth Amendment, which was adopted in 1868. Besides overturning *Dred Scott* (1857) by granting blacks American citizenship, Section 2 of the Fourteenth Amendment provides a mechanism for punishing obstructionist states by potentially reducing congressional representation for abridging the vote of eligible voting-age males.

In 1870 the country ratified the Fifteenth Amendment, which simply reads:

> Section 1: The right of citizens of the United States to vote shall not be denied or abridged by the United States or any State on account of race, color, or previous condition of servitude.
> Section 2: The Congress shall have power to enforce this article by appropriate legislation.

The purpose of the Fifteenth Amendment could not be clearer. The Union did not want individual states denying suffrage to former male slaves and black citizens. Section 2 is critical because it provides the grant of authority for congressional action to implement Section 1 of the Fifteenth Amendment. During Reconstruction, blacks voted and even elected their own to state legislatures and Congress. Hiram Revels (R-MS) even served in the U.S. Senate from 1870 to 1871. Nonetheless, at the close of Reconstruction the North began to tire of the animus race caused in the country. Congress looked the other way as the whites-only Southern Democratic Party reasserted its dominance over the Republican Party and its supporters, especially blacks. This dominance came in the combined form of Jim Crow laws and laws designed to deny blacks their Fifteenth Amendment rights. After Reconstruction, whites completely shut blacks out of the Southern political system. Despite pockets of progressivism, this system essentially lasted until the 1960s.

Even though whites dominated the Southern political system, the Fifteenth Amendment required Southern political elites, Bourbon Democrats, to resort to subterfuge and establish a variety of mechanisms in the late 1800s and early 1900s to prevent and dissuade blacks from voting. Although the details differed from state to state and even county to county, throughout the South this period saw a combination of poll taxes, literacy tests, grandfather clauses, white primaries, gerrymandering, and the disfranchisement of felons. Many previously elected positions became appointed. This allowed political elites to consolidate their power. Some of these "reforms" had the effect of reducing the number of white voters. Limiting the reach of the franchise certainly had the imprimatur of Southern elites because it ensnared almost all blacks and some poor whites. Yet to stanch the effect of limiting too many whites from voting, many states and localities enacted literacy tests with understanding clauses. Provided a white voter, even an illiterate one, could *understand* the relevant clause, he could vote. Local or county officials administered these tests, and they alone determined the sufficient level of understanding.[1]

Article 12 of the 1890 Mississippi Constitution required voters (1) to pay a poll tax, (2) to read and decipher a portion of the state constitution, and, failing that, to understand it if read to them, and (3) to prove that their antecedents could vote. In addition, Article 12 disbarred from voting those convicted of bribery, burglary, theft, arson, obtaining money or goods under false pretenses, perjury, forgery, embezzlement, or bigamy.[2] This one article of the Mississippi Constitution managed to combine a poll tax, a literacy test, a grandfather clause, and felon disfranchisement. When these provisions were challenged in *Williams v. Mississippi* (1898), the Supreme Court held, as written by Justice Joseph McKenna, that although Mississippi was "refrained by the federal constitution from discriminating against the negro race, the convention discriminates against its characteristics."[3] In other words, Mississippi's constitution did not discriminate based on race. Blacks could not vote only because—in the eyes of the framers of the Mississippi Constitution—they suffered disproportionately from poverty, illiteracy, poor choice of antecedents, and a criminal nature.

Future Mississippi governor James Kimble Vardaman's proud assertion "There is no use to equivocate or lie about the matter. Mississippi's constitutional convention was held for no other purpose than to eliminate the nigger from politics; not the ignorant—but the nigger" did not persuade the Supreme Court to rule contrariwise.[4]

PRE–VOTING RIGHTS ACT CHALLENGES TO THE DENIAL OF SUFFRAGE

Achieving real change at the legislative level via state legislatures and Congress was often hopelessly beyond reason; therefore, most precursors to the 1965 Voting Rights Act took place at the judicial level. For instance, in *Guinn v. United States* (1915) the Supreme Court held that the Fifteenth Amendment was violated by voter registration requirements containing "grandfather clauses" that made voter registration in part dependent upon whether the applicant was descended from men enfranchised before enactment of the Fifteenth Amendment.[5] This case developed in Oklahoma, and at first results were fleeting. Oklahoma simply passed a new statute giving African Americans twelve days in which to register or avoid permanent disenfranchisement. This provision was not overturned for another twenty-three years. Therefore, even after *Guinn*, Oklahoma effectively disfranchised another generation of black Oklahomans.[6]

The white primary was very effective at providing a semblance of political participation while simultaneously denying blacks the ability to have a meaningful voice in the political process. Because the South was a one-party polity dominated by the Democratic Party, its primaries were the only elections of significance for much of the area. The Supreme Court validated use of the white primary in *Newberry v. United States* (1921) by ruling that political parties were private organizations and not part of the government election apparatus.[7] *Newberry* was made possible by the earlier landmark decision in *The Civil Rights Cases* (1883) in which the Supreme Court held that the Fourteenth Amendment's Equal Protection Clause prohibited only government discrimination, and not individual discrimination.[8] If the Supreme Court had considered political parties in *Newberry* an official arm of the government, it would have triggered judicial review under the Fourteenth Amendment's Equal Protection Clause. Not until *Smith v. Allwright* (1944) did the Supreme Court rule that although the Democratic Party was a voluntary organization, because Texas statutes governed the selection of county-level party leaders and the Party conducted its primary elections under state statutory authority, and state courts were given exclusive original jurisdiction over contested elections, parties were "organs of the state."[9] As with *Guinn*, Texas Democrats attempted to circumvent the Supreme Court's wishes. This time Texas Democrats tried an end around with respect to *Allwright* by holding "preprimary" elections to select candidates for the Democratic primaries. The "preprimary" was held unconstitutional in 1953.[10]

In 1957 President Dwight Eisenhower signed into law the Civil Rights Act of 1957. Its goal was to increase voter turnout among African Americans, especially in the South, where local registrars continued to deny a large number of blacks their suffrage. Although it was the first civil rights legislation to pass since Reconstruction, —despite South Carolina Senator Strom Thurmond's record 24-hour, 18-minute filibuster—Southern Democratic senators gutted the bill considerably. Judiciary Committee Chairman James O. Eastland of Mississippi led the Southern effort to weaken the legislation. Not only did Southern Democrats reduce funds available to prosecute alleged civil rights violations, but they also gutted the Act by allowing persons charged with civil right violations to receive a jury trial instead of a trial by a federal judge. All-white juries in the South ensured that punishment would be nonexistent or weak. Nonetheless, the Act created a Civil Rights Division within the Justice Department, although it received minimal funding. The 1960 Civil Rights Act, also signed into law by Eisenhower, provided for federal inspection of local voter registration polls and established penalties for obstructing anyone's attempt to register to vote or for obstructing anyone's actual vote.

The 1964 Civil Rights Act attempted to tackle voting and housing discrimination, but resistance, again led by Southern Democrats, forced the bill's backers to strip meaningful provisions regarding voting and housing from the Act. Title 1 barred unequal application of voter registration, but the Act provided no enforcement mechanism.

Despite the efforts of the Civil Rights Acts of 1957, 1960, and 1964, registration and voting by blacks in the South barely changed. Black registration in Mississippi went from 5 percent in 1956 to 7 percent in 1964. Comparable figures for Alabama were 11 percent and 20 percent; for Georgia, 27 percent and 27 percent; and for Louisiana, 31 percent and 32 percent.[11]

LEGAL REQUIREMENTS OF THE VOTING RIGHTS ACT

The civil rights movement was the ultimate impetus for passing the 1965 Voting Rights Act. Despite passage of the Twenty-fourth Amendment in 1964, which outlawed poll taxes, voting rates by blacks still greatly lagged those by whites. A peaceful procession of demonstrators in Selma, Alabama, on March 7, 1965, turned particularly brutal when law enforcement beat and teargassed the marchers. This helped to finally set the stage for broad, sweeping reform that would come as close as constitutionally possible to guaranteeing the right to vote. President Lyndon B. Johnson signed the Voting Rights Act into law on

August 5, 1965, and Congress passed the Act pursuant to its authority found in Section 2 of the Fifteenth Amendment. The Voting Rights Act addresses two primary concerns: disfranchisement and vote dilution.

Section 2 of the Voting Rights Act of 1965 prohibits voting practices or procedures that discriminate on the basis of race, color, or membership in one of the language groups identified in Section 49(f)(2).[12] This section covers the entire nation, and it does not confine itself to certain jurisdictions, as do other sections of the Act. This section has no expiration date, unlike certain other provisions of the Act.

Section 3 of the Act strengthened the ability of the federal government, through the attorney general, to use federal courts to enforce the voting guarantees of the Fifteenth Amendment. Federal courts could now authorize "the appointment of federal examiners and observers, suspend the use of tests and devices, or require preclearance in any jurisdiction in the United States—regardless of whether or not the jurisdiction was covered by the 'triggering' formula of special provisions (found in Section 4 of the Act)."[13]

Section 4 of the Act originally covered local jurisdictions if "the jurisdiction maintained on November 1, 1964, any test or device as a precondition for voting or registering, and less than 50 percent of its total voting-age population were registered on November 1, 1964, or voted in the presidential election of 1964."[14] This provision lasted for five years, but reauthorization in 1970 and 1975 amendments changed the dates.[15] Tests included literacy tests; protections for language minorities were later included.[16] Since its inception, Section 4 covers Alabama, Georgia, Louisiana, Mississippi, South Carolina, and Virginia; Alaska, Arizona, and Texas have been covered since 1975. Parts of California, Florida, Michigan, New Hampshire, New York, and South Dakota are covered too. This is the "trigger" section of the legislation because it is nondiscretionary in its applicability. If a jurisdiction meets the conditions of Section 4, it is automatically covered. Section 4(a) allows covered jurisdictions to petition the U.S. District Court for the District of Columbia to be exempt from special coverage, provided the jurisdiction can prove that it has not used discriminatory devices for five years.

Section 5 of the Act concerns vote dilution, and it is a temporary measure, requiring reauthorization. This section requires preclearance from either the federal Justice Department or the U.S. District Court for the District of Columbia of any changes to local voting laws. It was important to Congress that decisions to change voting procedures in a covered jurisdiction not be made locally "because past experience indicated that local officials and district courts in the South frequently hindered efforts to ensure blacks' voting rights."[17] As later adjudicated, the point of Section 5 is to prevent "retrogression."[18] This means that any change to a jurisdiction's voting laws—whether as minor as polling place relocation or as major as decennial redistricting—must not make the voting environment for minorities worse than it was before the change. The governmental body is responsible for proving that the change does not have a retrogressive "purpose." In other words, the state cannot dilute minority voting strength.

Section 6 of the Act allows the federal Civil Service Commission to appoint examiners where the attorney general deems it necessary. Examiners determine if a voting applicant is eligible to vote. If an applicant is deemed eligible to vote, the examiner will place him on a list of eligible voters. Section 8 allows for federal election observers. The Civil Service Commission appoints these observers, essentially poll watchers, to make sure that all persons voting are eligible and to ensure the accurate counting of ballots.

Finally, Section 10 directs the attorney general to sue states that retain the poll tax. Supporters of the Voting Rights Act were unsure of the constitutionality of banning state poll taxes. To ensure that the entire Act was not declared unconstitutional, Congress directed the attorney general to test the constitutionality of the poll tax rather than ban the practice outright.[19] Writing for an 8-1 majority in *South Carolina v. Katzenbach* (1966), Chief Justice Earl Warren made the following remarks:

> Congress had found that case-by-case litigation was inadequate to combat widespread and persistent discrimination in voting, because of the inordinate amount of time and energy required to overcome the obstructionist tactics invariably encountered in these lawsuits. After enduring nearly a century of systematic resistance to the 15th Amendment, Congress might well decide to shift the advantage of time and inertia from the perpetrators of the evil to its victims.[20]

In other words, only sweeping congressional legislation could effectively combat discrimination in voting. Case-by-case litigation was too slow and too expensive, and it did not carry the gravitas of legislation.

EFFECT OF THE VOTING RIGHTS ACT ON REGISTRATION AND VOTE TURNOUT

The Voting Rights Act had an immediate impact on voter registration among African Americans. In Dallas County, Alabama, home of the Selma protests, voter registration had increased from 383 to 8,000 by November 1965.[21] In Mississippi between 1964 and 1976, "black voter registration increased from 29,000 to 286,000, an 886.2 percent increase."[22] By 1972 282,337 additional blacks had registered in Georgia, and 197,320 more blacks had registered in Alabama.[23] As presented in Table 4.1, the gap in black registration and white registration in six southern states decreased considerably between pre–Voting

Table 4.1
Differences in Black Registration and White Registration over Time

		Alabama	Georgia	Louisiana	Mississippi	North Carolina	South Carolina	Virginia
1965	Black	19.3	27.4	31.6	6.7	46.8	37.3	38.3
	White	69.2	62.6	80.5	69.9	96.8	75.7	61.1
	Gap	49.9	35.2	48.9	63.2	50.0	38.4	22.8
1967	Black	51.6	52.6	58.9	59.8	51.3	51.2	55.6
	White	89.6	80.3	93.1	91.5	83.0	81.7	63.4
	Gap	38.0	27.7	34.2	31.7	31.7	30.5	7.8
1970	Black	69.7	58.3	59.7	75.5	53.6	58.6	58.7
	White	82.5	70.0	75.0	78.9	66.3	60.2	63.3
	Gap	12.8	11.7	15.3	3.4	12.7	1.6	4.6
1980	Black	62.2	59.8	69.0	72.2	49.9	61.4	49.7
	White	73.3	67.0	74.5	85.2	63.7	57.2	65.4
	Gap	11.1	7.2	5.5	13.0	13.8	−4.2	15.7
1988	Black	68.4	56.8	77.1	74.2	58.2	56.7	63.8
	White	75.0	63.9	75.1	80.5	65.6	61.8	68.5
	Gap	6.6	7.1	−2.0	6.3	7.4	5.1	4.7

Cell entries are percent registered. Adapted from Bernard Grofman, Lisa Handley, and Richard Niemi, *Minority Representation and the Quest for Voting Equality* (Cambridge: Cambridge University Press, 1992), Tables 1 and 2.

Rights Act time and 1988. By 1988, a full political generation later, black registration and white registration was nearly even.

Research indicates that once we account for differences in education and income, differences in black registration and white registration are statistically insignificant.[24] Nationally, overall voter turnout in presidential elections declined slightly between 1964 and 1968, but turnout in Alabama, Georgia, Louisiana, Mississippi, North Carolina, South Carolina, and Virginia increased by an average of 8 percent. First-time black voters drove this increase.[25]

EFFECT OF THE VOTING RIGHTS ACT ON NUMBER OF BLACKS ELECTED TO PUBLIC OFFICE

The effect of the Voting Rights Act on the number of black elected officials is similarly impressive. Nationally, in 1970 there were 1,469 black elected officials, 169 were in state legislatures, and 623 occupied municipal offices. By 1980 nationally

Table 4.2
Blacks Elected to State Legislative Seats in Six Southern States, as of November 15, 1974

	Percentage of State Legislative Seats Held by Blacks	Black Percentage of the Population (1970)
Alabama	10.6	26.3
Georgia	9.3	25.9
Louisiana	6.3	29.8
Mississippi	0.6	36.8
North Carolina	3.5	22.2
South Carolina	7.6	30.7
Virginia	1.4	18.5

there were 4,912 black elected officials, 323 in state legislatures and statewide offices and 2,356 in municipal offices. By 1990 there were 7,370 black elected officials, 423 elected to state legislatures and statewide offices and 3,671 elected to municipal offices. By 2000 nationally there were 9,040 black elected officials, 598 elected to state legislatures and statewide offices and 4,465 elected to municipal offices.

Table 4.2 shows the percentage of state legislative seats held by blacks in six Southern states compared with the black percentage of the population in each of those states in 1970. Although some states—such as Alabama—made significant progress in just ten years, states such as Mississippi and Virginia continue to lag even their Southern peers in electing African Americans to their state legislatures. By 2001, however, Mississippi, the state with the largest black proportion of the population—over one-third—showed considerable progress and led the nation, with 892 black elected officials. Alabama was second, with 756 black elected officials, and Louisiana was third, with 705 black elected officials.[26]

Table 4.3 shows the number of blacks elected to Congress since the Voting Rights Act. The effects were not as immediate as with voter turnout because of incumbency. Additionally, it is not immediately clear how states should tackle the process of redrawing legislative lines in a nondiscriminatory manner while factoring in the new "one person, one vote" mandate.[27] Seven years after the Voting Rights Act, Barbara Jordan of Texas and Andrew Young of Georgia became the first African Americans elected to Congress from the South since 1901.

CONTROVERSIES AND CHALLENGES TO THE VOTING RIGHTS ACT

Not all states welcomed the Voting Rights Act. In 1966 the Mississippi legislature passed legislation allowing at-large districts instead of single-member districts for county supervisor elections. Clearly, the intent was to dilute the

Table 4.3
Blacks Elected to Congress

Congress	Year	Blacks in U.S. House	Blacks in U.S. Senate
87th	1961–1963	4	0
88th	1963–1965	5	0
89th	1965–1967	6	0
90th	1967–1969	5	1
91st	1969–1971	10	1
92nd	1971–1973	13	1
93rd	1973–1975	16	1
94th	1975–1977	17	1
96th	1979–1981	17	0
97th	1981–1983	19	0
98th	1983–1985	21	0
100th	1987–1989	23	0
101st	1989–1991	24	0
102nd	1991–1993	27	0
103rd	1993–1995	39	1
107th	2001–2003	39	0
108th	2003–2005	37	0
109th	2005–2007	42	1
110th	2007–2009	42	1

Adapted from Mildred L. Amer, *Black Members of the United States Congress: 1789–2001* (CRS Report for Congress).

potential for successful black candidates as well as minimize black political influence at the local level, although there is no mention of race in the legislative record. This particular scheme did not last long; the Supreme Court held that Section 5 governed this type of legislation.[28] Nonetheless, thirteen Mississippi counties still held at-large county supervisor elections in 1971. On the heels of the at-large changes, Mississippi attempted to switch to an open primary system, but Justice Department objections prevented its implementation.

VOTE DILUTION

Besides legislative obstinacy, a theoretical and pragmatic debate between descriptive and substantive representation has enveloped the application of the Voting Rights Act. Descriptive representation occurs when people elect their legislators based on physical, demographic-type characteristics, most often conceptualized in terms of race. Proponents of descriptive representation argue that only legislators sharing certain defining characteristics can have true empathy with their constituents.[29] As a result, they will be more likely to devote their time and resources to problems neglected by previous legislators, who do not share these characteristics. The benefits are twofold. Claudine Gay reports that blacks in districts with a black legislator are more likely to approach their legislator for help.[30] Jane Mansbridge suggests that because of uncrystallized interests people turn to descriptive indicators as a signal of quality representation.[31]

Nonetheless, some scholars take the counter-argument, in favor of substantive representation. Proponents of this position contend that quality representation occurs when a representative has similar ideology and policy goals as his or her constituents.[32] Supporters of substantive representation believe it should not and does not matter if certain descriptive characteristics are in alignment.

The debate leaves the theoretical and enters the pragmatic when the issue of racially polarized voting is addressed. This occurs when an overwhelming majority of one racial group votes counter to a large majority of another racial group. Today blacks and whites often vote in a racially polarized manner, especially in the South, where whites are largely Republican.[33] How courts treat descriptive versus substantive representation directly relates to how they view claims of vote dilution. If courts sympathize with the idea of descriptive representation, vote dilution (i.e., redistricting cases) will proceed in a manner conducive to the creation of majority-minority legislative districts, as opposed to districts where minorities will merely have "influence."

The first case addressing these issues was *United Jewish Organizations v. Carey* (1977). In *UJO* plaintiffs argued that New York's redistricting plans—done in accord with Section 5 of the VRA—diluted the voting strength of the Hasidic Jewish vote even though the plan devised by the state preserved the white-black balance in the state assembly. Plaintiffs claimed that the state assigned voters to voting districts solely by racial standards because the state redrew certain districts in Manhattan and the Bronx to create a majority-minority district and in the process divided the Hasidic Jewish community. The court held that there was nothing in the Constitution prohibiting the use of race in preserving nonwhite electoral majorities.[34]

As another way of looking at Section 5, take Hypothetical City, with 10,000 voting-age eligible residents and 100 percent turnout in an at-large election. Seventy percent of its residents are white and 30 percent are black. If the black residents vote for Candidate X and the white residents support Candidate Y, the white-supported candidate will win every election. Assume a large majority of the black residents vote for the Democratic candidate, as often happens with blacks in the South. It is quite possible that the quality of their representation will be minimal. Thirty percent of the population will be without substantive representation. Take this same scenario and multiply it by the number of council or commissioner seats in the local jurisdiction and you have the scenario the Supreme Court faced in *City of Mobile v. Bolden* (1980). Justice Potter Stewart, writing for a disjointed plurality, ruled in Mobile's favor because the government did not maintain the practice with racially discriminatory *intent*,[35] and "only if there is purposeful discrimination can there be a violation of the Equal Protection Clause of the Fourteenth Amendment."[36] The 1982 reauthorization of the Voting Rights Act overturns *City of Mobile* by requiring only discriminatory *effect*, not discriminatory *intent*, to win a lawsuit under Section 2.

The 1982 reauthorization is important because it signaled a shift in the focus of the Voting Rights Act. In 1965, when it was enacted, the primary purpose of the Act was to register as many blacks as possible and get them to become active in the political process. By 1982, the registration of black voters having largely been accomplished, efforts shifted to combating vote dilution. In essence, the focus went from Section 4, used to register black voters in the South, to Section 5, used to combat vote dilution.

Thornburgh v. Gingles (1986) attempted to make headway in this debate. Black residents in North Carolina used Section 2 of the Voting Rights Act to claim that North Carolina's redistricting plan regarding the state legislature diluted minority voting strength both by needlessly packing minority voters into one district and by thinly spreading the remaining blacks across multiple districts where they could not constitute a voting majority. The Supreme Court agreed with the plaintiffs. Justice Brennan put forth a three-pronged test for vote dilution: (1) The minority must be large enough and compact enough to compose a majority in a single-member district. (2) The minority group must be politically cohesive. (3) The white majority must be cohesive enough to defeat, usually, the minority's preferred candidate.[37] The point of emphasis is that racial bloc voting is the most important criterion in establishing a vote dilution claim.

In another vote dilution case in North Carolina, *Shaw v. Reno* (1993), the Supreme Court rejected drawing congressional lines strictly based on race because drawing these lines constitutes government efforts to separate voters into different districts based on race. Because Section 5 of the VRA covers forty North Carolina counties, North Carolina was required to submit its 1990 decennial congressional redistricting plan to the United States attorney general. The Justice Department rejected the plan because it provided just one black-majority district even though blacks represented 20 percent of North Carolina's voting-age population. Upon revision, the state designed two districts that would be majority black. One of these looked like a "bug splattered on a windshield."[38] For long stretches, District 12 was no wider than I-85. Justice O'Connor, writing for a 5-4 majority, opined that in instances where *only* race can explain the shape of a district, courts should hold such maps to an exacting standard of strict scrutiny.

Using the precedent set in *Shaw v. Reno*, Justice Kennedy, writing for a 5-4 majority in *Miller v. Johnson* (1995), said that Georgia's efforts at adding a new black-majority congressional seat was racial gerrymandering and a violation of the Fourteenth Amendment's Equal Protection Clause. Race cannot be the "predominant factor" in drawing district lines.[39] Similarly, in *Shaw v. Hunt* (1996), the Supreme Court said North Carolina did not narrowly tailor its plans to serve a compelling state interest justifying racially gerrymandered districts.[40]

In *Bush v. Vera* (1996), Texas added three new congressional seats following reapportionment in 1990. One district was majority Hispanic and two districts were majority black. African American voters claimed that race had been but one factor of many in drawing the district lines; just as important were concerns of partisanship and incumbency protection. Additionally, the districts were much more compact and contiguous than the North Carolina districts that were at the heart of *Shaw v. Reno* (1993). Nonetheless, the effect, supported by then Governor George Bush, was to increase Republican opportunities in adjacent districts that underwent bleaching. Justice O'Connor found that race subsumed the interests of partisan politics and incumbency protection and that political identity should not be racial.[41]

Reno v. Bossier Parish School Board (2000) limited the reach of Section 5 by ruling that a jurisdiction can violate Section 2, and the Department of Justice can preclear it provided the violation does not impair the minority community's ability to elect their preferred candidate. The Bossier Parish School Board had never had a black member on its twelve-member board despite a black district population of 20 percent. Board members conceded that the district boundaries were designed in a manner consistent with perpetuating the status quo. Justice Scalia, writing for a 5-4 Court, allowed it because "in vote dilution cases [Section 5] prevents nothing but backsliding, and preclearance under [Section 5] affirms nothing but the absence of backsliding." In other words, the Justice Department cannot fix past wrongs, only new wrongs.[42] The descriptive versus substantive representation debate came nearly full circle when black legislators in Georgia supported a plan in *Georgia v. Ashcroft* (2003) in which mapmakers drew minority voters out of majority-minority districts and into districts of "influence."[43]

VOTER IDENTIFICATION

In January 2008 the Supreme Court will hear an appeal of Indiana's voter identification law.[44] In 2006 Indiana, like twenty other states, passed legislation requiring voters to bring photo identification with them to the polls. The question at issue is whether the interests of the state in preventing voter fraud outweigh the additional burden placed on voters. Proponents of the law argue that it is nondiscriminatory and only prevents voter fraud. Opponents claim its real purpose is to dissuade the poor and ethnic minorities from voting while also diminishing turnout among the elderly and disabled, all of whom are less likely to carry driver's licenses or other approved forms of voter identification. An estimated 13 million to 22 million Americans of voting age do not have driver's licenses, passports, or other official forms of government-approved photo identification.[45] Opponents of the law point out that there is little actual evidence of people committing voter fraud by impersonating a voter. In fact, no one in the history of Indiana has ever been charged with impersonating a voter.

The voter identification cases illustrate an important partisan dynamic in the evolving debate on voting in America. Republicans in Indiana's and Georgia's state legislatures champion the voting ID statutes, and judicial appointees—primarily Republicans—have approved their use. In contrast Democrats in the legislature and on the bench oppose their use. Judge Posner, a Republican appointee writing for a two-to-one panel majority of the U.S. Court of Appeals for the Seventh Circuit, acknowledged the Democratic Party's standing in the case, arguing that most people without photo identification are "low on the economic ladder and thus, if they do vote, are more likely to vote for Democratic than Republican candidates." In dissent, Judge Terrance, a Democratic appointee, wrote, "Let's not beat around the bush: The Indiana voter photo ID law is a not-too-thinly-veiled attempt to discourage Election Day turnout by certain folks believed to skew Democratic." Adding to the controversy is the fact that although twenty states have similar statutes, the Missouri Supreme Court recently struck down that state's law requiring photo identification for voters.[46]

CONCLUSION

In 2006 the United States Congress renewed the 1965 Voting Rights Act for an additional twenty-five years. The Senate passed the measure, renamed the Fannie Lou Hamer, Rosa Parks, and Coretta Scott King Voting Rights Reauthorization and Amendments Act of 2006, 98-0. Conservatives sought amendments to Section 2, claiming the Voting Rights Act still unfairly singles out some states, such as Georgia, even though black Georgians now register and vote in numbers on par with whites. Another amendment sought to limit the time horizon of the Voting Rights Act to ten years instead of twenty-five. Overwhelming bipartisan majorities defeated these amendments.

NOTES

1. V.O. Key Jr., *Southern Politics in State and Nation* (New York: Knopf, 1949).
2. 1890 Constitution of Mississippi.
3. *Williams v. State of Mississippi*, 170 U.S. 213 (1898).

4. Jerrold M. Packard, *American Nightmare: The History of Jim Crow* (New York: St. Martin's Press, 2003), 69.

5. *Guinn v. United States*, 238 U.S. 347 (1915).

6. *Lane v. Wilson*, 307 U.S. 268 (1939).

7. *Newberry v. United States*, 256 U.S. 232 (1921).

8. *Civil Rights Cases*, 109 U.S. 3 (1883).

9. *Smith v. Allwright*, 321 U.S. 649 (1944).

10. *Terry v. Adams*, 345 U.S. 461 (1953).

11. Ronald Walters, "Political Participation: A Study of the Participation by Negroes in the Electoral and Political Processes in 10 Southern States since the Passage of the Voting Rights Act of 1965," in *Freedom Is Not Enough: Black Voters, Black Candidates, and American Presidential Politics* (New York: Rowman and Littlefield, 2005).

12. The Voting Rights Act of 1965, 79 Stat. 437 (1965), 42 U.S.C.

13. Bernard Grofman, Lisa Handley, and Richard Niemi, *Minority Representation and the Quest for Voting Equality* (Cambridge: Cambridge University Press, 1992).

14. The National Commission on the Voting Rights Act, *Protecting Minority Voters: The Voting Rights Act at Work 1982–2005* (Washington, DC: Lawyers' Committee for Civil Rights Under Law, 2006).

15. The 1970 reauthorization used 1968 instead of 1965, and the 1975 reauthorization used 1972 instead of 1968. The 1970 reauthorization also limited residency requirements to no more than thirty days.

16. Including a provision to eliminate literacy tests was critical to overturning the Supreme Court decision in *Lassiter v. Northampton County Board of Elections*, 360 U.S. 45 (1959), in which it ruled that North Carolina's literacy tests for voting did not violate the Fourteenth or Fifteenth Amendment.

17. Handley et al., *Minority Representation and the Quest for Voting Equality*.

18. *Beer v. United States*, 425 U.S. 130 (1976). While *Beer* establishes the principle of "retrogression," it is still a defeat for voting rights because it preserves the status quo by prohibiting only changes that make things worse.

19. The resulting court case was *South Carolina v. Katzenbach*, 383 U.S. 301, 327–328 (1966). This case upheld the constitutionality of the Act, particularly the ability to suspend literacy tests and the preclearance provisions found in Section 5. Also, see *Harper v. Virginia State Board of Elections*, 383 U.S. 663 (1966), where the Supreme Court ruled Virginia's use of the poll tax an infringement of the Fourteenth Amendment.

20. *South Carolina v. Katzenbach*, 383 U.S. 301, 327–328 (1966).

21. http://www.votingrights.org/timeline/?year=1951

22. Don Edwards, "The Voting Rights Act of 1965, as Amended," in *The Voting Rights Act: Consequences and Implications*, edited by Lorn S. Foster (New York: Praeger, 1985).

23. *The Voting Rights Act: Ten Years After*, United States Commission on Civil Rights, January 1975.

24. Jan E. Leighley and Arnold Vedlitz, "Race, Ethnicity, and Political Participation: Competing Models and Contrasting Explanations," *Journal of Politics* 61 (1999):1092–1114; Peter Wielhower, "Releasing the Fetters: Parties and the Mobilization of the African American Electorate," *Journal of Politics* 62 (2000):206–222.

25. Handley et al., *Minority Representation and the Quest for Voting Equality.*

26. David A. Bositis, *Black Elected Officials: A Statistical Summary* (Washington, DC: Joint Center for Political and Economic Studies, 2000). As a side note, Hawaii, Montana, North Dakota, and South Dakota were the only states with no black elected officials in 2001.

27. A critical but tangential case to racial redistricting occurred in 1962. In *Baker v. Carr,* 369 U.S. 186 (1962), the Supreme Court ruled that malapportionment was an issue on which courts no longer had to defer to state legislatures. *Reynolds v. Sims,* 377 U.S. 533 (1964), and *Wesberry v. Sanders,* 376 U.S. 1 (1964), pick up on this theme and end malapportionment at the state and congressional levels, respectively. In *Reynolds,* the court develops the "one man, one vote" standard. Also, see *Gray v. Sanders,* 372 U.S. 368 (1963), in which the Supreme Court invalidated Georgia's "county unit" system of voting.

28. *Allen v. State Board of Elections,* 393 U.S. 544 (1969).

29. Jane Mansbridge, "Should Blacks Represent Blacks and Women Represent Women? A Contingent 'Yes'," *Journal of Politics* 61 (1999):628–657. Also, see David T. Canon, *Race, Redistricting, and Representation: The Unintended Consequences of Black Majority Districts* (Chicago: University of Chicago Press, 1999).

30. Claudine Gay, "Spirals of Trust? The Effect of Descriptive Representation on the Relationship between Citizens and Their Government," *American Journal of Political Science* 46 (2002):717–732.

31. Mansbridge, "Should Blacks Represent Blacks."

32. Charles Cameron, David Epstein, and Sharyn O'Halloran, "Do Majority-Minority Districts Maximize Substantive Black Representation in Congress?" *American Political Science Review* 90 (1996):794–812; David Lublin, "The Election of African-Americans and Latinos to the U.S. House of Representatives," *American Politics Quarterly* 25 (1997):269–286; David Lublin, *The Paradox of Representation: Racial Gerrymandering and Minority Interests in Congress* (Princeton, NJ: Princeton University Press, 1997); David Lublin, "Racial Redistricting and African-American Representation: A Critique of 'Do Majority-Minority Districts Maximize Substantive Black Representation in Congress?'" *American Political Science Review* 93 (1999):183–186; Rodney E. Hero and Caroline J. Tolbert, "Latinos and Substantive Representation in the U.S. House of Representatives: Direct, Indirect, or Nonexistent?" *American Journal of Political Science* 39 (1995):640–652.

33. It is not, however, just during recent history that this has occurred. During Reconstruction, when blacks briefly enjoyed political rights prior to Jim Crow, blacks overwhelmingly identified as Republican while Southern whites engaged the political system as Democrats.

34. *United Jewish Organizations of Williamsburgh, Inc., et al. v. Carey,* 430 U.S. 144 (1977).

35. *City of Mobile v. Bolden,* 446 U.S. 55 (1980).

36. Handley et al., *Minority Representation and the Quest for Voting Equality,* 35.

37. *Thornburgh v. Gingles,* 478 U.S. 30 (1986), pg 50–51.

38. *Wall Street Journal,* February 4, 1992, p. A14.

39. *Miller v. Johnson,* 515 U.S. 900 (1995).

40. *Shaw v. Hunt*, 517 U.S. 899 (1996).

41. *Bush v. Vera et al.*, 517 U.S. 952 (1996). In a disjointed decision, Justice Sandra Day O'Connor wrote the majority opinion and a concurrence, to go along with concurrences by Justices Kennedy and Thomas and dissents by Justices Stevens and Souter.

42. *Reno v. Bossier Parish School Board*, 528 U.S. 320 (2000).

43. *Georgia v. Ashcroft*, 539 U.S. 461 (2003).

44. *Crawford v. Marion County Election Board*, No. 07-21 and *Indiana Democratic Party v. Rokita*, No. 07-25.

45. Adam Liptak, "Fear but Few Facts in Debate on Voter I.D.'s," *New York Times*, September 24, 2007, http://www.nytimes.com/2007/09/24/us/24bar.html.

46. *Jackson County, Missouri, et al. v. State of Missouri, Dale Morris and Senator Delbert Scott* (2006) and *Kathleen Weinschenk, et al. v. State of Missouri, Robin Carnahan, Secretary of State, Dale Morris and Senator Delbert Scott* (2006).

5

Registering to Vote and Getting Your Vote Counted

Captain Samuel F. Wright

In all but a handful of states, it is necessary to register to vote *before* casting a ballot. If you are not registered, and if the voter registration deadline has passed, you will not be able to vote. The deadline varies, but it is usually about four weeks before the election.

North Dakota does not have and has never had voter registration. It is a largely rural state—they pretty much know who everyone is and who is eligible to vote, and they don't need voter registration. Wisconsin, Minnesota, and a few other states require voter registration but have made provisions allowing an unregistered person to register and then vote on Election Day. In all the other states, you will not be able to vote if the day of the election has arrived and you are not registered.

In election administration and in drafting election laws, the constant battle, over many decades, has been between those (generally Democrats) who stress the need to make voting as easy and convenient as possible and those (generally Republicans) who stress the need to build in safeguards to prevent cheating and voting by persons who are not eligible (those who are not United States citizens, who are not at least 18 years of age, or who have already voted in the election).

Everyone recalls the thirty-five days of uncertainty regarding the outcome of the 2000 presidential election in Florida. In the final count, just 537 votes separated George W. Bush from Al Gore. To paraphrase Winston Churchill, "Never in the course of political elections has so much been decided for so many by so few."

Republicans and Democrats enacted the Help America Vote Act (HAVA) of 2002, in a rare display of bipartisanship in our nation's capital. There is a new paradigm and a new mantra: "Let's make it easier to vote and harder to cheat." With the use of modern technology, safeguards to ensure the integrity of the outcome need not increase the inconvenience to the individual voter.

But there is still the problem of identifying eligible voters. It must be known that the person presenting himself or herself to vote on Election Day, or applying for an absentee ballot in advance of the election, is in fact the individual that he or she claims to be. And it must be confirmed that the person meets the requirements for voting: legal age, United States citizenship, residence in the jurisdiction, and so on.

Someday, perhaps during the lifetime of the next generation if not this one, there will be a national all-purpose identification card, including biometric identifiers (fingerprint, retina scan, etc.). Such a card could be used to identify those persons who are eligible to vote, as well as those permitted to drive motor vehicles, enter commercial airliners, and practice other restricted activities. Until that day, a system of voter registration is required, except in rural areas where the population is small and population turnover is low.

The United States is a very mobile society. The Census Bureau reports that more than 40 million Americans move each year. A voter registration system requires constant maintenance to keep track of registered voters moving, as well as dying or becoming ineligible for other reasons (felony conviction, judicial declaration of mental incompetence, etc.).

In all states that require voter registration, the burden is on the individual registered voter to notify the voter registrar when he or she moves, whether across the street or across the nation. Such notification does not need to be difficult or inconvenient.

Once a person moves, there is a limited time within which he or she can return to the old precinct to vote. For example, in Virginia one can lawfully return to the old precinct to vote in the November general election that follows the move, and in any intervening election, such as a primary or special election. (Virginia holds an election every November, because its state elections fall in odd-numbered years.) Other states have even shorter deadlines—such as within 30 days after the move. In planning for and making a move, updating one's voter registration should be near the top of the checklist of notifications.

Despite common assumptions, it is not necessary to wait before registering to vote in a new county or state; a person can register to vote on the very day of arrival—for *all* offices, not just federal offices, if registration occurs before the deadline. Some state constitutions still require that an individual live in the county for at least six months and in the state for at least a year before registering, but the United States Supreme Court struck down all such durational residence requirements thirty-five years ago. (See *Dunn v. Blumstein,* 405 U.S. 330 (1972).)

ABSENTEE VOTING AND EARLY VOTING

In absentee voting, like voter registration, there is some unavoidable tension between voter convenience and ballot integrity. Absentee voting by mail is the aspect of election administration that is the most susceptible to cheating. Because the applicant for an absentee ballot does not appear in person before an election official, it is inherently more difficult to prevent impostor voting (voting with a fictitious name or in the name of another person, living or dead).

Members of the United States Armed Forces and their families generally must vote by absentee ballot, if they are to vote at all. Because of their service to our country, they cannot return to their home precincts to vote in person on Election Day. Similarly, persons who are confined to hospitals, nursing homes, or their own residences because of serious illness or disability will find it most difficult, if not impossible, to get to their precinct polling places on Election Day. There is general consensus that eligible voters who find it difficult or impossible to vote in person on Election Day should be given the opportunity to vote by absentee ballot, even if that accommodation necessarily detracts somewhat from confidence in the integrity of the election outcome.

In recent years, California, Texas, and several other states have instituted eligibility to vote by absentee ballot. In those states, it is no longer necessary for the voter to offer a reason or justification for voting by absentee ballot. Anyone who is registered and eligible to vote and who wishes to vote by absentee ballot is permitted to do so in those states.

California is famous (or infamous) for its long ballots, including many complicated propositions. Truly conscientious voters in a long-ballot state might prefer to vote by absentee ballot. In this way, they can spend all of Sunday afternoon reading the pro and con literature on each proposition, and for and against each candidate, before marking their ballots, without keeping their neighbors waiting at the precinct polling place.

Most states still limit absentee voting to certain classes of registered voters who can demonstrate a "need" to vote by absentee ballot. Depending on the state law, absentee voting may be limited to military and overseas voters, voters who state an expectation of being out-of-town on Election Day, and persons who find it difficult or impossible to get to the precinct polling place because of advanced age, illness, or disability. In recent years, state legislatures have broadened some of the categories of persons permitted to vote by absentee ballot, thus reducing the distinction between "closed" absentee voting states (like Virginia) and "open" states (like California).

There is one big downside to absentee voting by mail: there will always be a nontrivial percentage of eligible voters who will be disenfranchised in a system that relies upon the United States Postal Service (USPS). Absentee voting by mail involves three steps that are time consuming and that offer significant opportunities for disenfranchisement. First, the absentee ballot *request* must travel from the voter to the election official. Second, the *unmarked* absentee ballot must travel from the election official to the voter. Finally, the *marked* ballot must travel from the voter back to the election official. At each step, the application or the ballot can be lost or delayed, through no fault of the voter.

In military and civilian absentee voting from outside the country, the disenfranchisement rate exceeds 50 percent in some places. Even if the individual is voting by mail from a nursing home in the county where he or she has lived for the last eight decades, there is a nontrivial possibility (perhaps greater than 1 percent) that the ballot or the application will be lost and the voter thereby disenfranchised. In an exceedingly close election, like the 2000 presidential election, even the rare inadvertent disenfranchisement of an eligible voter could affect the outcome.

Most states make a distinction between early voting and absentee voting. In early voting, the voter goes to the county courthouse or some other location where early voting is being conducted and votes in person, a few days or weeks before Election Day. In absentee voting, the voter requests an absentee ballot by mail, receives the unmarked ballot by mail, and returns the marked ballot by mail.

There are several advantages to early voting, in states where it is available and for voters for whom this is a viable option. (Of course, Sgt. Jones, serving in Iraq, cannot come home to vote at the county courthouse three weeks before Election Day any more than she can come home on Election Day to vote at her precinct polling place.) In early voting, there is no risk to ballot integrity because the voter is presenting himself or herself to an election official, in person. In fact, there are probably better safeguards for early voting than for voting on Election Day. The election officials are generally better trained and less rushed. On Election Day, necessary safeguards are sometimes given short shrift because hundreds of other voters are waiting in line. In early voting, there are likely to be short lines or no lines at all. And in early voting, it is not necessary to entrust one's application and one's ballot to the USPS.

If absentee voting by mail is necessary, it is important to start the process, by submitting the absentee ballot application, as early as possible. Time must be allowed for the absentee ballot application to get to the election official, for the unmarked ballot to get to the voter, and for the voter's marked ballot to get back to the election official by the deadline. In most states, the deadline for the *receipt* (not the postmark) of a mailed absentee ballot is the close of the polls on Election Day. About fifteen states have extended that deadline to a few days after Election Day, but the ballots arriving after Election Day are generally counted only if they are from military or civilian voters *outside the United States.*

PROVISIONAL VOTING

An individual voting in person on Election Day must do so at the polling place for the specific precinct where he or she resides and is registered to vote. A voter who arrives at the polling place and is told by the clerk that the voter's name does not appear on the poll list should ask, "Am I at the correct polling place?" In urban areas, precincts are small and polling places may be only a few blocks apart. Remember that the polling place that is closest to home is not always the polling place for one's home precinct.

Voters who are certain that they are at the right place, and yet are told that election officials still cannot find their names on the list, are entitled by federal law to cast a *provisional ballot.* This is a separate paper ballot that is marked and to which the voter attaches a statement (under oath) explaining the circumstances. Within a few days after Election Day, the election official is required to investigate and to count the provisional ballot if the investigation establishes the voter's eligibility. Casting a provisional ballot is *not* a waste of time; the election official is required to count the vote, assuming eligibility, even if the election is not close. And there have been several cases of congressional elections and other important contests remaining in doubt for a few days after Election Day as election officials reviewed and counted the provisional ballots.

There is considerable variation among the states as to the circumstances under which a provisional ballot will be counted. Suppose that on Tuesday, November 4, 2008 (Election Day), a voter is away from his home in Arlington, Virginia, on personal business; the voter is in Norfolk (200 miles away), and the polls will close in just one hour. The voter cannot possibly get to his Arlington polling place in just one hour, but he can get to a polling place in Norfolk. He wants to cast a provisional ballot at the Norfolk polling place, and he wants his ballot to be counted for the statewide offices that are common between his home precinct and the Norfolk precinct where he actually voted. Virginia does not count provisional ballots cast under these conditions, but some states do.

6

The Disenfranchisement of Felons

Alec C. Ewald

The United States is unique among democracies in that one cannot fully understand its elections without knowing a bit about its criminal justice system. The U.S. incarcerates a much larger portion of its population than does any of its peers—in fact, six or seven times as many as most other industrialized democracies. Meanwhile, almost everywhere in the United States, people in prison temporarily lose the right to vote—and in most states people on probation or parole do so as well. In a small but notable number of states, some people who have finished their sentences entirely still cannot vote. The United States appears to be the only country in the world that disenfranchises a significant number of people who are not incarcerated. All told, almost 5 million Americans lack the right to vote because of a felony conviction. The majority of these people are no longer incarcerated, and over a million have completed their sentences entirely.[1]

Criminal disenfranchisement—or "felony disenfranchisement," since felony conviction is the most common cutoff—brings together a potent blend of questions related to law, history, political philosophy, race, and voting behavior. In the last ten years academics, advocates, legislators, and the media have brought new scrutiny to laws barring people convicted of crime from voting, making this one of the central disputes in U.S. voting rights today. American suffrage offers a long catalog of voting restrictions: in different states at different times, students, soldiers, women, men without sufficient property, blacks, Asians, Mormons, native peoples, Catholics, Jews, and those who couldn't pass literacy tests have been barred from the polls. Felony disenfranchisement is the last standing restriction on the voting rights of adult U.S. citizens, and there is increasing evidence that it has helped decide some close elections in recent decades. Indeed, scholars and advocates are only now grasping just how deep the effects of these laws go. For example, our most basic political measurements, such as voter turnout figures, now need correction because the voting-age population on which those figures are based includes so many people who are actually *ineligible* to vote.[2]

Like many areas of U.S. election law, disenfranchisement law varies from one state to the next. In two states, Maine and Vermont, felons retain the right to vote even while incarcerated. About one-fifth of the states disqualify only those currently serving time in prison. In most states, people in prison as well as those sentenced to probation or on parole following release from prison, cannot vote—but everyone who has completed their sentence may vote. And in eleven states, at least some people are disqualified from voting indefinitely, even after all aspects of their sentences have been discharged.[3]

Because disenfranchisement laws are found in state constitutions and suffrage statutes instead of the penal code, the loss of the vote is legally not part of an offender's sentence: it is a "collateral consequence" of conviction. Indeed, U.S. courts have disagreed over whether disenfranchisement is properly understood as a punishment or as "a nonpenal exercise of the power to regulate the franchise," as the Supreme Court has described the policy. However, historical and contemporary sources strongly suggest that American disenfranchisement laws were designed with punitive purposes, from the colonial period through the nineteenth century and into the present.[4]

The 1970s and 1980s saw significant litigation challenging state disenfranchisement laws. As explained below, the Supreme Court ruled in each decade on the constitutionality of laws barring people with criminal convictions from voting—and did so in ways that continue to shape the debate over the issue. The most recent legal campaign challenging disenfranchisement began in the early 1990s, with a prominent law review article and a lawsuit charging that New York's disenfranchisement law violates the Voting Rights Act. A landmark report published by Human Rights Watch and the Sentencing Project in 1998 familiarized many political observers with the topic for the first time, but it was not until the presidential election of 2000 that felony disenfranchisement truly moved to center stage in American politics.

Two different aspects of Florida's disenfranchisement policy came to light after that election. First was Florida's botched attempt to clean up counties' voter rolls, removing from the lists those who had died, moved away, or been convicted of a felony. State and county election officials, together with a private company hired to help out, failed to communicate about the need to double-check a draft list, and purged everyone on it—and in the process, any number of live, local, non-felonious citizens lost the right to vote.[5]

But there is a far more profound way disenfranchisement helped determine the 2000 election. While only 537 votes decided the presidential election in Florida, about half a million *non*-incarcerated Floridians—one thousand times the margin by which then-Governor George Bush won the state—were prohibited from voting because of a felony conviction, owing to the indefinite post-sentence disenfranchisement law then in effect.[6]

If those figures are not startling enough, studies also suggest that almost one-third of black men in Florida were disqualified from voting. Indeed, the policy's remarkable impact on African Americans—who are disqualified at a rate about seven times that of whites—is an important reason why it has drawn so much critical attention. Of course, electoral institutions in the United States have a deep and clear history of racial discrimination, and the apparent disproportion in disenfranchisement's effect on communities of color has become one of the policy's most contentious attributes.

HISTORY

Laws barring people convicted of a crime from political activity have deep roots in European history and political thought. Ancient Greeks and Romans prevented "infamous" criminals from speaking in assemblies, and medieval Europeans developed the concepts of "civil death" and "outlawry," by which convicted criminals lost all the protections of the law.

Colonial America adopted the idea that some offenders should be excluded from politics. The Plymouth Colony refused to admit as a freeman "any opposer of the good and wholsome laws of this colonie," and one could lose freeman status by behavior that was "grossly scandalouse, or notoriously vitious." Fearing that "some corrupt members may creep into the best and purest societies," Plymouth in 1651 provided that any person judged to be "grossly scandalouse as lyers drunkards Swearers & C. shall lose theire freedome of this Corporation." In Massachusetts Bay Colony, disenfranchisement was authorized as an additional penalty for conviction of fornication or any "shamefull and vitious crime." Further south, Maryland declared that a third conviction for drunkenness incurred loss of suffrage.[7]

Barring offenders from voting has a long history in America, but there are important differences between colonial and contemporary policies. In colonial times, removal of criminals from the suffrage had a visible, public dimension, since the penalty was imposed at sentencing. Its moral purposes were explained in the law, and the sanction usually applied only to egregious violations of the moral code. Modern disenfranchisement laws—automatic, invisible in the criminal justice process, considered "collateral" rather than explicitly punitive, and applied to broad categories of crimes with little or no common character—lack these characteristics.

Of course, early U.S. state laws barred most adults from voting, and many states explicitly excluded people convicted of a crime, either by constitutional provision or by statute. Between 1776 and 1821 eleven state constitutions disqualified criminals from voting; by 1868 eighteen more states excluded serious offenders from the franchise. However, one historian has concluded that these prohibitions were laxly enforced in the nineteenth century.[8]

The next major development in the history of American criminal disenfranchisement took place in the post–Civil War South. After Reconstruction, some Southern lawmakers openly employed disenfranchisement law exactly as they had used the literacy test and the poll tax: as a policy neutral on its face, but with the intent and effect of barring blacks, but not whites, from the polls. Previously, most U.S. states stripped ballot rights from anyone convicted of a crime punishable by incarceration in the penitentiary. But in their search for facially neutral ways to remove blacks from the rolls, several Southern states actually *narrowed* their criminal disenfranchisement provisions to target not all crimes, but the petty property infractions for which blacks were most often convicted.

In 1896 the Mississippi Supreme Court articulated the discriminatory nature of these policies. The 1890 state constitution, the court observed, "swept the circle of expedients to obstruct the exercise of the franchise by the negro race." That race was composed of "a patient, docile people, but careless, landless, and migratory within narrow limits, without forethought, and *its criminal members given rather to furtive offenses than to the robust crimes of the whites.*" Those "furtive offenses"—including burglary, theft, and obtaining money under false pretenses—were now grounds for disqualification, while "robust crimes" such as robbery and murder were not.[9]

CONSTITUTIONAL AND LEGAL ISSUES

A 1973 challenge to the constitutionality of California's disenfranchisement law initially met with success in that state's supreme court. In the United States, any law restricting a fundamental right fails unless it can meet what is called the "compelling state interest" test. When a court applies that test, the challenged law is presumed to be unconstitutional, and the government can defend the challenged restriction only if it can show that the restriction is *necessary* to achieving some specific, vital public objective. Ideas alone will not suffice; the state must show that it has some extremely important practical objective it is pursuing, and that only the challenged policy will achieve that objective. California argued it needed to disenfranchise convicts in order to prevent voter fraud; the state's supreme court agreed that preventing fraud was an important objective, but noted that other means are available to achieve that goal and struck down the law.[10]

The state appealed to the U.S. Supreme Court. And with its 1974 decision in the *Richardson* case, the Supreme Court placed an almost insurmountable obstacle in front of contemporary court challenges to disenfranchisement. Plucking a phrase from a long-slumbering and outdated section of the Fourteenth Amendment, the Court found explicit constitutional approval for state laws barring people convicted of a crime from voting. Although legal scholars have documented serious problems with the Court's reasoning in *Richardson*, the grounds it chose means that almost all state laws barring offenders from voting are constitutional.[11]

There is one important exception, however. A decade after *Richardson*, the U.S. Supreme Court struck down the egregiously racist state laws described above. In the 1985 *Hunter* case, the Court held that where they were enacted with clear discriminatory intent, laws barring convicts from voting violate the Equal Protection Clause of the Fourteenth Amendment. *Hunter* involved the permanent disenfranchisement of two Alabama men convicted of writing bad checks. The state considered that to be a crime of "moral turpitude," and thus subject to loss of voting rights under Section 182 of the Alabama Constitution of 1901. The Supreme Court threw out the "moral turpitude" clause, which it found was intentionally adopted to disenfranchise blacks, would not have been included without that discriminatory purpose, and had achieved its intended effect.[12]

Although *Hunter* did invalidate part of Alabama's disenfranchisement law, on the whole the ruling may actually have strengthened the policy against constitutional challenges. The *Hunter* Court explicitly declined to reconsider *Richardson*, and by striking down *only* that narrow portion of Alabama law that it could trace to explicit racist intent, the Court allowed more broadly written provisions to stand—despite evidence that the sanction continues to have a disproportionate impact on blacks in many states.

Those effects are at the heart of contemporary legal challenges to felony disenfranchisement in the United States. Even as the Supreme Court handed down its *Richardson* decision, state and federal laws were in place that punished those convicted merely of drug possession much more severely, and studies consistently show that the results have hit black and Latino Americans at levels out of proportion to actual drug use in those communities. Indeed, one scholar concludes that "[t]aken together, the drug war and felony disenfranchisement have done more to turn away black voters than anything since the poll tax."[13]

Most legal critics of disenfranchisement agree, and they focus their attention on the nexus of discriminatory criminal justice laws and voting rules. In the United States, a policy or practice that deprives a person of voting rights "on account of race" violates the federal Voting Rights Act (VRA). Challenges brought in courts across the country have tried, so far unsuccessfully, to convince federal judges that felony disenfranchisement is such a policy. Though one federal court did observe sympathetically that disenfranchisement has "the effect of shifting racial inequality from the surrounding social circumstances into the political process," courts have to date been reluctant to bring felony disenfranchisement fully under the reach of the VRA.[14]

POLICY ARGUMENTS

Racial history and contemporary effects aside, there are two primary arguments for disqualifying people convicted of a crime from voting. The first is *punitive*. As one prominent defender of the policy writes, "[N]ot allowing criminals to vote is one form of punishment." And a Massachusetts state legislator declared that the loss of the vote "is part of the penalty—you are in jail, you don't pass go, you don't collect the $200, you don't vote until you get out."[15]

There is also a *political* case for disenfranchisement. This logic says that disenfranchisement is intended not to achieve any punitive goals, but to protect what is sometimes called "the purity of the ballot box" from the pollution of those unfit to participate. Drawing on another strand of American political thought, the political argument sometimes invokes the "social contract," claiming that those who break the rules should not get to help make the rules. From this perspective, the primary objective of such policy is to keep U.S, political life healthy, not punish wrongdoers.

Critics attack both grounds for the policy. Any form of punishment must achieve one of four objectives: incapacitation, deterrence, rehabilitation, or retribution. Incapacitation justifies policies disqualifying those who commit election fraud from voting, but not blanket laws. Deterrence is a weak claim: it is hard to imagine that someone not deterred from crime by a long prison sentence would stay his hand for fear of losing the vote. The objective of rehabilitation would seem to argue against policies that further alienate the offender from civil society. And although it is tempting to use retributive aims as an easy catch-all, Americans have always insisted on a measure of proportionality between infraction and penalty, and it is not clear that automatic, blanket disenfranchisement fits.

Responses to the political arguments for disenfranchisement emphasize that Americans no longer tolerate restrictive policies based on such gauzy abstractions as the "purity of the ballot box" and the "social contract." After all, the "purity" objective was long associated with racial limitations on suffrage; later, "purity" arguments targeted voter fraud, which is now criminalized by a variety of state and federal laws. The idea of a "social contract," meanwhile, originally helped restrict political participation only to those who owned property and could write. (It is, after all, a business metaphor.)

To put a sharper point on it, Americans across the political spectrum today believe that a property-less, illiterate, non-taxpaying person has the right to vote. This statement would have been utter gibberish to those who developed the idea of the "contract," because our deep belief in equality has led us to leave behind most of the political ideas of the men who developed the social contract concept almost four centuries ago.

Public opinion data suggest that proponents of disenfranchisement still have the upper hand, at least when it comes to disenfranchising people still under sentence. But critics of disenfranchisement seem to be making headway, given the amount of change state laws have seen in recent years. Since 1997 sixteen states have implemented policy reforms making their disenfranchisement laws less exclusionary.[16]

IMPACT ON ELECTIONS

One fascinating aspect of criminal disenfranchisement is its effect on the partisan landscape. At first blush, re-enfranchisement seems likely to help Democrats, given that offenders share many of the socioeconomic characteristics of Democratic voters and that left-leaning interest groups have led the recent wave of reform. Indeed, sociologists Chris Uggen and Jeff Manza have concluded that increasingly restrictive laws implemented in the last thirty years have helped Republicans win several close elections—including not only the 2000 presidential election, but prior contests that determined partisan control of the U.S. Senate. Certainly, the media accepts the premise that rights restoration will help Democrats, some even referring to the policy as their "secret weapon."[17]

Yet many Republicans appear to believe that the issue is a political winner for them, precisely *because* they share the belief that former inmates are likely Democratic voters. Criticizing a post-sentence restoration bill, one politician said, "As frank as I can be, we're opposed to it because felons don't tend to vote Republican."[18] For this speaker, linking felons with Democrats in the public mind benefits Republicans. When a judge temporarily suspended Alabama's disenfranchisement laws and it appeared that inmates might be allowed to vote, the state's Republican Party chair said, "If the public sees voting machines being rolled behind the walls of Alabama's prisons, the Democrats will see some serious repercussions at the ballot box."[19] Some Republicans seem to have concluded that talking about voting by offenders is a good way to burnish their "tough on crime" credentials, and that raising the specter of pro-Democratic votes by offenders may help motivate their own supporters to go to the polls.

CONCLUSION

Contemporary research and public advocacy on American felony disenfranchisement now focuses on the big picture and the small. The big picture concerns international context, and the fact that so many other democracies allow most or all *inmates* to vote. For decades, a deep skepticism toward laws restricting fundamental individual rights—speech, property, voting, religious exercise—has been a proud intellectual and political export of the United States. But whereas dozens of democracies insist that prisoners retain the right to vote, most American states continue to bar from the franchise even some people living in the community on probation or parole. Most U.S. courts are quite unlikely to be influenced by such comparative facts, but some advocates believe legislators and the public may be willing to reexamine the issue once they learn how unusual American policies are.[20]

At the same time, many reform advocates are now working at the micro level, trying to untangle what voting rights historian Morgan Kousser calls "the bureaucracy of disfranchisement": the web of disqualifications, restoration procedures, waiting periods, and documentary requirements that often confuse even the state and local election officials directly responsible for enforcing them. Advocates, corrections, and election officials in a number of states are now working together to clarify existing policies and to help former inmates navigate them. This is particularly important given evidence that many election officials do not know even basic aspects of voter eligibility laws in this area and may well be enforcing them in exclusionary ways.[21]

Criminal disenfranchisement occupies an uncertain place in American election law today. First, it fits only awkwardly in contemporary American political thought. To be sure, it is consistent with a variety of other popular measures stigmatizing offenders and justified by "tough on crime" rhetoric. And as noted above, it can claim a deep pedigree in Western thought. But in terms of voting rights now, criminal disenfranchisement stands alone. Unlike other controversial measures, such as whether voters should be required to present photo identification or what balloting technology should be used, felony disenfranchisement formally and totally bars a person from the polls. Yet this restriction has been exempted from the kind of rigorous scrutiny the Fourteenth Amendment and Voting Rights Act together bring—again, unlike virtually every other rule, procedure, or practice related to voting in the United States today. Today, when Americans examine restrictive policies—regarding property, speech, guns, religion, or voting—we emphasize the standards and terms of individual rights. And most Americans understand that key rights can only be denied when a real and pressing danger to society exists, and only when a specific, necessary purpose is achieved by doing so. Mere ideas are not enough: we must know what concrete purposes can be achieved only through the exclusion. And although there are certainly strong *theoretical* premises supporting disenfranchisement, there is no clear *practical* objective that only this policy can achieve.

Perhaps because it stands outside core doctrines protecting voting rights, even some of our wisest legal minds fall into surprisingly sloppy logic when analyzing the issue. For example, in a recent book federal judge and law professor Richard

A. Posner swings back and forth on core questions raised by criminal disenfranchisement. Posner calls the idea that disenfranchisement is a deterrent "ludicrous," notes that "felons have interests like everybody else," and mocks the idea that felons can be denied the vote because they are "bad people." But Posner then blithely endorses the "bad people" argument in advocating a five-year post-sentence waiting period, and argues that allowing inmates to vote would be "inimical to prison discipline." Judge Posner does not offer empirical support for this claim, and there is none: where inmates of jails and prisons vote in the United States and elsewhere, prison discipline is unaffected. On no other voting rights issue could a sitting federal judge meander back and forth on key questions—and ultimately rest a complete deprivation of rights on a hunch, unsupported by evidence.[22]

Yet Judge Posner's approach to the issue is not unusual, and his reasoning captures the puzzle of American criminal disenfranchisement law today. As Posner tacitly acknowledges, the policy is incompatible with our fundamental view that elections must express the interests of all citizens, and its connections to punitive purposes are shaky at best. But Judge Posner, like most Americans today, seems to conclude that people convicted of a crime have sacrificed their status as full citizens, and that preventing them from voting is therefore unobjectionable.

NOTES

1. The United States incarcerates about 700 people per 100,000 population. The corresponding figure for the UK is 139, for Canada 116, for Germany 91, and for Japan 53. For incarceration rates, see the International Centre for Prison Studies, online at www.prisonstudies.org. For the most current data on felony disenfranchisement, see the online resources of the Sentencing Project, at www.sentencingproject.org.

2. On voter turnout studies, see Michael P. McDonald and Samuel L. Popkin, "The Myth of the Vanishing Voter," *American Political Science Review* 95 (2001): 963. For a summary of voting restrictions in U.S. law, see Alexander Keyssar, *The Right to Vote* (New York: Basic Books, 2000), particularly the appendices.

3. See the resources of the Sentencing Project, at www.sentencingproject.org.

4. *Trop v. Dulles*, 356 U.S. 86, 96–97 (1958).

5. See Andrew L. Shapiro, "Note: Challenging Criminal Disenfranchisement under the Voting Rights Act: A New Strategy," *Yale Law Journal* 103 (1993): 537; B*aker v. Pataki*, 85 F.3d 919 (2d Cir. 1996); Jamie Fellner and Marc Mauer, "Losing the Vote: The Impact of Felony Disenfranchisement Laws in the United States" (1998), report for Human Rights Watch and the Sentencing Project.

6. See Jeff Manza and Christopher Uggen, "Punishment and Democracy: Disenfranchisement of Nonincarcerated Felons in the United States," *Perspectives on Politics* 2 (2004): 498.

7. See Alec C. Ewald, "'Civil Death': The Ideological Paradox of Criminal Disenfranchisement Law in the United States," *Wisconsin Law Review* (2002): 1060.

8. For figures, see Keyssar, *Right to Vote*, Appendix 7 ("Suffrage Exclusions for Criminal Offenses: 1790–1857") and Appendix 9 ("Summary of Suffrage Requirements in Force: 1855"). The term "laxly enforced" is in Richard F. Bensel, *The American Ballot Box in the Mid-Nineteenth Century* (New York: Cambridge, 2004), 29.

9. *Ratliff v. Beale*, 20 So. 865, 867 (1896). Emphasis added.

10. *Ramirez v. Brown*, 507 P.2d 1345 (1973).

11. *Richardson v. Ramirez*, 418 U.S. 24 (1974). For a more complete explanation of the decision and its problems, see Ewald, "'Civil Death,'" pp. 1064–1071.

12. Hunter v. Underwood, 471 U.S. 222 (1985).

13. David Cole, "Denying Felons Vote Hurts Them, Society," *USA Today*, February 3, 2000. For a good survey of disparities, see Paul Butler, "Racially-Based Jury Nullification: Black Power in the Criminal Justice System," *Yale Law Journal* 105 (1995): 677.

14. *Farrakhan v. Washington*, 338 F.3d 1009 (2003).

15. Roger Clegg, "Who Should Vote?," *Texas Review of Law & Policy* 6 (2001): 177; Frank Phillips, "Lawmakers Push to Ban Inmate Votes," *Boston Globe*, June 28, 2000, p. B1 (quoting House Minority Leader Francis Marini).

16. For public opinion data, see Brian Pinaire et al., "Barred from the Vote: Public Attitudes Toward the Disenfranchisement of Felons," *Fordham Urban Law Journal* 30 (2003). On recent changes, see Ryan King, "A Decade of Reform: Felony Disenfranchisement Policy in the United States" (Sentencing Project, 2006); Erik Eckholm, "States Are Growing More Lenient in Allowing Felons to Vote," *New York Times*, October 12, 2006.

17. Christopher Uggen and Jeff Manza, "Democratic Contraction? Political Consequences of Felon Disenfranchisement in the United States," *American Sociological Review* 67 (2002): 777; Emily Bazelon, "The Secret Weapon of 2008," *Slate*, April 27, 2007; Carl Bialik, "Figuring the Impact of Allowing Felons in Florida to Vote," *Wall Street Journal*, May 4, 2007.

18. Kim Chandler, "Felon Voting Bill Ensnares Riley," *Birmingham News*, June 22, 2003.

19. Tim Howe, "Alabama GOP Says Judge's Ruling on Registering Felons Is Attempt to Bolster Democratic Voting Rolls," Press Release, August 24, 2006.

20. For an authoritative survey of criminal disenfranchisement laws around the world, see Laleh Ispahani, *Out of Step with the World: An Analysis of Felony Disfranchisement in the U.S. and Other Democracies* (ACLU, 2006).

21. Morgan Kousser, "Disfranchisement Modernized," *Election Law Journal* 6 (2007): 112; Alec Ewald, *A Crazy-Quilt of Tiny Pieces: State and Local Administration of American Criminal Disenfranchisement Law* (Sentencing Project, 2005).

22. Richard A. Posner, *Law, Pragmatism, and Democracy* (Cambridge, MA: Harvard University Press. 2003), 234–235.

7

Where We Vote

Polling Place Location and Its Impact on Elections

Moshe Haspel and H. Gibbs Knotts

On Election Day, millions of Americans visit a local school, church, or other public building intending to vote for their preferred candidates and positions. Voting is the most common form of political participation, and for many citizens it is the only form of political participation in which they engage. If elections are the "stuff" of which democracy is made, then precincts are the factories where democracy is built. Yet people give little thought to where they vote except when they have difficulty locating a polling place or when their designated polling place changes. But the characteristics of a polling place can determine who votes and, in a very close election, perhaps even decide the winner.

The 2000 presidential election demonstrated the importance of the seemingly minor administrative details of an election. Before that election, no one had heard of "hanging chads." Few had considered that different voting technologies such as punch cards or optically scanned ballots would make a difference in the final vote count.[1] And although few gave much thought to a ballot's physical design, the "butterfly ballot" in Palm Beach County, Florida, has been shown to have changed the outcome of the election in favor of George W. Bush.[2]

So if administrative details matter, what do we know about where people vote? Polling places have been an accepted feature of American elections for as long as our country has existed. Article II, Section 1 of the U.S. Constitution specifies that electors meet in their respective states to cast ballots for president. But because Article I, Section 4 provides that, unless regulated by federal law, the time, places, and manner of holding elections for Congress is left up to each state, there can be and often is a good deal of variation in how these issues are handled. A survey of election officials conducted by the National Association of Secretaries of State (2006) found that only forty-three states[3] mandate statewide opening and closing times for the polls.[4] Among these states, polls most commonly open at 7 a.m. and close at 8 p.m., for a total time open of thirteen hours.[5] A total of nine states have state holidays and eleven close schools on Election Day.[6] The National Federation of Independent Business (2006) surveyed state legislation and found that thirty-one states require employers to allow employees time off to vote. Another study of precinct locations in Arizona found that the highest percentages of residents voted in churches (40 percent), followed by schools (26 percent) and community centers (11 percent).[7]

This chapter takes a closer look at administrative details related to polling place locations. Because the location of polling places can affect the costs of voting, it begins with a brief discussion of the costs of voting commonly associated with the decision of whether or not to participate in an election. Grounded in the discussion of costs, the focus turns to a newly identified yet important cost of voting: the distance a person must travel to a polling place. Next the discussion shifts to another distance-related concern, the consolidation and expansion of polling place locations. Given the costs associated with locating and traveling to polling places, there have been a number of electoral reforms designed to move away from precinct voting. The next section discusses efforts to reduce these types of costs through absentee voting, vote by mail, and online voting. We then consider the effectiveness of precinct-less voting and highlight a new option for voters, the Election Day Voting Center (EDVC). An evaluation of the effects of precincts on election outcomes is presented before some concluding remarks about general voting reforms and the need to increase the levels of civic engagement in the United States.

THE COSTS OF VOTING

Though the poll tax was outlawed by the Twenty-fourth Amendment, voting is still a costly activity. Consider this: in order to vote, one must invest time to learn about the candidates and issues, and also take time out from what is, for most people, a workday. The polling place itself may not be on the way to work or school, it may not have convenient parking, and there will likely be at least a short wait before voting. And without a car, the act of voting becomes even costlier. So it is no wonder that, since the publication of Anthony Downs's *An Economic Theory of Democracy* in 1957, scholars who study voter turnout commonly frame the decision of whether or not to vote as a cost-benefit analysis.[8]

What are the consequences of high voting costs? The higher the costs of voting are, the greater the likelihood that the benefits of voting will be outweighed by those costs, and the less likely citizens will be to vote. And if a democracy requires consent of the governed,[9] how much legitimacy does a system enjoy if voter turnout flirts with 50 percent levels even in presidential election years?[10]

Moreover, the costs of voting are harder to "pay" for some citizens than others: the burden weighs most heavily on poorer, less educated citizens.[11] Because this threatens the concept of "one person, one vote," some scholars refer to voting as a socioeconomically biased form of political participation.[12]

It should be no surprise, therefore, that concerns about reducing the costs of voting have provided much of the impetus behind major electoral reforms and experiments of the last fifteen years, including "Motor Voter"[13] and "convenience voting" measures: early voting, voting by mail, Internet voting, and the EDVC. Given the socioeconomic division in voting patterns, one might expect higher costs to favor Republicans. But the findings on this score are, in fact, mixed.[14]

DISTANCE TO THE POLLS

As mentioned above, the distance a person lives from his or her polling place affects the costs of voting and thus the decision of whether or not to vote. With a couple of exceptions, this cost had largely been overlooked in the literature until fairly recently. Richard Niemi proposed that "a small increase in the costs of voting—such as driving a mile instead of a half-mile to the polls—would significantly reduce turnout" but he did not test this idea.[15] Along the same lines, Elizabeth Sanders recognized the costs associated with travel, arguing that "getting to the polls is more difficult in rural areas where distances may be larger."[16] Fortunately, advances in Geographic Information Systems (GIS) software has made research evaluating the impact of distance much more practical.

Perhaps the first study to empirically verify the impact of distance on voter turnout was conducted by James Gimpel and Jason Schuknecht.[17] These scholars evaluated aggregate precinct-level data from over 300 locations in suburban Maryland. They found that reducing the average distance to a polling place by five miles increases turnout between 1.7 and 2.3 percent. In addition, the authors suggest a nonlinear relationship between distance and turnout, arguing that the effects of distance are greatest in suburban precincts where voters travel between two and five miles to the polling location.

A second study evaluated individual voter file data to determine the impact of distance to the polling place on turnout in the 2001 Atlanta mayoral election.[18] The voter file provided the home address for each of the registered voters in the city of Atlanta. Transportation modeling software was used to compute the distance between the home address and the appropriate voting precinct—imagine conducting a MapQuest search between the home address and polling place for each of the city's nearly 200,000 registered voters. In this election, the average citizen living directly next door to a polling place had about a 50-50 chance of voting. For a citizen living just two blocks away, the chance of voting dropped to about 35 percent. Moreover, the less likely a citizen was to have access to a vehicle, the steeper the decline in likelihood of voting.

A third study examined individual voter records in Clark County (Las Vegas), Nevada, to determine the effect proximity to the polls had on nonvoting, precinct voting, and nontraditional voting.[19] The researchers found that voters living greater distances from the polls had an increased likelihood both of nonvoting and of voting by mail. Specifically, they found that a 1.75-mile increase in distance increases absentee voting by 0.9 percent, decreases precinct voting by 2.3 percent and increases nonvoting by 1.3 percent.

A fourth study focused specifically on the impact of distance on early voting.[20] The authors analyzed voter file information from Bernalillo County (Albuquerque), New Mexico, and Clark County, Nevada. Overall, they found a 4 to 5 percent increase in convenience voting for voters in Bernalillo County living within one-half mile of a site. In addition, the authors concluded that voters living in suburban areas with long commutes are more likely to engage in convenience voting.

Although the four studies examined the impact of distance to the polls on voter turnout in different parts of the country using varied methods, the findings are quite similar. Distance is a tangible cost of voting, and scholars must account for this cost when explaining the decision of whether or not to vote. The results also suggest that policymakers must be cognizant of the impact of distance and continue to develop strategies for decreasing the distance a voter must travel to the polls.

CONSOLIDATION AND EXPANSION OF POLLING PLACE LOCATIONS

Both practical and economic factors lead to the alteration of voting locations, and these changes often increase voters' travel distances and information costs. Suppose that a voter gets a note in the mail indicating that the polling place location has been changed. She used to vote at the neighborhood library but is now instructed to vote at an Episcopal church in a nearby neighborhood. Does she know where the church is? Might she forget and go to the old polling place out of habit? Is the new site farther away?

Henry Brady and John McNulty evaluated the effects of polling place closures in Los Angeles County during the 2003 gubernatorial recall election.[21] Prior to this election, the number of voting precincts had decreased from about 5,000 to about 1,800. The researchers found an overall 1.5 percent decrease in turnout when the precinct was changed. Changes in polling places resulted in a 3.3 percent decline in voting at the polling place and a 1.8 percent increase in absentee voting.

A study of an election where the number of precincts increased from 160 to 168 provided further evidence of the impact of polling places.[22] Turnout for voters in new precincts actually increased, and the study concluded that gains from moving precincts outweigh the likelihood of lower turnout because of information costs associated with locating new polling places.

Although limited, research on this topic indicates consistent and politically relevant findings about the consolidation and expansion of polling place locations. In the case of consolidation, the evidence suggests that turnout will decrease. Other data, however, provide strong evidence that an increase in the number of polling places causes an increase in voter turnout.

ELECTORAL REFORMS

Citing a question from the 2005 Current Population Survey, Robert Stein and Greg Vonnahme indicate that time pressures are the most common reason given for nonvoting.[23] As a result, election administrators and elected officials have searched for ways to make voting less costly in terms of time.

Precinct-less Voting

Any discussion of where people vote would be amiss without an overview of the growing trend toward precinct-less voting. Early voting, vote by mail, and Internet voting demonstrate that the precinct may be going the way of the VCR and the landline telephone. Such reforms entail both positive and negative outcomes that need to be evaluated by scholars and policymakers.

An increasingly popular option in many states is early voting. The majority of states now allow no-excuse pre–Election Day in-person voting.[24] Three states and the District of Columbia allow in-person absentee voting where an excuse is required.[25] Another trend that could signal an end to precincts is vote by mail. A majority of states (twenty-nine) allow no-excuse absentee vote by mail, and in Oregon all voting is done by mail.[26] Internet voting provides a final alternative to traditional polling places. The 2000 Arizona Democratic Primary was conducted online and experienced an increase in voter turnout.

Do These Policies Work?

As discussed above, a major purpose of electoral reform was both to increase turnout and to decrease the socioeconomic bias in turnout by decreasing the cost of voting. But evaluation of these reforms indicates that they are not having the desired effect. Studies have found that in-person early voting did not increase the likelihood that an individual would vote and concluded that the demographic characteristics between Election Day voters and early voters were similar.[27] A study of vote by mail in Oregon concluded that this method does not increase turnout or make the electorate more representative of the general population.[28] Other studies suggest that mandatory voting by mail could actually lead to lower levels of participation.[29] In addition to security issues associated with Internet voting, a subsequent examination of the Arizona election demonstrated that Internet voting increased the likelihood of voting only among higher-status individuals.[30]

In a review of the studies examining the impact of these reforms, Adam Berinsky concludes that there is no evidence that reducing the cost of voting decreases the socioeconomic bias in turnout.[31] Indeed, these reforms largely appear to exacerbate the bias. Turnout goes up, according to Berinsky, but only among people predisposed to vote.

A New Innovation

One new innovation that may help is the EDVC, an idea piloted in Larimer County, Colorado, but one that will likely spread to other localities.[32] An EDVC is similar to a precinct in that there are locations spread throughout a county where people may vote. But unlike precinct-based voting, which requires citizens to cast ballots at a single place determined by where they reside, EDVC voting allows people to vote at any of the sites.

How does it reduce the cost of voting? First, it increases the time span within which a person can vote. Except for the nine states that declare Election Day a holiday, a person is typically near his or her home precinct only early in the day and in the evening. But there is probably an EDVC near the person's school, workplace, or shopping center. Thus, voting becomes an activity that is "complementary rather than competing with other demands."[33] The lines to vote are likely shorter as well, because voting (concentrated in the morning and evening under a precinct system) is spread out over the day under an EDVC system. And by reducing the number of sites needed to meet voter demand, the locality is able to reinvest the resources it saves into better equipment and more and better-trained election place personnel. This last point is crucial, because a positive overall voting experience is part of what is needed to encourage habitual nonvoters to go to the polls. Indeed, comparing individual vote histories from Larimer County and a neighboring control county, Stein and Vonnahme find that EDVCs increase voter turnout not just overall, but especially among infrequent voters.[34]

POLLING PLACE LOCATION AND ELECTION RESULTS

There are two ways polling place location can alter election outcomes. First, turnout should be higher in more compact precincts, controlling for other factors. If there is a regional component to voter preferences, this turnout differential could sway a close election. Indeed, a study of the 2001 Atlanta mayoral race examines such an instance.[35] The outcome of the 2001 mayoral race—a particularly close election—was re-estimated, with each polling location placed at the center of its precinct. Findings indicate that the eventual winner, Shirley Franklin, would have had to face a runoff under these conditions. The election results were also re-estimated assuming that everyone lived next door to the polling location. Once again, the election results would have changed only slightly—but enough to have forced a runoff.

A second way that polling locations can affect election results concerns the characteristics of the places where people vote. Jonah Berger, Marc Meredith, and S. Christian Wheeler built on the priming literature in marketing to study the impact of polling places on election results.[36] According to this literature, consumers primed with a stimulus may alter their purchasing behavior. For example, when German music is played in a wine store, shoppers are more likely to select a German wine than when French music is being played. The authors conclude that support in Arizona for Proposition 301, a 2000 measure to raise the state sales tax from 5 to 5.6 percent for education, increased when voters cast ballots in schools. The scholars found that 55 percent of the people who voted in schools supported the initiative, compared with 53 percent of people who voted in nonschool locations. In the same study, the authors report the results of an experiment where participants were primed with images of churches and schools and then asked questions about policy issues. The scholars confirmed the Arizona initiative findings, demonstrating increased support for an education initiative when participants were primed with school images rather than church images or control images. The authors also reported less support for a stem cell initiative when respondents were primed with images of a church as opposed to school or control group images.

CONCLUSION

Where people vote remains an important albeit understudied feature of American politics. Polling place location has a substantial impact on the costs of voting. And simple administrative features, such as the number of precincts in a municipality or the location of precincts, can have a significant effect on the decision of whether or not to vote. There are also new alternatives to traditional polling place voting, a phenomenon that is motivated in part by a desire to reduce the costs of voting. Early voting, vote by mail, and Internet voting all represent important alternatives to precincts; these potential reforms need additional study by scholars and policymakers. Initial evidence suggests that these types of precinct-less voting make frequent voters more likely to vote but they also increase socioeconomic biases in the electorate.[37] However, a recent study of

EDVC voting provides evidence of increased turnout among infrequent voters. Finally, polling place location can have an impact on election outcomes.

Even with reduced costs of voting, the American political system will likely continue to have a substantial number of nonvoters. A remaining challenge is to engage nonvoters in the larger political process. As Adam Berinsky notes, "[I]nstead of making it incrementally easier for citizens to participate in politics, we should make people *want* to participate."[38] He calls on political leaders to reframe issues and expand mobilization efforts to diversify the electorate. Compelling candidates and competitive elections may also drive additional voters to the polls. Finally, a renewed focus on civic education may increase the likelihood of voting and engage greater numbers of citizens in the democratic process.

NOTES

1. Stephen Ansolabehere and Charles Stewart III, "Residual Votes Attributable to Technology," *Journal of Politics* 67 (2005): 365–389.

2. Alan Agresti and Brett Presnell, "Misvotes, Undervotes and Overvotes: The 2000 Presidential Election in Florida," *Statistical Science* 17 (November 2002): 436–440.

3. For the purpose of this discussion, the District of Columbia will be counted as a state.

4. Maine, Montana, Tennessee, and Vermont regulate only the closing time; New Hampshire, North Dakota, and Rhode Island grant latitude to localities for both opening and closing times. Oregon votes entirely by mail, so issues related to polling places do not apply.

5. Polls in Hawaii are open the shortest length of time (7 a.m. to 6 p.m.), and polls in New York are open the longest (6 a.m. to 9 p.m.).

6. These figures include Illinois, which does so only in even-numbered years, but not states that leave these issues up to the localities. In addition to Illinois and the District of Columbia, the states are Delaware, Georgia, Hawaii, Kentucky, New Mexico, New York, Rhode Island, South Carolina, and West Virginia.

7. Jonah Berger, Marc Meredith, and S. Christian Wheeler, "Can Where People Vote Influence How They Vote? The Influence of Polling Location Type of Voting Behavior" (Research Paper Series, Stanford Graduate School of Business, February 2006).

8. John H. Aldrich, "Rational Choice and Turnout," *American Journal of Political Science* 37 (1993): 246–278.

9. See John Locke, *Two Treatises of Government*, edited by Peter Laslett (Cambridge: Cambridge University Press [1689] 1988), §96.

10. It is worth noting, however, that most studies show little difference in policy preferences between voters and nonvoters (Wolfinger and Rosenstone, *Who Votes?* New Haven, CT: Yale University Press, 1980); Stephen Bennett and David Resnick, "The Implications of Nonvoting for Democracy in America," *American Journal of Political Science* 34(3) (August 1990): 771–802). Jonathan Nagler and Jan A. Leighley (paper pre-

sented at the Annual Meeting of the Southwestern Political Science Assocoiation, March 2007) find differences in voters and nonvoters in relation to opinions on the role of government in redistributive policies, showing that voters are more conservative than nonvoters.

11. Anthony Downs, *An Economic Theory of Democracy* (New York: Harper & Row, 1957); Wolfinger and Rosenstone, *Who Votes?*

12. Arend Lijphart, "Unequal Participation: Democracy's Unresolved Dilemma," *American Political Science Review* 91 (1997): 1–14; Ruy Teixeira, *The Disappearing American Voter* (Washington, DC: Brookings Institution, 1992).

13. The National Voter Registration Act of 1993 gave people the option of registering to vote when they renew or obtain a driver's license. The act was supported by Democrats and opposed by Republicans. Research indicates that, at best, the law has had only a modest impact on turnout (Stephen Knack, "Does 'Motor Voter' Work? Evidence from State-Level Data," *Journal of Politics* 57(3) (1995): 796–811).

14. James DeNardo, "Turnout and the Vote: The Joke's on the Democrats," *American Political Science Review* (June 1980): 406–420; James DeNardo, "Does Heavy Turnout Help Democrats in Presidential Elections?" *American Political Science Review* (December 1986): 1298–1304; Jack Citrin, Eric Schickler, and John Sides, "What If Everyone Voted? Simulating the Impact of Increased Turnout in Senate Elections," *American Journal of Political Science* 47 (January 2003): 75–90; Zoltan Hajnal and Jessica Trounstine, "Where Turnout Matters: The Consequences of Uneven Turnout in City Politics," *Journal of Politics* 67 (May 2005): 515–535; Jack H. Nagel and John E. McNulty, "Partisan Effects of Voter Turnout in Senatorial and Gubernatorial Elections," *American Political Science Review* 90 (December 1996): 780–793.

15. Richard G. Niemi, "Costs of Voting and Nonvoting," *Public Choice* 27 (1976): 115–119.

16. Elizabeth Sanders, "On the Costs, Utilities, and Simple Joys of Voting," *Journal of Politics* 42 (1980): 854–863.

17. James G. Gimpel and Jason E. Schuknecht, "Political Participation and the Accessibility of the Ballot Box," *Political Geography* 22 (2003): 471–488.

18. Moshe Haspel and H. Gibbs Knotts, "Location, Location, Location: Precinct Placement and the Costs of Voting," *Journal of Politics* 67 (2005): 560–573.

19. Joshua J. Dyck and James G. Gimpel, "Distance, Turnout, and the Convenience of Voting," *Social Science Quarterly* 86 (2005): 531–548.

20. James G. Gimpel, Joshua J. Dyck, and Daron R. Shaw, "Location, Knowledge, and Time Pressures in the Spatial Structure of Convenience Voting," *Electoral Studies* 25 (2006): 35–58.

21. Henry E. Brady and John E. McNulty, "The Costs of Voting: Evidence from a Natural Experiment" (paper presented at the annual meeting of the Midwest Political Science Association, Chicago, Illinois, 2004).

22. Haspel and Knotts, "Location, Location, Location."

23. Robert M. Stein and Greg Vonnahme, "Engaging the Unengaged Voter: Vote Centers and Voter Turnout," *Journal of Politics* 70 (2008).

24. According to electionline.org, thirty-one states allow no-excuse pre–Election Day in-person voting ("Pre-Election Day and Absentee Voting by Mail Rules," available

online at http://www.electionline.org/Default.aspx?tabid=474, accessed September 28, 2007). Early voting states include Alaska, Arizona, Arkansas, California, Colorado, Florida, Georgia, Hawaii, Idaho, Illinois, Indiana, Iowa, Kansas, Louisiana, Maine, Montana, Nebraska, Nevada, New Mexico, North Carolina, North Dakota, Ohio, Oklahoma, South Dakota, Tennessee, Texas, Utah, Vermont, West Virginia, Wisconsin, and Wyoming.

25. The states are Kentucky, Minnesota, and Virginia.

26. States that allow no-excuse absentee voting by mail are Alaska, Arizona, Arkansas, California, Colorado, Florida, Georgia, Hawaii, Idaho, Iowa, Kansas, Maine, Maryland, Montana, Nebraska, Nevada, New Jersey, New Mexico, North Carolina, North Dakota, Ohio, Oklahoma, Oregon, South Dakota, Utah, Vermont, Washington, Wisconsin, and Wyoming.

27. Robert M. Stein, "Early Voting," *Public Opinion Quarterly* 62 (1998): 57–69; Robert M. Stein and Patricia A. Garcia-Monet, "Voting Early, but Not Often," *Social Science Quarterly* 78 (1997): 657–671.

28. Adam J. Berinsky, Nancy Burns, and Michael W. Traugott, "Who Votes by Mail? A Dynamic Model of the Individual-Level Consequences of Vote-by-Mail Systems," *Public Opinion Quarterly* 65 (2001): 178–197.

29. Matt A. Barreto and Barry Pump, "Closing the Polls: How Switching to All Vote-By-Mail Elections Affect Public Confidence and Turnout" (paper presented at the annual meeting of the American Political Science Association, Chicago, Illinois, 2007).

30. Michael R. Alvarez and Jonathan Nagler, "The Likely Consequences of Internet Voting for Political Representation," *Loyola Law Review* 34 (April 2001): 1115–1153.

31. Adam J. Berinsky, "The Perverse Consequences of Electoral Reform in the United States," *American Politics Research* 33 (2005): 471–491.

32. According to Larimer County (2007), other Colorado counties as well as Illinois, Florida, Texas, Michigan, and North Carolina have investigated the vote center model.

33. Stein and Vonnahme, "Engaging the Unengaged Voter."

34. Stein and Vonnahme, "Engaging the Unengaged Voter."

35. Haspel and Knotts, "Location, Location, Location."

36. Berger, Meredith, and Wheeler, "Can Where People Vote Influence How They Vote?"

37. Berinsky, "The Perverse Consequences."

38. Berinsky, "The Perverse Consequences."

8

Absentee Voting in the Twenty-first Century

Dotty LeMieux

Call it absentee voting, early voting, or convenience voting, but offering voters a method to cast their ballots prior to Election Day is slowly but surely changing the way Americans vote.

As old as the vote itself, absentee voting made its first appearance in this country while the "colonies" were still under the English Crown. In the seventeenth century, the practice was used by farmers and frontiersmen, who were busy tending their far-flung herds or blazing trails in the back country on Election Day. Later, the right to cast an early vote was extended to soldiers whose duties took them far from home for extended periods.[1]

By the end of World War I, twenty states allowed absentee voting to those who presented a valid excuse for being absent from the jurisdiction or were unable to get to the polls on Election Day. Currently, all fifty states and the District of Columbia allow some type of absentee voting.

Although many states have instituted "no-excuse" absentee or early voting for any voter who wants it, some still require an excuse such as illness, service in the armed forces, college attendance, advanced old age or infirmity, and being out of the country. According to information provided by Electionline.org, as of July 2006, some thirty-one states offered no-excuse early voting. Some states require the voter to show up at a designated location; in other states, voters may cast their votes by mail.[2]

PERMANENT ABSENTEE VOTING

One of the newest and most interesting changes in absentee voting is the practice of allowing no-excuse permanent absentee voting (PAV). While most states require the voter to reapply for early or absentee status on a regular basis, a few states have begun allowing voters to register once as a permanent absentee, no excuses needed. (In most states, permanent absentee voting is permitted only with a doctor's excuse or for advanced age.)

In California, PAV has changed the electoral landscape for all the players, including the county registrar of voters, who must monitor and count each absentee ballot received; the voters, who now have the option of casting their ballots at their leisure; and the candidates, who must cope with an election cycle that maintains its fever pitch for as long as six weeks to ensure that their messages reach all voters at the most effective time. Even with many states now offering early in-person voting to anyone, permanent absentee mail-in balloting appears to be preferred and has brought the most radical changes to the way campaigns are run.

The state of Washington has had no-excuse PAV for many years, since the passage of the National Voter Registration Act ("Motor Voter" law) in 1993. Because so many of the state's voters were using the system, many counties opted to go to all mail-in ballots. According to the official site for the Washington Secretary of State's office, currently thirty-four of the state's thirty-nine counties use all mail-in balloting, with no polling places open on Election Day. The other five counties offer both mail-in and in-person voting options.

Because this expansion of early voting is still so new, there has to date been no comprehensive analysis of its effect.[3] For instance, does it increase voter turnout? Some say it does, but others say it has no effect at all. Most say it is simply too soon to tell.

THE OREGON EXPERIMENT

By public vote, Oregon initiated its vaunted vote-by-mail program in 1998, following a seventeen-year series of experiments with a trial program. (Ballot Measure 60 passed by 69 percent of the public vote.) Today all elections in the state are conducted by mail, making all Oregonians absentee voters. Unlike other states where vote by mail begins close to a month before Election Day, ballots in Oregon are not available until fourteen to eighteen days before an election.[4]

According to a survey conducted by the University of Oregon five years following the passage of Measure 60, vote by mail increased turnout among about one-third of all voters. Women, younger people, and the disabled said they voted more often. The breakdown shows that among women, voting was up 32.9 percent; among working people, it was up 33 percent; among young people,

40 percent; among the disabled, 48 percent; among homemakers, 51.9 percent; and among the minorities, the vote went up a whopping 78 percent.[5]

However, Paul Gronke of Reed College's Early Voting Information Center found that voter turnout in Oregon increased only by 10 percent, and that resulted more from voter retention than from new voter registration.[6] That means that although historically large numbers of voters had showed up to vote in the general election, there had been a drop-off in voting in primaries and local elections. The all-mail voting system has resulted in increased participation in the latter elections, as voters are more likely to cast their ballot by mail than go to the polling places in those elections they had previously avoided. Whether this leads to a more educated voting population or just to more votes cast remains an open question.

In the same report, Gronke found that election integrity appeared to be the most dramatic result of an exclusively mail-in ballot. Whereas other reports cited massive problems with the increased use of absentee ballots in jurisdictions that utilized both absentee and ballot box voting options, the conversion to an all-mail ballot (as opposed to what Gronke calls a "hybrid" method) seemed to remedy many of these difficulties.

The main problems with "hybrid" elections is that those administering them—elections officials at the local registrar of voters and secretary of state offices—are in essence charged with conducting two simultaneous elections, one for the poll voters and one for absentee voters. With the addition of early voting, which often takes place also at the registrar of voters office, the workload of the office increases and, along with it, the likelihood of misplaced ballots, hastily decided disputes, and undetected voter fraud. "Under the old system we were putting out fires all over the county on Election Day," a voting official said.[7]

The only drawback in terms of election integrity, according to Gronke, is the potential for election fraud in the use of "drop-off locations" for mail ballots. Although ballots are mailed to every voter in Oregon, there is no requirement that they be mailed back, so long as they are delivered to the elections office or one of many designated or unofficial drop-off points. Often campaign workers collect ballots for delivery. The lack of oversight to confirm the actual delivery of these ballots has led some Oregon officials to consider requiring that all ballots either be mailed or dropped off only at designated locations. However, no fraud has been documented, unlike the case in some jurisdictions still using the hybrid method.[8]

THE CURRENT STATE OF AFFAIRS

Over the past fifteen years there has been an overall increase in early voting across the country—up from about 2 percent to close to 20 percent in 2004, according to R. Doug Lewis, Executive Director of Houston's nonprofit Election

Center, an organization made up of government elections employees.[9] In California, absentee balloting accounted for some 47 percent of all ballots cast in the 2006 primary election, nearly double the level in 2002, the year no-excuse permanent absentee voting was passed.[10]

In the 2006 California general election, late absentee votes caused the turnout rate statewide to jump from 43.8 percent on the night of the election to 56.1 percent once all the votes were counted nearly a month later.[11] More than one of every five votes was not counted until at least several days after the election, leaving many races up in the air.

Since that time, an increasing number of permanent absentee voters have behaved more like traditional voters who cast their ballots at the polling place. Prior to the recent changes, conventional wisdom taught that absentee voters were generally more conservative. The Republicans have taken advantage of that fact for years, urging churchgoers and other constituents to vote early to ensure that the vote was locked up.[12] Now Democrats have caught up, and even in nonpartisan races strategies targeting absentee voters are receiving their primary attention, which has diminished the Republican's advantage among absentee voters.

Projections from some early voting numbers appeared to show a Republican edge in 2006.[13] Republicans had benefited from aggressive pushes for absentee voting in the 1990s, leading to their dramatic midterm victory in 1994 and their long hold on national offices.[14] That early lead did not hold, as the changes in the House and Senate show.

In 2006 an aggressive push by Republicans in Michigan appeared to be responsible for a 61 percent advantage in absentee votes a few days before Election Day. The local Republican operatives used tools such as micro-targeting and encouraging voters to cast their ballots early. Their campaign plan involved identifying those with a high propensity to vote Republican and using that list (as well as a second list of lower-propensity voters) to deliver absentee ballots right to the selected voters' doorsteps. Follow-up consisted of repeat phone calls and targeted mail.[15]

However, this aggressive strategy did not result in Republican gains in the House of Representatives, although no Democrat won a traditionally Republican seat in Michigan either. Michigan's governor and two U.S. senators remain Democrats. This seems to bolster the findings of recent studies that show no discernible partisan advantage to the vote-by-mail process.[16]

The most dramatic outcome occurred in the 2006 California election to replace State Senator Joe Dunn of Orange County, who had reached his term limit. A slim election night lead for the Republican candidate turned into a nearly 1,400-vote loss once all 20,000 late absentee and provisional ballots (those ballots given to voters who did not show up on the voter rolls or who had other issues with registration) were counted weeks later.[17]

There are many useful tools available to help the potential absentee voter or campaign strategist learn what options are available on a state-by-state basis. Besides individual secretary of states' offices, several online tools exist. One is the state guide to absentee voting, put out by students at the Institute of Politics at the John F. Kennedy School of Government at Harvard University. It was prepared with the college student in mind but is a useful guide for anyone interested in learning how absentee voting is conducted in every state. The guide contains dates for voting in 2006, but the general guidelines for applying for and returning an absentee ballot can be applied to other years by identifying the date of Election Day and working backward from there.

THE EFFECT ON ELECTIONS AND CAMPAIGNING IN THE FUTURE

In general, absentee voters have tended to be older and more conservative than Election Day voters. However, with more and more people joining the ranks of the early and absentee voters, the profile has changed, requiring all campaigns to develop methodologies for capturing that vote. This new focus has led to increased use of micro-targeting, including aiming particular messages at voters based on their propensity for early voting. Secretaries of state and local registrars of voters keep detailed voter rolls, often showing the voting history for each voter and whether or not the voter has been a habitual or permanent absentee voter.

Micro-targeting has been less effective for down-ballot local races or underfunded grassroots candidates. It is standard fare for candidates to target all permanent absentee voters in their district with an early mailing. But candidates are finding that is not enough. As issues unfold and more voters hold their ballots until later in the race, the candidate needs to make sure the campaign's messages are still being heard by those who have not yet voted. There is a fine line between getting the message out early and peaking too soon. Ways of addressing this problem involve updating voter lists, removing the names of voters who have already cast their votes, adding voters who apply for absentee ballots, and personalizing messages for those who cast their ballots in the last few days of the race.

Even with such targeting efforts, projecting who is likely to vote by mail (among those not already registered as permanent absentee voters) remains speculative.[18] The voter rolls—generally available from the secretary of state, party, and local elections offices—provide information on voting patterns that allow the savvy campaigner to make an educated prediction, but there are no statistics on when previous absentee voters cast their ballots. There is still a paucity of data for predicting which absentee voters are likely to cast their ballots early in the process and which later. Very few studies looking at the effects of early voting address this crucial element.[19] Another wrinkle for campaigns is that many states, in addition to offering absentee voting or vote by mail, allow voters to cast an early ballot in person either at the local elections office or at other designated locations.

What all this means for campaign strategy is still being determined, although more and more campaigns are being front-loaded to catch the absentees who vote early. Gone are the days when campaigns could count on absentee voters being more conservative, older, and less influenced by tactics such as direct mail, television and radio ads, and "robo" calls. Those party loyalists usually had their minds made up as soon as they knew who the candidates were. In nonpartisan races, they tended to vote based on incumbency, name recognition, or candidates' positions on issues that were easily identifiable early on in the campaign.

Now, with a larger proportion of the population casting their ballots in the privacy and leisure of their own homes, the late absentee voters are more likely to match the poll voters, and the later they cast their votes, the more they resemble their Election Day counterparts. Such voters become more susceptible to late advertising and pitches over the phone. The downside of this is that because campaigns still need to ensure that their message reaches the traditional early voting absentees, these later voters may be barraged with campaign slogans and mudslinging at an increasingly frantic pace as Election Day nears. Consultants and campaign managers concerned about reaching every possible voter at every stage of the game sometimes overplay their hand and sabotage their candidate's chances by bombarding the voters with too much material. Knowing what to send out when requires the finesse and balance of a tightrope walker.

Because of the large number of absentee voters who hold on to their ballots until close to Election Day, campaigns cannot afford to let up on their messaging. In a recent campaign for a California school board seat, a candidate was devastated by his narrow loss. However, once the exhausted elections officials finished counting the late absentee and provisional ballots two weeks later, it turned out he had squeaked out a victory. His campaign team had pushed him to make last-minute phone calls and literature drops, which appear to have paid off.[20] Of course, there was no way to know for sure how many of the late absentee voters had been influenced by the late campaigning. But with the use of more sophisticated software and voting data retained by counties and states, future campaigns should be able to predict voter behavior with more certainty.

Early voters may be more persuaded by slick campaign materials from better-funded candidates and miss out on late-breaking campaign messages, scandals, and news articles about the campaign. As an example of how early voting may have skewed a recent presidential election, a *Washington Post* article cites the late-breaking revelation about George W. Bush's 1976 drunk-driving arrest, which hit the airwaves a mere five days before the 2000 election. Would this information have changed enough voters' minds to have made a difference? The writers imply that it may have in states such as Tennessee, where a large number of absentee votes had been cast before the news broke.[21]

Less dramatic may be the results of debates, newspaper editorials and endorsements, and the knock on the voter's door when the candidate comes to call in person, all of which an early voter may also miss.

Whether the system is a hybrid system, which most states have, or a complete vote-by-mail system, as used in Oregon and many Washington counties, early voting poses particular problems for campaigns in terms of money and energy spent to reach voters. Another downside is that, while attempting to reach the voters before they cast their ballots, campaigns run the risk of alienating the very voters they rely on for victory. Every candidate has had at least one phone receiver slammed down by a frustrated voter screaming, "Why won't you people leave me alone!"

This is being seen more and more in lower-profile, down-ticket races, such as contests for the local school board, fire district, and city council. Because these races lack the news buzz of a presidential or even a gubernatorial race, more of these new absentee voters will mail in their ballots early. If things do heat up, a smaller percentage of voters will be left to benefit from changing events. Early voters in these local races will more likely vote along party lines or perhaps vote for the better-known candidate, whereas later voters are more likely to be influenced by the results of debates and other late campaign efforts. The limited data that exist on this topic show that campaigns need to pay equal attention to the early and late voters in order to judge the effectiveness of their campaign strategy.[22]

CONCLUSION

Early voting is here to stay. Although a measure to allow all-mail voting in Arizona was soundly defeated last year, with the Help America Vote Act (HAVA) being implemented in every state, it is likely that more and more states will opt for no-excuse absentee voting, early balloting, and all-mail voting. Federal legislation introduced by U.S. senators Ron Wyden, Barack Obama, and John Kerry to provide funding for states and localities to switch to all-mail voting—legislation that was defeated last year—is being reintroduced in the new Democratic-led Congress.[23]

All these trends point to a longer campaign period in more races, with the resulting need for new techniques to capture the vote without turning off the voters. The trick, then, for consultants and campaigns is to develop finer targeting methods, while elections officials may need better tracking mechanisms to predict voter turnout. If more states develop exclusive mail-in balloting, some of these problems will ease, as people grow more accustomed to voting by mail and states and counties make more efficient use of their resources to count votes quickly. Whatever developments are put into place, long campaign seasons may be here to stay.

NOTES

1. "No Excuse One-Stop Absentee Voting Sites," North Carolina State Board of Elections (http://www.sboe.state.nc.us/pdf/law/NEOSVoting.PDF).

2. For early and absentee voting laws as of 7/26/06, see http://electionline.org/Default.aspx?tabid=474.

3. Hal Malchow, "Opinion: Strategies for Reaching Voters Who Cast Ballots Early and by Mail," *Campaigns and Elections Magazine* (July 2004).

4. Multinomah County Web site (http://www.co.multnomah.or.us/dbcs/elections/election_information/voting_in_oregon.shtml).

5. Priscilla L. Southwell, "Five Years Later: A Reassessment of Oregon's Vote by Mail Electoral Process," University of Oregon–Eugene, Dept. of Political Science (2003).

6. Paul Gronke (Director, EVIC at Reed College), "Ballot Integrity and Voting by Mail: The Oregon Experience. A Report for the Commission on Federal Election Reform," June 15, 2005 (http://www.reed.edu/~gronkep/docs/Carter%20Baker%20Report-publicrelease.pdf), p. 2.

7. Gronke, "Ballot Integrity," p. 3.

8. Gronke, "Ballot Integrity," p. 4.

9. See http://www.electioncenter.org/.

10. California Secretary of State's Office (http://www.ss.ca.gov/elections/hist_absentee.htm).

11. John Wildermuth, "Ballot Counts Stretch Days, Weeks—Delay Final Election Results," *San Francisco Chronicle*, February 2, 2006.

12. Pete Winn, "Getting Out the Church Vote: Absentee Ballots and Early Voting," Citizen Link, 10/15/2004 (http://www.citizenlink.org/CLFeatures/A000000395.cfm).

13. John D. McKinno and Erika Lovly, "Republicans See Edge from Early Voting," *Wall Street Journal*, October 31, 2006.

14. McKinno and Lovly, "Republicans."

15. Saul Anuzis, "Turnout Watch: Behind the Scenes of the 72 Hour Program," The Hotline (http://hotlineblog.nationaljournal.com/archives/2006/11/turnout_watch_b.html).

16. Gronke, "Ballot Integrity," p. 2, footnote 10.

17. Gronke, "Ballot Integrity."

18. Malchow, "Opinion Strategies," p. 3.

19. Paul Gronke, "Early Voting Reforms and American Elections," August 2004 (http://www.reed.edu/~gronkep/docs/Gronke-EarlyVoting-APSA2004.pdf).

20. Dotty LeMieux, "The Changing Role of the Absentee Voter in Local Elections," *Campaigns & Elections Magazine* (September 2006).

21. Jo Becker, "Voters May Have Their Say before Election Day," *Washington Post*, August 26, 2004 (http://www.washingtonpost.com/ac2/wp-dyn/A33796-2004Aug25?language=printer).

22. Gronke, "Early Voting," p. 15.

23. Jeff Mapes, "Vote by Mail Spreads Across U.S.," *The Oregonian*, January 1, 2007.

9

Americans Abroad and Voting at War

Captain Samuel F. Wright

In a 1952 letter to Congress, President Harry S Truman wrote:

> About 2,500,000 men and women in the Armed Forces are of voting age at the present time. Many of those in uniform are serving overseas, or in parts of the country distant from their homes. They are unable to return to their states either to register or to vote. Yet these men and women, who are serving their country and in many cases risking their lives, deserve above all others to exercise the right to vote in this election year. At a time when these young people are defending our country and its free institutions, the least we at home can do is to make sure that they are able to enjoy the rights they are being asked to fight to preserve.

What President Truman wrote of the brave young men and women who were fighting the Korean War in 1952 is equally true of their grandsons and granddaughters, and great-grandsons and great-granddaughters, fighting today. Unfortunately, today, as in 1952, military personnel and their family members are often disenfranchised through no fault of their own. In the twenty-first century, most states still conduct absentee voting essentially as they did during the Korean War: by shipping pieces of paper around the world via "snail mail."

Whether one is voting from a nursing home in his or her home county or from Iraq or Afghanistan, there are three time-consuming steps in absentee voting. First, the absentee ballot application must travel from the voter to the local election official. Second, the unmarked absentee ballot must travel from the election official to the voter. Finally, the marked absentee ballot must travel from the voter back to the election official and must be received (not just postmarked) by the deadline imposed by state law. In most states, the deadline is the time set for the close of the polls on Election Day.

Each of these steps can take weeks if the mail must be used, but would take only seconds if secure electronic means were authorized. Every day, huge sums of money are transmitted by electronic means. In the military, *classified* information is transmitted electronically, via a Department of Defense (DoD) system called SIPRNET (Secure Intranet Protocol Routing Network). If electronic systems are secure enough to transfer billions of dollars and our nation's most sensitive secrets, it should be possible to establish a system enabling a service member to vote by electronic means, no matter where the service of our country has taken him or her. Unfortunately, there is still a lot of resistance to this necessary capability, both among election officials and within DoD itself.

Federal law gives overseas citizens the right to vote and to register to vote by absentee process in primary, general, runoff, and special elections for federal offices (president, U.S. senator, and U.S. representative). The pertinent federal law is called the Uniformed and Overseas Citizens Absentee Voting Act (UOCAVA), and it is codified in Title 42 of the United States Code, sections 1973 and following (42 U.S.C. §§1973 et seq.).

UOCAVA applies to "absent uniformed services voters" and to "overseas voters." An absent uniformed services voter is a member of the uniformed services (Army, Navy, Marine Corps, Air Force, Coast Guard, Public Health Service commissioned corps, or the National Oceanic and Atmospheric Administration commissioned corps), or the spouse or family member of a uniformed services member. The absent uniformed services voter has the right to vote under UOCAVA *whether inside or outside the United States.* The individual does not even need to be absent from his or her home state—just from the county or other local election precinct where the individual is eligible to vote. For example, a sailor from Arlington, Virginia, who is serving on active duty in Norfolk, Virginia, is an "absent uniformed services voter" for purposes of UOCAVA. The law applies only to federal elections, but most active-duty service members and their voting-age family members are eligible under state law to vote for *all* offices, including governor, state representative, mayor, and so on.

WHERE TO VOTE?

Members of the military serving at sea or anywhere outside the United States must, of course, vote by absentee ballot, if they are to vote at all. If they are serving within the United States, they have a choice to make: register to vote at the place where they are serving, or vote in their hometown by absentee ballot. Of course, they are limited to one vote per election. There is a single place that constitutes a person's *domicile,* and the person must vote only in that place.

Every human being has one and only one domicile, even if it is something of a legal fiction. The billionaire who owns twenty houses and sleeps in all twenty over the course of a year has one domicile; she does not earn additional votes by buying additional houses. The sailor who sleeps and keeps all his worldly possessions in a rack and wall-locker on a submarine likewise has one and only one domicile.

An individual entering active duty starts with a *domicile of origin,* which is the place where the person lived and was domiciled immediately before entering active duty—the place that is also called the *home of record.* Some career service members remain on active duty for twenty years or more and keep the domicile of origin at the home of record for the entire time. They have the right to do that.[1]

Military personnel can change domicile while on active duty, but to do so they must *simultaneously* have a *physical presence for a significant time* at the place where they wish to establish their new domicile (called a *domicile of choice*) and the *intent* to make that place their home. Neither intent alone nor physical presence alone is sufficient to bring about a change in domicile.

A tangible example may help to clarify the legal mumbo-jumbo. Seaman Joe Jones, U.S. Navy, grew up and graduated high school in Boston, Massachusetts. He joined the Navy while in his senior year, and he reported to boot camp a few days after the graduation ceremony. The home in Boston where he lived with his parents is his domicile of origin. When he votes by absentee ballot, he must list that address as his "voting residence address" in item 3 of the Federal Post Card Application (FPCA).

Jones's domicile and voting residence address is the place where *he* lived and was domiciled just before entering active duty. It is not necessarily the current domicile of his parents. It is likely that at some point during Jones's military service, if he remains on active duty for a full career, his parents will move away or even pass away. Such a change does *not* affect Jones's domicile. Jones can maintain his domicile of origin and voting residence address at that address for his entire career, even thirty years. It does not matter that Jones no longer has relatives living at that address. It does not matter that Jones cannot receive mail at that address. It does not matter that the house was torn down to make room for a new commercial development.

Now let us say that Jones completes boot camp and is assigned to the naval station in Corpus Christi, Texas, for his first duty station. Whereas Massachusetts has a high state income tax, Texas has no state income tax. Jones can change his domicile to Texas and avoid paying the Massachusetts state income tax, and many service members do something like this. But there are other important consequences of changing domicile. State income tax liability is an important consideration, but it is not the only consideration.

For example, suppose that instead of remaining on active duty for his career, Jones decides to leave active duty at the end of his four-year commitment. He returns home to Massachusetts and enrolls in the University of Massachusetts. He seeks the in-state tuition rate, which is substantially lower than the rate charged to students who were not residents of Massachusetts immediately before enrolling. The university informs Jones that he is not eligible for the in-state tuition rate because he was domiciled in Texas, not Massachusetts, for the last three years prior to enrollment.

The point is that no one should change domicile lightly, just to save a few bucks on state income tax. They must think this decision through carefully, and may need legal advice. So long as they are on active duty, they are eligible for military *legal assistance* from a military legal assistance attorney.[2]

A military legal assistance attorney is a judge advocate, or in some cases a civilian attorney employed by DoD, whose specific assignment is to assist service members and their families with *civilian* legal problems. Not all judge advocates are legal assistance attorneys—some are prosecutors or defense counsel in courts martial, some serve as staff judge advocates advising military commanders, and some serve in other important ways.

Now back to Seaman Jones, the sailor from Boston who changed his domicile to Corpus Christi, Texas, while assigned there on active duty. Suppose he decides to reenlist at the end of his initial four-year active-duty commitment. He remains on active duty for twenty-eight years and retires as a warrant officer. Having made a bona fide change of his domicile, from Boston to Corpus Christi, he is entitled to *maintain* his new domicile in Texas for the entire period he is on active duty. He has the right to continue voting by absentee ballot in Nueces County, Texas, until the day he leaves active duty by retiring. This assumes, of course, that he remains on active duty continuously and does not establish a new domicile of choice at some other place during his military career.

Every person has *one and only one* domicile, for all legal purposes. A person in military service cannot simultaneously vote in Virginia, where he or she is stationed, and claim to be exempt from Virginia state income tax because of being domiciled in Texas. The service member, by registering and voting in Virginia, became a Virginian and gave up the Texas domicile.

Under a law formerly known as the Soldiers' and Sailors' Civil Relief Act (SSCRA), and now (since a 2003 rewrite) as the Servicemembers' Civil Relief Act (SCRA), the active-duty service member cannot be required to pay state income tax on military salary and benefits to the state where he or she physically resides *unless that place is the member's domicile.* The SCRA also exempts the service member from having to pay personal property tax (on a vehicle, for example) to the state where the member physically resides but is not domiciled. This assumes that the vehicle is titled in the service member's name alone and is not utilized in a trade or business.

Consider Colonel Mary Smith, on active duty in the Marine Corps for the last twenty-five years and domiciled in California. She is transferred from

Okinawa to Marine Corps Base Quantico, in Prince William County, Virginia. She buys a house in Stafford County, two exits south of Quantico on I-95. The SCRA precludes Virginia and Stafford County from taxing her military salary or her personal automobile. But if she registers to vote in Stafford County, she thereby waives her claim to California domicile and her exemption from the Virginia state income tax and the Stafford County personal property tax.

Now take Joe Smith, Mary's husband. He lives with Mary and the children in the Stafford County house. Unlike Mary, Joe is not on active duty in the armed forces; maybe he has already retired, or maybe he never served. It does not matter for this purpose. Joe commutes every day to Washington, DC, where he has a good job.

Because Joe is not on active duty, the SCRA does not protect him from having to pay Virginia state income tax on *his* salary. He must pay that tax regardless of whether he votes in Stafford County, or votes somewhere else, or does not vote at all. Accordingly, Joe seeks to register and vote in Stafford County. He has every right to do so, and his choice to register to vote in Stafford County has no effect on Mary's domicile or her exemption from having to pay Virginia state income tax on her salary.

It may seem anomalous, but it is entirely possible for a married couple to live together in the same house but be domiciled in different states, if one or both of them are on active duty in the armed forces. And the result would be no different if the husband were the active-duty colonel and the wife the civilian. All of these issues are gender neutral. The domicile of the husband does *not* control the domicile of the wife, and vice versa.[3]

When one is voting by absentee ballot, while on active duty or while married to an active-duty service member, the voting residence address is required in item 3 of the FPCA and the "mail my ballot to" address in item 4. The election official receiving the completed FPCA needs the *exact address* of the domicile, even if the voter has no relatives living there today and cannot receive mail at that address. The election official needs the exact address to "precinct" the absentee ballot application, in order to send the correct ballot for that precise location. Within the city of Boston, for example, there are parts of three congressional districts and multiple state legislative and other districts.

Say that Bob Williams, an active-duty soldier, is from a rural area in western Massachusetts. He had no street address (just a rural route number and box number) at the home where he lived with his parents when he graduated from high school and joined the Army, more than twenty years ago. Williams has maintained his domicile at that location for his whole career and is still on active duty. When he completes his FPCA, he needs to provide a concise description of the location of his permanent home, even if the house at that place no longer exists—for example: "On the south side of State Highway 14,750 yards west of the Conoco station."

HOW TO VOTE?

If a serviceman is within the United States and has chosen to become a domiciliary of the place where he physically resides, as described above, then he must register and vote in the same way that all other eligible voters vote. In such a situation, he is not an "absent uniformed services voter" as defined by UOCAVA, because he is not absent from the county or other local election unit where he is eligible to vote.

Except in a handful of states, it is necessary to register to vote before Election Day. The voter registration deadline is generally about four weeks before Election Day, and it is a hard deadline: if the deadline passes the voter will be disenfranchised. And a voter who moves must register to vote in the new county or change his or her voter registration to the new precinct within the same county. Any voter who fails to do this by the voter registration deadline will likely be disenfranchised.[4]

On the other hand, anyone on active duty in the uniformed services, and the voting-age spouse or family member of an active-duty service member, who is away from the county or other local election jurisdiction (city, township, parish, etc.) that qualifies as that person's domicile, qualifies as an absent uniformed services voter under UOCAVA. Such voters are eligible to use the FPCA as a *simultaneous* voter registration application and absentee ballot request.

For example, Airman Barney Barnes is on active duty in the U.S. Air Force and stationed at Elmendorf Air Force Base in Alaska. Barnes graduated from high school in Florida eighteen months ago and reported to boot camp the next month. He has maintained his Florida domicile. He has never voted or even registered to vote. But if he submits a properly completed FPCA to the county supervisor of elections in his home county in Florida, the supervisor is required by federal law to send him an absentee ballot for each federal election (including primaries and special elections, as well as the November general elections) through the next two biennial general elections.

Assume that Barnes submitted the completed FPCA in February 2006. The election official must send him (without any new applications on Barnes's part) absentee ballots for the 2006 and 2008 primaries and general elections, and if there is a special election for a federal office (for example, if his U.S. representative were to die or resign), the election official must send him an absentee ballot for that election as well, all resulting from that one completed FPCA.

Federal law requires the election official to send multiple absentee ballots, for multiple elections, all from a single completed FPCA, but because of the high potential for problems in many cases a person should submit a new FPCA for each election, or at least for each year. Two years later, you are likely to have a new duty station, and a new mailing address, if you are even still on active duty.

As mentioned previously, there are three time-consuming steps involving the mail and absentee voting: the ballot request, the unmarked ballot, and the marked ballot. Most states still conduct all three steps entirely by "snail mail." Accordingly, voters must allow sufficient time for all three steps to be completed by Election Day. UOCAVA permits voters to apply for an absentee ballot, using the FPCA, *at any time during the calendar year of the election.* The problem is that voters may not know in January, or even in July, where they will be in October, when the general election ballot must be delivered. It is still beneficial to apply early in the year and to try to make contact with the local election official. In this way, the voter might be able to inform the election official by e-mail or telephone if they are deployed or redeployed, making it necessary for the election official to mail the ballot to a different address.

Every state is required by federal law to accept the FPCA, if the applicant is an "absent uniformed services voter" or an "overseas voter" as defined by UOCAVA. But the instructions for completing that federal form vary from state to state. Military units are required to have a voting assistance officer (VAO), usually a junior officer or a mid-grade noncommissioned officer. The VAO keeps blank FPCAs and copies of the *Voting Assistance Guide*, published by DoD every two years, to be distributed to interested service members. The *Guide* gives detailed instructions on how to complete the FPCA for the voter's home state, and it provides the mailing address for the election official in the voter's domicile.

Thanks to the nonpartisan Overseas Vote Foundation (OVF), there is now a new and better way to complete the FPCA voter registration form. Go to www.overseasvotefoundation.org to access online registration and absentee voter application (RAVA) tools and instructions. The OVF Web site provides everything necessary to register to vote, request a ballot, obtain the correct mailing address, and more—all in simple, easy-to-follow steps with no special training required. The OVF Voter Help Desk (VHD) will also answer individual voters' questions.

OVF has the most current database available for election jurisdiction addresses—the OVF Election Official Directory (EOD), which provides mailing and physical addresses, e-mail addresses, and fax and telephone numbers for all election jurisdictions in the United States. The EOD is the most up-to-date directory listing available.

Of the three time-consuming steps in absentee voting, the most problematic step, especially for the military voter, is the second—the transmission of the unmarked ballot from the election official to the voter—for two reasons. First, until all uncertainties about the candidates and issues on the ballot have been resolved, the election official cannot print, much less mail, the ballots. Late primaries, ballot access lawsuits, and other problems often delay the printing and mailing of absentee ballots and result in their delay in getting to the voter. This can result in overseas voters (military and civilian) losing their effective right to vote. Improvements may come in 2008, with earlier primaries scheduled in many states. There is also the new Federal Write-in Absentee Ballot (FWAB), an alternative voting method for military and overseas voters whose ballots do not arrive on time.

Complicating things is the fact that the military voter is often in transit or in the process of redeployment. Lance Corporal Connie Cox is on active duty in the Marine Corps and is serving in Iraq. She is eligible to vote in Sayner, a very small town in far northern Wisconsin. In July, while in Baghdad, she mails her completed FPCA to the town clerk back home. On October 1, on the same day that the town clerk mails the absentee ballot to Cox in Iraq, Cox suffers a serious injury when an improvised explosive device detonates near the vehicle in which she is traveling. She is transported to the National Naval Medical Center in Bethesda, Maryland. The ballot is in Iraq, but Cox is not. It may be months before that ballot catches up with her.

THE FEDERAL WRITE-IN ABSENTEE BALLOT: THE LAST-CHANCE OPTION

Fortunately, there is a solution to the late-ballot problem. It is called the Federal Write-in Absentee Ballot (FWAB). This is a special federal ballot provided for by federal law and made available at U.S. military installations at home and abroad. The blank FWAB is also available on the FVAP Web site, www.fvap.gov, or through OVF at www.overseasvotefoundation.org. The FWAB is not a complete ballot: it is limited to federal offices. The FWAB is a legal ballot in any state or territory, and voters can download it at any time.

In October 2007 OVF instituted improved, online, automated FWAB services. If a voter doesn't receive the absentee ballot by one month prior to Election Day, the FWAB is an option for voting.

The FWAB is a blank ballot: it does not contain names of candidates. You mark the ballot by writing in the names of candidates or by expressing a party preference. For example, you can write that you want to vote for the "Republican Nominee" or "Democratic Nominee" for the U.S. House of Representatives. The local election official must count that ballot for the nominee of the party in the general election.

The FWAB is a pretty poor substitute for a ballot, but it beats being wholly disenfranchised. The beauty is that voters do not have to give up on the regular ballot when they submit the FWAB. A voter who submits the FWAB and later receives the regular absentee ballot should complete and submit that ballot as well. If the regular absentee ballot arrives on time to be counted, the FWAB will be set aside and ignored. The regular absentee ballot is clearly preferable to the FWAB because it includes all offices, not just federal offices, and it lists names of candidates, not just titles of offices.

In 2004 Congress amended UOCAVA to permit the absent uniformed services voter (including military family members) to submit the FWAB *from either within or outside the United States.* Because of this 2004 amendment, Lance Corporal Cox can submit her completed FWAB from the National Naval Medical Center in Bethesda, Maryland.

Voting Information Center

Voters on active duty and voting by absentee ballot are hundreds if not thousands of miles away from the community where they vote, on Election Day and in the weeks leading up to the election. This distance means that they miss out on a lot of the sources of information about candidates and elections that other voters take for granted. These voters do not have the opportunity to watch local television, listen to local radio, or read local newspapers from the community. During the campaign season, these voters will not receive "get out the vote" calls from political phone banks. Political volunteers will not knock on their doors with campaign literature, and they probably will receive little if any political mail.

In 1988 DoD established the Voting Information Center (VIC) to give military personnel and family members the opportunity to learn about elections and public affairs in their home states and congressional districts, enabling them to engage in *informed* voting via their absentee ballots. Service personnel and family members can call the VIC toll-free from all over the world at DSN (Defense Switched Network) 425-1584 or at 1-800-438-VOTE.

Callers have the opportunity to listen to messages recorded by incumbent U.S. senators, U.S. representatives, and governors. If your senator, representative, or governor has not bothered to record a message for this free service, you will hear the default statement "No message has been recorded." During the last thirty days before the election, you can also hear, in a different part of this same system, from *challenger candidates* for senator, representative, and governor. Candidate messages are available only for a few days before the election, but incumbent messages are available all the time, in odd-numbered as well as even-numbered years.

The VIC also allows voters to communicate with their U.S. senators, U.S. representative, and governor at no cost. After hearing the official's message or the default message, callers can press 1 on a touch-tone phone, and they will be connected with the main office of the senator, representative, or governor.

NOTES

Captain Wright recently retired from the Navy Reserve Judge Advocate General's Corps, with more than thirty-seven years of active and reserve service. In 1981 he initiated an ongoing effort to reform absentee voting laws to facilitate the enfranchisement of military personnel and their families. He has recruited more than 3,000 volunteers, mostly military reservists and retirees, and each state has made some progress toward simplifying absentee voting procedures and providing more ballot transmission time. You can reach him by e-mail at samwright50@yahoo.com.

1. See Law Review 144.
2. See Law Review 125.
3. See Law Review 204.
4 See Law Review 0601.

10

PRESIDENTIAL NOMINATION VOTING

The Caucus versus the Primary

Christopher C. Hull

The major U.S. parties' presidential nominees are selected by a series of state-level contests culminating in a national convention. The states' contests come in two basic flavors: caucus-to-convention systems, like that used in the first-in-the-nation Iowa caucus, and primary elections, like that used in the first-in-the-nation New Hampshire primary.

Each state party, using one of these two voting styles, selects delegates to the national convention, which technically nominates the candidate, although since 1976, when President Gerald Ford edged California Governor Ronald Reagan at the Republican Convention, the nominee has typically become apparent earlier and earlier in the process. Republican and Democratic presidential candidates then face each other in the general election, along with third-party and independent candidates.

Though the caucus-to-convention system and the primary election both culminate in the selection of delegates to the national convention, they are very different in their procedures, in their origins, and in their impact.

CAUCUS AND PRIMARY PROCEDURES: ACTIVIST CONFAB VERSUS PARTY PLEBISCITE

A caucus is a local party meeting that conducts business, including the selection of delegates to continue on through a process that culminates in a state convention. The local caucus—usually held at the precinct level or its equivalent—performs functions such as plotting electoral strategy, determining the local party leadership, considering resolutions, and, of course, electing delegates to go on to the next level of party meeting, usually a county convention. The county convention would perform similar functions, including selecting delegates to the (congressional) district or state convention.

Ultimately, it is the state convention that once every four years determines which delegates to send to the party's national presidential nominating convention. This entire process is referred to as a "caucus-to-convention system," with only the original, local meeting bearing the shorter moniker, "caucus."

In presidential election years, some state parties conduct a straw poll at local caucuses to gauge candidate support. In Iowa this straw poll has become a major production, watched closely by the media as an early test of campaigns' relative strength. However, it should be emphasized that these straw polls are in no way binding on the process and do not necessarily reflect the candidate affiliations of national convention delegates.

Caucuses stand in contrast to the primary's formal voting process, which mirrors a general election. In a primary election, state parties open the polls and allow either party regulars or voters in general to cast a ballot over the course of an entire day. In "closed" primaries, only voters registered as affiliated with the party are allowed to participate. In "open" primaries, any voter may cast a ballot.

Closed primaries generally strengthen political parties. They encourage supporters to identify themselves, which promotes party-building contact. They reward party regulars by giving them a voice in candidate selection, and they help ensure that those participating are committed to the party's success. Open primaries, by contrast, allow the participation not only of voters who consider themselves independents, but also members of the other party—who may cast ballots for those most closely aligned with their own beliefs or, theoretically, for candidates they consider weaker and whom they would prefer that their candidate face in the general election.

ORIGINS OF THE CAUCUS AND THE PRIMARY: THE ROOTS OF THE REPUBLIC AND THE PROGRESSIVE ERA

In the United States, caucuses once dominated the nomination landscape. Originally, closed, elite-dominated "king caucuses" consisting of party regulars convened to select nominees. But those "smoke-filled rooms" led reformers to turn toward alternatives, including open caucuses, where any party member could participate, and ultimately toward primaries.

From the legislative caucuses of the 1790s, in which elected leaders and party elites selected candidates to carry their banner, caucuses evolved into strategy sessions at which party activists wrestled with each other for partisan control.[1] But during this evolution, the caucus faded relative to primaries, which have become the standard for the major U.S. political parties. The first primary nominating election was held in 1842 in Crawford County, Pennsylvania, from where the practice spread to nearby counties. However, the idea did not catch on broadly until the progressives of the late nineteenth and early twentieth centuries began pushing it as a reform measure to do away with the "smoky back rooms" dominated by party bosses.[2]

Primaries were especially popular in the post-Civil War South, where the Democratic Party had grown so muscular that no true contest took place in the general elections. The GOP, on the other hand, lagged in picking up primaries, and it was mainly after World War II that the party moved more aggressively to adopt them.[3]

In the 1970s the United States took a giant step away from caucuses toward primaries. Frustrated by the loss of activist favorite Senator George McGovern (D-SD) to party insider Vice President Hubert Humphrey in 1968, the Democratic Party adopted a resolution that ultimately led to a landslide of electoral reforms within the party's nomination system.

An extended—and extraordinary—debate in American political science concerns what the impact of these reforms has been on the U.S. presidential election process.[4] In one study, Austin Ranney makes the contention that although these Democratic nomination process reforms were intended not to promote primaries over caucuses, but rather to simply open up the process, the strict conditions required of caucuses to ensure that they were open and proportional had the effect of steering states away from them and toward primaries.[5]

The Republican Party's adoption of the primary after World War II and the Democratic Party's reforms of the 1970s swung the balance dramatically against caucuses and toward primaries. In 1948 only fourteen states held primaries, with only 5 million voters participating; in 1996 forty states held primaries, with nearly 25 million votes cast. In the 2008 cycle, Republicans held only five caucuses and Democrats only seven.[6]

THE IMPACT OF CAUCUSES AND PRIMARIES: GRASSROOTS ORGANIZING VERSUS MEDIA ADVERTISING

In caucuses a candidate's goal is to organize as many party supporters as possible to attend a lengthy meeting at a particular time. In primaries, by contrast, the goal, as during a general election, is to mobilize as many supporters as possible, while demobilizing as many nonsupporters as possible, to show up at the polls for a relatively brief process that can be conducted at any time over the course of Election Day.

Both caucuses and primaries are open to any party member (or any voter, depending on the requirements of the state and its parties). However, according to Barbara Norrander, the structural difference between primaries and caucuses leads to important results in U.S. presidential nomination contests:

> Besides channeling considerably more resources to primary than to caucus states, in caucus states candidates concentrate on organizational structures to reach party or issue activists. In primary states, advertising costs soar in attempts to reach the average voter. Candidates who are successful at one tactic may not be successful at the other.[7]

Given that caucuses tend to promote grassroots organization efforts to lure activists and primaries tend to promote advertising to all voters, it may be said that in caucuses the tone is more positive than that in primaries. Recent research has explored the impact of the move to primaries on campaign tone in American presidential nomination contests, with preliminary findings demonstrating that in the 2000 presidential election, political ads run in U.S. primary states were three times as likely to be attack ads compared with caucus states and that, controlling for other factors, primaries were associated with far more negative TV ad tone than were caucuses.[8] However, because advertising is not usually the primary method of voter contact in caucuses, these results may be misleading, as caucus competitors might be more negative in other media, such as direct mail or paid phone calls.

Caucuses are local party meetings, populated largely by committed supporters rather than the general public. They are attended mainly by those who are or who become in the process loyal partisans, only later culminating in conventions attended by their chosen representatives.

As a result, caucuses tend to insulate the broader public from a party's internal squabbles and debates—and potentially discourage them more generally, as they may encourage candidates to build up their own organizations rather than tear down an opponents public image. That said, whether divisive primaries necessarily translate into disaster in the general election is very much open to debate. Also open to debate is whether it is preferable for a party to test a candidate's meddle in grassroots support building as opposed to engaging in media sword fighting, given that the general elections have traditionally been dominated by the latter (which, moreover, likely gained strength in 2000 and 2004).

CONCLUSION

The caucus and the primary, the two main tools used to allocate state delegates in presidential races, also serve a broader function. Caucuses, local party meetings, also are used to select local party leadership and in part to determine local party strategy. Primaries, intra-party (or occasionally nonpartisan) elections, also determine which candidates go on to contests for other offices, from city council to U.S. Senate. The quadrennial presidential nomination process does not and has never overlapped perfectly with states' processes for these other offices. As a result, the existing state presidential nominating systems regularly shift in their timing—especially forward, as in the "front-loading" that appears to be culminating in a virtual national primary for the 2008 cycle—and change in their character.

The trend toward presidential primaries may continue until no caucuses remain, although Iowa in particular may find it difficult to give up its century-and-a-half-old tradition. For the time being, however, the presidential nomination process for the two major parties will continue to include both tools, the caucus and the primary, in its progression toward a final decision.

NOTES

1. Hugh Winebrenner, *The Iowa Precinct Caucuses: The Making of a Media Event*, 2nd ed. (Ames: Iowa State University Press, 1998), 227.

2. James H. Booser, "Origins of the Direct Primary," *National Municipal Review* 24 (1935): 222–223, quoted in V. O. Key, Jr., *Politics, Parties, and Pressure Groups* (New York: Crowell, 1946), 371. Cited in Harold F. Bass, Jr., "Partisan Rules, 1946–1996," in *Partisan Approaches to Postwar American Politics*, edited by Byron E. Shafer (Chappaqua, NY: Chatham House, 1998), 227. See also Christopher C. Hull, *Grassroots Rules: How the Iowa Caucus Helps Elect American Presidents* (Palo Alto, CA: Stanford University Press, 2007).

3. Bass, "Partisan Rules," 228.

4. See Randall E. Adkins and Andrew J. Dowdle, "How Important Is Early Organization to Winning Presidential Nominations? An Analysis of Pre-Primary Campaign Organization in the Post-Reform Era," Conference paper, Midwest Political Science Association, Chicago, IL, 2001; Randall E. Adkins and Andrew J. Dowdle, "How Important Are Iowa and New Hampshire to Winning Post-Reform Presidential Nominations?" *Political Research Quarterly* 54(2) (June 2001): 431–444; Bass, "Partisan Rules"; Jim Lengle and Byron Shafer, "Primary Rules, Political Power, and Social Change," *American Political Science Review* (1976): 26–40; James I. Lengle, *Representation and Presidential Primaries: The Democratic Party in the Post-Reform Era* (Westport, CT: Greenwood Press, 1981); Barbara Norrander, "Presidential Nomination Politics in the Post-Reform Era," *Political Research Quarterly* 49(4) (December 1996): 875–915; Nelson W. Polsby, *Consequences of Party Reform* (New York: Oxford University Press, 1983); Steven E. Schier, *The Rules of the Game: Democratic National Convention Delegate Selection in Iowa and Wisconsin* (Washington, DC: University Press of America, 1980).

5. Austin Ranney, "Changing the Rules of the Nomination Game," in *Choosing the President*, edited by James David Barber (Englewood Cliffs, NJ: Prentice-Hall, 1974), cited in Norrander, "Presidential Nomination Politics."

6. Bass, "Partisan Rules," 245.

7. Barbara Norrander, "Nomination Choices: Caucus and Primary Outcomes, 1976–88," *American Journal of Political Science* 33(3) (August 1989), 344.

8. See Christopher C. Hull, "Sharp Elbows on the Airwaves: Are Presidential Primary Process 'Reforms' Provoking More Negative Television Advertising?" Conference Paper, 2006 Annual Meeting of the Midwest Political Science Association, Chicago, IL, Section 24, Panel 1: New Technologies of Persuasion in Federal Politics, April 20, 2006; Christopher C. Hull, "Bringing Democracy Back to the Grassroots: The Caucus vs. the Primary as Participatory Electoral Systems," Conference Paper, 20th Annual Congress of the International Political Science Association, Fukuoka, Japan, Special Session SS01: Candidate Selection: Consequences and Strategies, July 14, 2006.

11

Casting Votes by Mail

Will Other States Follow Oregon's Lead?

Priscilla L. Southwell

In the fall of 1995 the state of Oregon was in the national limelight for two reasons: first, Senator Bob Packwood's dramatic exit from the U.S. Senate and second, Oregon's method of replacing him. The special Senate election in Oregon marked the first time that an all-mail ballot was used to decide a federal election. Prior to this 1996 election, vote by mail had been used only for local contests or statewide ballot measures.[1] The decision to use this particular electoral method was controversial and has spawned considerable debate ever since.[2] Both proponents and opponents have made various assertions about the probable effects of vote by mail, often without much empirical evidence.

BACKGROUND ON VOTE BY MAIL

From 1981 to 1983 the Oregon state legislature tested vote by mail in local elections.[3] In 1987 the legislature made vote by mail an option for local and special elections.[4] A majority of counties then adopted vote by mail for local elections.[5] In 1993 vote by mail was used, for the first time, in a statewide ballot measure election.[6]

In 1995 the Republican-controlled state legislature passed a bill that would have used vote by mail for all types of elections.[7] The impetus for this bill was the high level of absentee voting (22 percent of all votes cast) in the 1994 general election, which delayed the certification of certain electoral outcomes for many weeks.[8] However, John Kitzhaber, Oregon's Democratic governor, vetoed this bill.[9] He argued that it was too early for Oregon to adopt such a drastic reform without further study or experimentation.[10]

Senator Packwood's resignation in the fall of 1995 gave Governor Kitzhaber the option of holding either a convention or a primary election to choose the party nominees. He opted for a primary election. The "special" nature of both this December primary and the general election in January 1996 allowed then Secretary of State Phil Keisling to adopt the vote-by-mail format for these two elections. Keisling chose the format because he was s a strong supporter of vote by mail and, given the governor's explanation for his veto of the vote-by-mail bill, this election provided an opportunity for the experimentation the governor felt was needed.[11] As secretary of state, Keisling had the right to determine the format of any "special" election—that is, any election not held on one of the four designated dates in the year.[12] Nearly 58 percent of eligible voters participated in the December 1995 primary, and approximately 66 percent of Oregon's registered voters cast a ballot in the January 1996 general election.[13]

The Oregon League of Women Voters led a successful petition drive to put vote by mail on the 1998 general election ballot, and this ballot measure passed with 69 percent of the vote. Since that time, all elections in Oregon have been conducted by mail.

THE DEBATE OVER VOTE BY MAIL

The arguments over vote by mail are varied and complex. Supporters of vote by mail make three main arguments.[14] First, the cost of conducting vote-by-mail elections is generally one-third to one-half less than the cost of conducting polling place elections.[15] Second, higher turnout typically occurs in vote-by-mail elections, although differences among elections make a pure comparison of the two types difficult.[16] Finally, proponents of vote by mail argue that by facilitating the participation of individuals who have difficulty getting to the polls, vote by mail extends the vote to a wider group of individuals.[17] Similar to the arguments presented in support of the National Voter Registration Act ("Motor Voter Bill"), its supporters argue that providing an expanded time frame for voting will reduce the impact of such obstacles as illness, childcare responsibilities, and inclement weather, which often prevent individuals from voting on Election Day.

Opponents of vote by mail question the desirability of making voting "too easy" thereby drawing uninformed individuals into the electorate.[18] The issue of fraudulent voting also concerns opponents—specifically, that someone other than the addressee will make use of undelivered or duplicate ballots.[19] Although such fraud would require the ability to forge the registered voter's signature, the possibility remains a concern for some. [20] A related concern is the prospect that someone might intimidate the voter into casting his or her ballot a certain way.[21] Finally, opponents warn about the dangers of "ballot parties," where group leaders may pressure rank-and-file members to vote as instructed.[22]

The question of partisan advantage adds another dimension to this debate. Research has shown that absentee voters who specifically request a mail-in ballot in lieu of going to the polling place tend to favor Republican candidates.[23] However, another body of research suggests that higher turnout leads to a higher probability of Democrats winning the election, although this conclusion has been challenged recently.[24] Concern over possible partisan advantage led state party leaders to swap positions on vote by mail between 1995 and 1997. Party leaders on both sides initially assumed that vote by mail would favor the Republican Party. Each party, however, reassessed its relative position after the election of a Democratic senator in the 1996 vote-by-mail election, and the parties switched views on vote by mail.[25]

ANALYSIS OF THE IMPACT OF VOTE BY MAIL

To address the question of partisan advantage as well as many other concerns surrounding vote by mail, the University of Oregon conducted two surveys—one immediately following the 1996 special election[26] and another, follow-up survey in 2003. These surveys focused on (1) general public opinion on vote-by-mail elections; (2) the possibility of election difficulties, irregularities, or undue influence occurring during this election period; (3) the probable effect on the makeup of the electorate from the inclusion of people who voted in this mail-in election but not in previous polling place elections; (4) the effect that the all-mail format may have had on the outcome of the Senate race, and (5) the influence of vote by mail on levels of participation (2003 only). The results of these surveys are analyzed next.[27]

Voter Preferences

A clear majority (76 percent) of the respondents favored the vote-by-mail type of election over the polling place in the 1996 survey, and this proportion increased to 80.9 percent by 2003. The majority preference for vote by mail was similar across all demographic categories but was strongest among women, those under 25, those over 65, those who had moved recently, and those who were paid by the hour. When asked to explain their preferences, those respondents who favored vote by mail cited its ease and convenience, the increased time available to read the ballot, and freedom from such problems as inclement weather and conflicting job responsibilities as the primary reasons. Those who preferred polling place elections, on the other hand, mentioned concerns about casual attitudes toward voting, possible voting fraud, the loss of sense of community, and excessively long voting periods as factors driving their distrust of vote by mail.

The Context of Vote by Mail

The 1996 survey also sought to identify where, when, and how people voted in the 1996 vote-by-mail election. As discussed previously, the possibility of undue influence is an important concern in vote-by-mail elections. A substantial proportion of voters (25.6 percent) indicated that another person was in the same room when they voted, but in nearly all cases this person was a member of their immediate family, often a spouse or partner. More important, only three individuals, or 0.3 percent of all voters, said that the presence of another person made them feel pressured to vote a certain way. Of these three, only one claimed to have voted differently as a result of this pressure. Moreover, the survey identified no examples of "ballot parties." An overwhelming majority of voters marked their ballots in their homes. Of the thirty-three individuals who voted elsewhere, most marked their ballots at the office or other place of employment.

A Profile of Voter Types

To assess the effect of vote by mail on the nature of the electorate, the survey identified three types of voters based on their previous voting behavior and their ability to get to the polls. The three categories were "traditional" voter, "vote-by-mail" voter, and "registered nonvoter." Traditional voters were defined as those registered voters who (1) voted both in the 1992 polling place election and in the 1996 vote-by-mail election; (2) indicated that they had no problems getting to the polls on Election Day; and (3) indicated that, in the past, they had voted all or most of the time ($N = 425$). Vote-by-mail voters were defined as those registered voters who (1) voted in the 1996 vote-by-mail election but not in 1992 election; (2) indicated that they had problems getting to the polls; or (3) indicated that, in the past, they had voted some of the time, rarely, or never ($N = 442$). Registered nonvoters were those who did not vote in either the 1992 or the 1996 election ($N = 150$).

A comparison of traditional voters and vote-by- mail voters suggests that the latter were more likely to be nonwhite, young, politically independent, and employed. They also were more likely to have households with children, to have moved recently, and to be paid hourly.

Vote-by-mail voters were slightly less likely than traditional voters to pay "a great deal" of attention to political events in Oregon (43.2 percent vs. 45.2 percent) or to correctly state the name of the governor (75.4 percent vs. 84.1 percent). However, they were no less educated than traditional voters and were as likely to correctly identify their U.S. representative. Furthermore, no significant differences were found in ideological makeup or gender distribution between these two groups.

The reported voting behavior in the special Senate election was nearly identical for the two sets of voters. That is, nearly identical proportions of the two groups indicated support for the Democratic or the Republican Senate candidate, respectively. This suggests that no partisan advantage accrued to either party as a result of the vote-by-mail format. However, the group of vote-by-mail voters contained more registered Independents than did the traditional voters.

Effect of Vote by Mail on Voter Turnout

The follow-up 2003 survey, conducted five years after Oregon began the use of vote by mail for all elections, showed even greater support for this method of conducting elections, as noted earlier. It also asked respondents whether they had voted "more often," "less often," or "about the same" since Oregon started conducting its elections by mail. Although a majority of respondents indicated that they voted at about the same frequency under either system, 24.5 percent indicated that they had voted more often under vote by mail. Multivariate analysis showed that female respondents or those who were employed were the most likely to claim that they voted more frequently since the advent of vote by mail.[28]

As for the actual overall turnout in Oregon elections from 1980 to 2006, research results show that the mobilizing impact of vote by mail on voter participation is seen primarily in special elections, rather than during the usual primary and general elections, as shown in Table 11.1. Although there appears to be a modest increase in presidential election turnout under vote by mail, this difference is primarily attributable to the closeness of the particular presidential elections (2000 and 2004) held since the adoption of vote by mail.[29]

Oregonians in general vote at higher rates than do residents of other states, so the effect of an electoral reform such as vote by mail is likely to be marginal in these normally scheduled elections. For Oregonians who are likely voters, vote

Table 11.1
A Comparison of Turnout of Registered Voters Across Electoral Format and Election Type, 1980–2006

	Polling Place	Vote by Mail
All elections (43)	57.5%	55%
Presidential elections (7)	78.5%	82.4%
Off-year general elections (7)	69.3%	70%
Primary elections (14)	46.5%	45.8%
Special elections (15)	43.9%	50.6%
N	(24)	(19)

Source: State of Oregon, Office of the Secretary of State, *Election Report*, 1960–2006.

by mail may prevent them from missing an election when they experience an unforeseen personal crisis on Election Day. However, it is unlikely to draw new voters into the electorate, except in the case of no-candidate, special elections, which have traditionally lacked the stimulus to draw voters to the polls. However, other states with typically lower rates of participation might experience a boost in turnout under vote by mail, because of the added convenience of voting under such a system.

CONCLUSIONS AND RECOMMENDATIONS

In general, the findings of these empirical analyses should assuage many of the concerns about vote by mail. Evidence of undue influence or pressure on voters from such a system is minimal or nonexistent. Nearly all voters cast their ballots under circumstances that closely resembled the privacy of a voting booth. The long-term effect of enfranchising additional citizens through vote by mail is not likely to change the characteristics of the electorate or to advantage one party over the other. And vote by mail is very popular, as it simply reduces the physical obstacles and eases the time constraints connected with the act of voting.

For those states considering the adoption of vote by mail, the following steps or system characteristics are recommended:

1. An initial "experiment" using local elections only, followed by the system's possible use in special elections, and finally moving to the federal election.
2. Use of the secrecy envelope and signature verification of the mailing envelope (see Note 20).
3. Consistent updating of the addresses of registered voters (Oregon does not send out ballots once a ballot is returned as "undeliverable" to a registered voter's address).
4. Require identification at the time of initial voter registration.
5. Notification of former county's election division when voter re-registers at another address in the state.
6. Establishment of civil penalties for undue influence or coercion of voter or for voter fraud.

As with any change in the "rules of the game," there is understandable concern about the unintended and unforeseen consequences of a proposed electoral reform, coupled with inevitable self-interested assessments, but Oregon's experience should dispel most of these doubts and concerns. The adoption of vote by mail has been gradual, with considerable input by election officials, practical politicians, academics, and the public along the way. The result has been a highly successful method of easing the burdens and costs of the simple act of voting.

NOTES

1. See Randy Hamilton, "American All-Mail Balloting: A Decade's Experience," *Public Administration Review* 48 (1988): 860.

2. See Harry Esteve, "Mail Vote Experiment to be Watched Closely," *Register Guard* (Eugene, OR), October 17, 1995, p. 1A; "Reading the Clues from Oregon," *Los Angeles Times*, February 1, 1996, p. 8.

3. See Act of August 21, 1981, ch. 805, 1981 *Oregon Laws* 1199. Vote by mail was made permanent in 1983. See Act of June 21, 1983, ch. 199, 1983 *Oregon Laws* 226.

4. See Act of June 23, 1987, ch. 357, 1987 *Oregon Laws* 624.

5. See Secretary of State, State of Oregon, *Oregon's Special Senate Election* (November 11, 1995) [hereinafter *Special Senate Election*].

6. See Nena Baker, "Mail Balloting Isn't in the Bag," *The Oregonian,* November 15, 1996, p. A1.

7. See S.B. 319, 68th Oregon Legislative Regular Session (1995).

8. See "Vote by Mail Gains Support after Delays in Ballot Count," *Register Guard* (Eugene, OR), November 19, 1994, p. 5B. This delay is caused by the need to check each absentee ballot against the polling place roster to ensure that no one has voted twice. See Oregon Revised Statute 254.470(10), (11) (1997).

9. See "Vote by Mail," p. 5B.

10. See Harry Esteve, "Voters Will Still Be Going to the Poll," *Register Guard* (Eugene, OR), July 15, 1995, p. 1A.

11. See Secretary of State, State of Oregon, *Oregon Blue Book* 15 (1997–1998) [hereinafter *Blue Book*].

12. See *Blue Book,* p. 15,338.

13. See *Blue Book* (2005–2006) for turnout in recent vote-by-mail elections.

14. See "Vote by Mail Is a Winner," *San Francisco Chronicle*, February 2, 1996, p. A20; "Oregon's New Idea," *Washington Post*, February 5, 1996, p. A20; "Mail-in Democracy," *New York Times*, February 8, 1996, p. A24.

15. For example, the May 1994 polling place election in Oregon cost $4.33 per ballot. *Special Senate Election*, p. 4.

16. See Priscilla Southwell and Justin Burchett, "The Effect of All-Mail Elections on Voter Turnout and the Composition of the Electorate," paper delivered at the Annual Meeting of the American Political Science Association, San Francisco (August 29–September 1, 1996); David Magleby, "Participation in Mail Ballot Elections," *Western Political Quarterly*, 40 (1987): 79–91.

17. See "Vote by Mail Is a Winner," p. A20.

18. See George Will, "Mail Vote Subverts Democracy," *Register Guard* (Eugene, OR), October 26, 1995, p. 11A; Norman Ornstein, "A Vote Cheapened," *Washington Post*, February 8, 1996, p. A25; Jeff Jacoby, "Election by Mail? Here's a No Vote," *Boston Globe*, February 1, 1996, p. 9.

19. See Brad Cain, "Senate Election Prompts Vote by Mail Worries," *Register Guard* (Eugene, OR), October 8, 1995, p. 4B.

20. In Oregon the voter marks the ballot, puts it into an unmarked "secrecy" envelope, and then puts this envelope in a separate mailing envelope. The voter must then sign the outside of this mailing envelope. This signature is initially compared with the

voter's original signature on the registrar's list. Then the secrecy envelope is separated from the mailing envelope and the ballots are subsequently tallied on Election Day. See Oregon Revised Statutes 254.470(10), (11) (1997). See also "Election Workers Do Just Fine without Those Fancy Gizmos," *Register Guard* (Eugene, OR), November 24, 1996, p. 8C. Voter fraud is a Class C felony in Oregon. See Oregon Revised Statutes 260.715(1)–(5), 260.993(2) (1997).

21. This scenario allegedly occurs most often in abusive relationships. See Cain, "Senate Election," p. 4B.

22. See Nena Baker, "Welcome to the Mail-Ballot Party," *The Oregonian*, October 18, 1995, p. A1.

23. See Samuel C. Patterson and Gregory A. Caldiera, "Mailing in the Vote: Correlates and Consequences of Absentee Voting," *American Journal of Political Science* 29 (1988): 766; J. Eric Oliver, "The Effects of Eligibility Restrictions and Party Activity on Absentee Voting and Overall Turnout," *American Journal of Political Science* 40 (1996): 498.

24. Among those concluding that higher turnout helps the Democratic Party are Walter Dean Burnham, *The Current Crisis in American Politics* (New York: Oxford University Press, 1983); Frances Fox Piven and Richard A. Cloward, *Why Americans Don't Vote* (New York: Pantheon, 1989); Benjamin Radcliff, "Turnout and the Democratic Vote," *American Politics Quarterly* 22 (1994): 259. But see also Ruy A. Teixeira, *The Disappearing American Voter* (Washington, DC: Brookings Institution Press, 1992), 137–143; and Jerry Calvert and Jack Gilchrist, "Suppose They Held an Election and Almost Everybody Came," *Political Science and Politics* 26 (1993): 695, 699 (who find that nonvoters do not differ from actual voters in their partisan preferences). James DeNardo in his articles "Turnout and the Vote: The Joke Is on the Democrats," *American Political Science Review* 74 (1980): 406, and "Does Heavy Turnout Help Democrats in Presidential Elections?" *American Political Science Review* 80 (1986): 1299, suggests that only a minority party benefits from elevated turnout. Recent analyses conclude that the overall relationship between turnout and partisan outcomes is insignificant. See Jack H. Nagel and John F. McNulty, "Partisan Effects of Voter Turnout in Senatorial and Gubernatorial Elections," *American Political Science Review* 90 (1996): 780; and Fran Quigley, "Social Welfare and Ideological Attitudes of United States Nonvoters: Assessing the Potential Impact of the National Voter Registration Act of 1993," *Journal of Political and Military Sociology* 23 (1995): 227.

25. See Baker, "Mail Balloting," p. A1.

26. Funding for this 1996 survey and subsequent analysis was obtained from the National Science Foundation. The National Science Foundation bears no responsibility for uses of this collection or for interpretations or inferences based on such uses.

27. See Priscilla L. Southwell and Justin Burchett, "Survey of Vote-by-Mail Senate Election in the State of Oregon," *Political Science and Politics* 91(1) (1997): 53–57.

28. See Priscilla L. Southwell, "Vote by Mail: Voter Preferences and Self-Reported Voting," *American Review of Politics* 39 (forthcoming).

29. See Paul Gronke and Priscilla Southwell, "Convenience Voting Reforms and Voting Turnout," paper presented at the 2007 Annual Meeting of the American Political Science Association, Chicago, IL, August 30–September 2, 2007.

12

The Rise of Ballot Initiatives

Kristina Wilfore

At the dawn of the twentieth century, progressive reformers wanted to exorcise the corruption and greed plaguing many state legislatures. These reformers saw the ballot initiative process as enabling ordinary citizens to shape public policy and regain power from the corporate interests, which were running roughshod over—or buying off—their elected officials. The activists also realized that the initiative process could have an "educative value," by which placing measures on the ballot would encourage citizens to become more civically and politically engaged.

Fast-forward 100 years. The original authors of the process may not recognize the system they so passionately advocated. First, ballot initiatives are not just about public policy anymore. In fact, the importance of ballot initiatives has never been greater within the purely political realm. No longer are citizen groups, individuals, corporations, and other vested interests using the initiative process solely to change public policy in the states. In fact ballot initiative sponsors today are often agnostic about the policy focus of their ballot measure campaigns—instead choosing to insert controversial or "wedge" issues into the election in order to drive certain voters to the polls and impact the outcome.

Second, issue committees may raise unlimited sums of "soft" money. As a result, some argue that candidates running for statewide office increasingly use initiatives to provide an alternative electoral vehicle outside restrictive candidate campaign contribution limits.

Regardless of the intent, voters increasingly respond to ballot measures, often claiming to be more mobilized by issues on the ballot than by candidates. Each year, voters in states across the country go to the ballot box for reasons other than proclaiming their support for an aspiring potential officeholder. They are motivated by the opportunity to decide for themselves how issues close to their lives are managed and resolved, instead of leaving it up to the promises of lawmakers. These key issues of the day—including raising the minimum wage, rolling back affirmative action, allowing the medical use of marijuana, and banning same-sex marriage, to name just a few recent trends—together comprise the fabric of daily life for millions of citizens.

Ballot initiatives represent the most direct form of democracy and civic participation that our country has to offer. Yet although they possess the power to draw voters to the polls, their significance is often overshadowed by the sometimes higher-profile parade "buzz" created by candidate races. Even as many conservative and progressive organizations for years have understood the power and potential of ballot measures, many national political operatives and candidates have been slow to see the benefits that initiatives can offer their campaigns. This is a mistake.

Voters have become increasingly cynical and disengaged from electoral politics. Ballot measures create a direct opening to talk with, identify, and turn out voters as well as provide a vehicle through which to define a message and influence national elections. Initiatives also present an early agenda-setting opportunity. The process of signature gathering alone places a campaign in a position to gauge and influence public sentiment on many issues prior to the heat of the election. Candidates and their gurus have a golden opportunity to use this inherently democratic process to mobilize activists and voters around a coherent issue agenda, keep opponents scattered and on the defensive, and swing crucial elections.

Throughout the years ballot measures have been used as a tool to:

1. Recruit, mobilize and energize activists on both sides of the political spectrum.
2. Increase turnout of key voters.
3. Frame the election cycle around particular controversial ideas.
4. Drain or divert resources from the opposition.
5. Help define issues and candidates in the eyes of voters.
6. Provide an effective use of soft money donations.

BALLOT MEASURE USAGE

The 2006 cycle was the third most active election cycle for ballot initiatives since the first measure was proposed in 1904. Voters decided 204 statewide measures in thirty-seven states last cycle. Seventy-nine of the 204 measures were from the people (citizen-petitioned) and 125 referred by government (legislative referenda). There were 22 more initiatives on the ballot than in 2004. Voters approved 29 initiatives and 108 legislative referenda. Figure 12.1 explains the differences between initiatives and referenda, and Table 12.1

Figure 12.1
Initiatives and Referenda: Definitions

According to the Initiative and Referenda Institute, *initiatives* involve citizens collecting a minimum number of signatures on a petition within a specified time, then placing advisory questions, memorials, statutes, or constitutional amendments on the ballot for their fellow citizens to adopt or reject. Twenty-four states allow the initiative process.

In many of the same states citizens have the ability to decide laws or amendments proposed by the state legislature. This process is commonly referred to as the *referendum process.*

There are two types of referenda in this country—*popular and legislative.*

The *popular referendum*, which is available in twenty-four states but is used much less frequently, allows the people to refer to the ballot specific legislation enacted by their legislature by collecting signatures on a petition for the people to either accept or reject.

A *legislative referendum*, which is allowed in all states, permits state legislatures, an elected official, state-appointed constitutional revision commission, or other government agency or department to submit propositions (constitutional amendments, statutes, bond issues, etc.) to the people for their approval or rejection.

Table 12.1
National Initiative and Referendum Activity, 1998–2006

Year	Initiatives or Citizen Vetoes	Legislative Referenda	Total Ballot Measures
2006	79 (29 passed)	125 (108 passed)	204 (137 passed)
2004	57	106	163
2002	53	147	200
2000	71	133	204
1998	61	174	235

shows the specific initiative and referendum activity over the last five elections.

Not only has the number of initiatives increased, but the intensity, coordination, and money spent make recent election cycles unique, with multi-state, single-issue strategies dominating the political dynamics in the states. Organizations and individuals supporting or opposing ballot measures in 2006 spent a significant amount of money on those measures. Although 2004 was a record-breaking year, with $393 million spent on ballot initiatives, in 2006 just twelve of the most expensive initiatives in the country spent $329,142,360. That includes the most expensive initiative campaign ever—$153 million spent by proponents and opponents on California's renewable-energy campaign.

Very few proposed initiatives make it to the ballot, and less than half of those pass. Incorporating results from the most recent election, a total of 2,212 initiatives have qualified for the ballot since the process began. Less than half of all measures have been approved by voters; 900 of the measures passed, or 40.7 percent. The passage rate of the 2006 initiatives was lower than the historical average, as only 29 out of 79 initiatives were approved by voters, or 36.7 percent.

THE IMPACT OF BALLOT MEASURES ON VOTER TURNOUT

Initiative campaigns focused on achieving larger electoral gains—targeted turnout, message framing opportunities for candidates, wedging political opponents based on past votes on the issue—have successfully changed the dynamic of state elections. When ballot measure campaigns in multiple states focus on these goals using the same issue, together they can force a national public conversation on a single issue. Conservatives accomplished this feat in 2004 using thirteen gay marriage bans, while progressives responded in 2006 with initiatives to raise and index the minimum wage in six states.

Peer-reviewed academic research has documented that ballot measures do increase voter turnout in midterm and even in presidential elections (though the impact is less significant in high-voter-turnout years). Research has shown that weak partisans are more likely to be mobilized to turn out and vote by ballot measures than are Independents, and that some ballot initiatives help to shape the electorate in favor of the proponents of those measures, while others help to mobilize opponents of the measures.

Turnout Facts and Figures

- Over the past twenty-five years states with the ballot initiative process have had higher voter participation than states without the process. On average each statewide initiative on the ballot increased a state's turnout by almost 1 percent in presidential elections and almost 2 percent in midterm elections, holding constant other state demographic information (high school graduation rates, region, racial diversity), and economic (income) and political (voter registration laws, U.S. Senate and gubernatorial races) factors.

- Between 1972 and 1996, holding other factors constant, the presence of "salient" initiative and legislative referenda led to an average increase in turnout in midterm elections by roughly 3 percent over states without measures on the ballot, but had no effect in presidential elections.
- Individual, survey-level findings on turnout have shown that citizens exposed to initiatives on their statewide ballot are more likely to vote, all else equal, in midterm elections and some presidential elections. Holding all other factors constant, national survey data show that in the 1998 midterm election, each additional initiative on a statewide ballot increased the likelihood of an individual voting by 1 percentage point. Thus, an individual residing in a state with four initiatives on the ballot was estimated to have a 4-point higher probability of voting than if the same individual resided in a state without an initiative on the ballot.

BALLOT MEASURE MONEY TRENDS

Because ballot issues do not provide voters with partisan cues, it is important for voters to understand what economic interests are involved in ballot measure campaigns and how these campaigns are often coordinated at the national level.

Each year, a handful of grassroots organizations that depend on a broad volunteer base and a large number of small donors use the initiative process to advance issues long ignored or blocked by legislative bodies. However, powerful special interests and wealthy individuals also use the process to circumvent state legislatures to advance their policy agendas.

Ballot measure campaign financing differs from candidate campaign financing in two significant ways. First, there are no state limits on contributions to ballot measure campaigns. Any individual or organization can spend unlimited money on a ballot measure issue. This was reinforced in the *Buckley v. Valeo* Supreme Court decision, which categorized legislative issues (i.e., ballot initiatives) as free speech and candidate campaigns as electioneering. As a result, the cost of ballot measure campaigns can skyrocket into the millions.

Second, ballot measure contribution and expenditure disclosure procedures are much weaker than candidate campaign disclosure practices. Voters in many states often struggle to acquire ballot measure funding information, and often only after the election do voters become aware of the economic interests behind the campaigns. Gathering comprehensive ballot measure donor data can be difficult even months after an election. Each state has its own campaign finance reporting laws, schedules, and disclosure procedures. Most state disclosure agencies—usually a division of the secretary of state's office—are severely understaffed and under-resourced. For a variety of reasons, many disclosure agencies readily admit that they process candidate donor data before ballot measure donor data, further delaying initiative donor disclosure. Moreover, states that do not require campaign finance reports to be electronically filed generally add weeks and sometimes months to disclosure schedules.

Unlike most competitive candidate campaigns, ballot measures are often characterized by lopsided spending. Ballot campaigns that pit one industry against a competing industry (Indian gaming vs. nontribal gaming, for example) often involve heavy spending on both sides. Spending patterns in ideological ballot fights (such as efforts to ban gay marriage) vary widely. Casual ballot initiative campaign observers and academics who study initiative campaign finance trends agree that overwhelming spending against an initially popular measure will practically guarantee its defeat whereas heavy spending in favor of an initiative does not ensure its passage.

Spending data gathered during the 2002 election confirm this theory also. Of the eight most expensive "yes" campaigns (those urging voters to approve a ballot measure) in which proponents outspent opponents by at least 21 to 1—overwhelming odds by any standard—only two were approved by voters. Meanwhile, of the eight most expensive "no" campaigns (those urging voters to reject a ballot measure) in which opponents outspent proponents only by at least 2.5 to 1, voters rejected all eight questions.

Though the financial composition of ballot measures varies widely from year to year, most ballot measure campaigns can be characterized in one of the following ways:

- Grassroots or issue advocates versus corporate or special interests (such as the effort to require labeling of genetically modified foods in Oregon and the measure to de-privatize hydroelectric dams in Montana)
- Industry versus industry (e.g., tribal gaming vs. corporate gaming)
- Ideological group versus ideological group

CONSIDERATIONS FOR BALLOT INITIATIVE CAMPAIGNS

Although the initiative process can be an effective way to embed important and just policies into state law, like all mechanisms for social change, ballot initiative campaigns are costly and time consuming. To increase the chance for success at the ballot box, initiative proponents should do the necessary work prior to filing an initiative to assess whether the process is right for their issue.

Following is a list of questions that potential ballot initiative proponents should ask themselves prior to sponsoring a ballot measure.

Does Your Initiative Have Voter Appeal?

If approved by voters, how would it affect the lives of the majority of the people in the state? As much as possible, ballot initiatives should be structured to appeal directly to voters' emotional or financial self-interest. Voters who do not have a personal stake in the outcome of a ballot measure are much more likely to be influenced by misleading information from opponents.

Initiatives to cut taxes have been extremely successful over the years—not necessarily because voters make an ideologically driven decision to shrink government, but because these measures almost always appeal to voter's short-term, pocketbook-based self-interest. On the flip side, self-interest has also made tobacco tax initiatives to expand healthcare equally victorious—nonsmokers vote to increase taxes on a product they do not use in exchange for something tangible, such as access to prescription drugs or healthcare for children.

This is not to suggest that policy issues embraced by Americans often do not engage their sense of fairness or empathy for others. However, an issue that does not appeal to a voter's self-interest is more appropriate for a lobbying or grass-roots mobilization campaign than for a ballot initiative.

Ballot initiatives to reform election procedures, for example, are often difficult to frame to appeal to a voter's self-interest. Campaign proponents in 2002 who wanted to allow same-day voter registration were unable to convince voters that it was in their self-interest to make it easier for nonregistered citizens to register to vote, even though it is difficult to oppose the notion of increasing civic participation in democracy by allowing more people to vote.

The only way to gauge popular support for an initiative is to poll on the proposed measure. Ballot initiative campaigns should begin with the support of at least 65 percent of voters. The lower the support at the start of a campaign, the higher the probability that opponents can move the vote below 50 percent. Most voters are predisposed to keep the status quo, especially if the opposition spends heavily against the measure. As mentioned above, less than half of all qualified ballot initiatives have been approved by voters.

Is It Simple and Straightforward?

Structuring too complex a ballot measure—such as by attempting to do too much in one law—is the death knell of an initiative. Complex social problems in this country often cannot be resolved by initiatives. Successful initiatives can always be explained in one succinct statement and often focus on populist themes. Simple ballot initiative concepts also lend themselves to effective advertising campaigns. Ballot initiatives are often lost in the sea of news coverage of candidates, and therefore campaigns should not rely solely on an earned media effort to communicate with voters.

The ballot initiatives in Oregon in 2002 and six states in 2006 to increase state minimum-wage levels and tie future increases to inflation are examples of simple and straightforward initiative issues. Despite being outspent in nearly every state in these elections, proponents have been successful the majority of the time. These measures are easy to understand—with a message emphasizing economic justice and fairness—and media campaigns focused on the lives of the individuals who benefit from an increase in wages and on the unjustness of members of Congress voting to increase their own wages eight times while refusing to increase the minimum wage over the last decade. Although most voters are not minimum-wage workers, the notion of adults working full-time for less than $13,000 a year intuitively does not make sense to most Americans.

Does It Have Strategic or Tactical Value?

Proponents must ask themselves whether the initiative will be difficult to beat. What are the implications of the proposed ballot measure if approved by voters? How far reaching is it? Has a similar law been approved in other states, and is there potential to replicate it? Campaign finance reform, legalization of medicinal marijuana, and term limits are examples of initiatives with both replicability and far-reaching implications. The mere suggestion of a ballot measure can also be an effective way to leverage legislative change for decision-makers that for a variety of reasons may not wish to see an issue put to a public vote.

Is the initiative diversionary—will it force the opposition to spend a lot of money and time on their campaign? Ballot initiatives have often been used to drain the resources of an adversary, or at the very least to distract them from their agenda. Does the presence of an initiative force the staunchest opposition to spend money against it? Conservatives have used this strategy to effectively force socially progressive groups to go on the defensive and use valuable resources on running "no" campaigns against initiatives that threatened reproductive freedom, affirmative action, equal rights, the environment, organized workers, nonprofit charities, public employees, public education, and an independent judiciary.

Can You Attract the Necessary Resources?

Can proponents attract the necessary resources to run an effective campaign? The chances of victory are directly correlated with the amount of money raised and are almost always proportional to the amount of money the opposition spends. It is vital to research the opposition's financial capacity and carefully assess how much money and resources they can devote to defeating an initiative. If opponents have the potential to overwhelm a campaign with opposition funds, an initiative may not be the best method to pursue. Successful initiatives tend to raise more funds and outspend their opposition. There are exceptions to this rule, but by and large if the opposition spends significantly more than the proponents, they are almost guaranteed to win.

Think clearly about actions that could be taken during the drafting of an initiative that could reduce the opposition, and start building alliances as soon as possible. For instance, the environmental organizations behind the 2002 water bonds initiative in California derived their success, in part, from effectively lobbying their opponents, such as the Chamber of Commerce, into backing away from running an opposition campaign well before the election.

Where initiative proponents were in a position to mount well-funded—or at least adequately funded, staffed, and strategized—ballot measure campaigns in the past, they have won some important victories. On the other hand, some well-publicized initiatives were never genuinely competitive, and their defeat was no real surprise. In 2002 Oregon's universal healthcare initiative faced 32 to 1 spending odds; Montana's "buy the dams" measure was outspent 41 to1; and Oregon's genetically modified foods labeling measure was outspent 61 to1, with the agricultural industry dumping more than $5 million into the campaign to defeat this measure. All three of these campaigns began with broad-based support, but they simply could not overcome their formidable opposition.

Initiatives are costly, in terms of both human resources and real dollars. Campaigns can cost anywhere from $100,000 to $160 million depending on the state, the issue, and the opposition. It is essential to have a feasible fundraising plan in place before attempting to qualify a measure. Most winning campaigns pay for at least a portion of the signatures to qualify a measure and organize a communications strategy that includes radio and television.

People power is equally important to factor in. Particularly for citizen-based ballot initiative efforts, it is imperative to have people on the ground across the state who are connected and invested in the initiative. Potential allies should be identified and brought into the campaign coalition early, especially members of the community who have credibility with the public, the opinion leaders, and the media. Campaigns with limited resources should also strive to attract support among organizations with a considerable membership and volunteer base.

Is It Cost-Effective—Will It Cost Relatively Little to Qualify?

In addition to determining whether resources are available, it is crucial to investigate whether investing resources in a ballot measure campaign is cost-effective in the long term. If the majority of campaign funds to qualify a measure need to be spent on signature gathering, then a ballot initiative is not the right approach to take. One of the first tactical considerations the campaign will undertake is deciding whether to utilize paid or volunteer signature gatherers. All-volunteer efforts are few and far between these days, but where possible they can be very effective. For example, the Humane Society successfully collected 500,000 signatures using incredibly committed volunteers to qualify an initiative to ban gestation crates for pregnant pigs in Florida. By the end of a signature gathering process lasting a year and a half, they also had a database of approximately 12,000 volunteers.

Like everything else in a ballot initiative campaign, a decision about the method for collecting signatures is often a budgetary one. Costs for qualifying measures vary from state to state, largely based on the number of signatures required. Most states required between 5 and 20 percent of voters in the last gubernatorial election to sign a petition. Several states call for geographic distribution of signatures. For example, in Utah, 10 percent of the required signatures must come from twenty of the twenty-nine counties. Some states even require signature gatherers to be residents of the state. North Dakota is one such example.

Paid signature-gathering campaigns can cost anywhere from $1 to $4 per signature, depending on the number of petitions being circulated in the state at the same time, geographic requirements, and several other factors, including complexity. The more complex the issue, the harder it is to obtain a signature because it takes more time to explain the issue to voters. For a state such as Florida it could cost around $1 million to qualify a measure if the effort was entirely driven by paid signature gathering.

Volunteer signature gathering also requires expenditures, for recruiting, training, and managing volunteers. Some experts believe that volunteer signature-gathering drives can be nearly as costly as paid signature-gathering efforts.

Is the Political Climate Right?

As in nearly every other aspect of life, timing matters in a ballot initiative drive. In many states ballot initiative proponents can choose which election they want their initiative to be a part of. Primary and general elections—and certain sets of competing candidates—draw different kinds of voters. Presidential elections tend to pull more "liberal" voters than off-year elections. Lower-turnout elections tend to bring out a disproportionate amount of white fiscal conservatives. Careful thought should be given to how this may affect the initiative issue in question.

Consideration should also be given to other issues in the public consciousness when a ballot initiative is launched. Firefighting and law enforcement organizations in Washington encountered little opposition to an initiative to increase control over their pensions. This is hardly surprising given the level of community support these public servants enjoy in a post-9/11 climate and the public's increasing understanding of how important it is for workers to have control over their retirement funds.

Will the Ballot Language Be in Your Favor?

Ballot initiative titles and summaries should be as simple and as succinct as possible. Many initiative veterans believe that no single factor is more important to the success or failure of a campaign than the language of the initiative, especially the title. Even with an effective outreach strategy some voters will know nothing about a ballot initiative until they read the language for the first time in the voting booth. Many otherwise strong initiatives have failed merely due to complex or confusing ballot language. Ambiguous or confusing language provides an opportunity for the opposition to exploit voter confusion. In states where proponents can write their own ballot title, most successful campaigns test alternative ballot language through public opinion polling and focus groups.

Fiscal notes, which are attached to the ballot summary in the states that require them, can complicate things. For example, Ohio is one of about twelve states that require fiscal information for initiatives. However, unlike California, Ohio does not include information on the cost savings of implementing a measure. This is believed to be the main reason that a recent measure favoring drug treatment over incarceration in Ohio failed. The ballot title included the cost for implementing the measure over seven years with no reference to cost savings. The "yes" campaign chose not to challenge the language because the Ohio Supreme Court justice who would have heard their argument was openly opposed to the measure. The campaign's polling showed that voter knowledge of the measure's projected cost—without the publicizing of cost savings—was the biggest factor in reducing support for the initiative from approximately 66 to 32 percent.

Ballot initiatives aimed at limiting the political participation of working-class people—so-called paycheck protection measures—have benefited from titles that read like traditional campaign finance reform initiatives or employee projections. The title of Oregon's 2000 paycheck protection measure read "AMENDS CONSTITUTION: PROHIBITS PAYROLL DEDUCTIONS FOR POLITICAL PURPOSES WITHOUT SPECIFIC WRITTEN AUTHORIZATION," which made it difficult for opponents to help voters understand the true intent and effect of this anti-union proposal.

Similarly, in Florida in 1990, the League of Cities convinced the legislature to refer a measure to ban unfunded mandates. The legislature, which was opposed to the referendum, drafted their own language for the measure, which was so confusing (the title had a triple negative) that voters, upon initial reading, thought it would have the opposite effect to what the law would actually do. It is important that ballot initiative proponents try to maintain control of the language, when possible.

Does It Help or Hurt Candidates?

Does the presence of a ballot initiative motivate a progressive base or drive a conservative one? Does it help or hurt candidates whom initiative proponents care about? Research shows that the presence and use of the initiative process is associated with higher voter turnout in both presidential and midterm elections. The presence of certain ballot initiatives, such as a minimum-wage increase or anti-abortion measure, can also compel a certain type of voter to come to the polls and dramatically affect the outcome of the rest of the election. The presence of controversial ballot initiatives, such as gun control, often leads opponents to pour money into extensive get-out-the-vote operations that can help or hurt certain candidates.

Ballot initiative results can sometimes have unintended political consequences. The Latino vote in California over the past twenty years has been greatly influenced by two particularly controversial and divisive ballot initiatives. Ronald Reagan and other Republicans in the state had as much as 40 percent of the California Latino vote until the 1994 governor's race, in which Pete Wilson, then the Republican incumbent, championed Proposition 187—the anti–immigrants' rights measure. Although Wilson won, since Proposition 187 the Republicans' share of the Hispanic vote in California has hovered at the 20–29 percent mark. Experts attribute this to the damaging effect of Wilson's association with this controversial measure.

The anti–affirmative action initiative in California—Proposition 209—had a similarly powerful effect on voter turnout. Approved by voters in 1996, Proposition 209 banned the consideration of race in public hiring, contracting, and school admissions. The California Republican Party supported the measure and Republican lawmakers aggressively raised campaign funds for it. A pro–Proposition 209 television advertisement used the words of Dr. Martin Luther King, Jr., to convince voters that the measure would lead to a color-blind society. But political observers say the campaign alienated minority voters from the Republican Party. The GOP lost its majority in the California Assembly that election, in part because minority voters incensed by Proposition 209 flocked to the polls. Governor Jeb Bush is said to have prevented the California proponents from sponsoring a similar measure in Florida in 2000 because he didn't want a racially divisive campaign to distract from the 2000 presidential election.

Does It Help or Hurt Other Ballot Initiatives?

How does the initiative impact other measures on the same ballot? In the state of Washington in 1996 gay rights activists collected the necessary signatures to qualify a nondiscrimination measure. During the same election campaign, Washington Citizens for Handgun Safety, a coalition of religious, civic, and education groups, placed an initiative on the ballot that required safety locks for handguns. The National Rifle Association spent a tremendous amount of money to defeat this measure, which attracted a significant number of gun advocates to the polls, who voted not only against the gun safety measure, but also against the gay rights initiative and for an initiative to eliminate affirmative action. Improved coordination between like-minded campaigns and strategic positioning of certain ballot measures in particular elections can help ensure success.

Are You Prepared to Win?

Losing is not winning. It is a grave mistake to think there is something beneficial to fighting the good fight for a ballot initiative without experiencing victory. Initiatives are difficult undertakings, and they should be waged only if proponents believe there is a strong chance of success. Have all administrative, legal, and legislative avenues to pass a law truly been exhausted? Policy issues in some states will never find success legislatively, which is why the process has been so important in instituting laws in favor of such things as physician-assisted suicide, clean elections, animal protection, and the creation of funding sources for open space and education. By and large, if an initiative fails, little good results. Ballot initiative campaigns can codify existing sentiments and beliefs that can either propel a movement or set it back.

13

The Unglamorous Elections

Getting People to the Polls for Down-Ballot Races

Phillip Stutts

Political campaigns that engage voters with a consistent message from numerous communication angles will create a multiplier effect that can lead to larger voter turnout and greater success on Election Day. This belief is grounded in experience and can be applied to the highest-profile races, like one for president, to the lowest-level campaign, like that for justice of the peace.

Lower-level elections, or down-ballot elections, hold a unique place in political campaign strategy, especially in relation to getting voters to the polls, and it is worth taking a broader look at them.

There is a big difference between high-profile and down-ballot races. High-profile campaigns usually gobble up the most experienced consultants and staff. Because of their ability to attract money, these campaigns can afford to be big and bold, making the maximum use of technology, high-quality TV ads and direct mail, big campaign events, and narrowly targeted grassroots operations.

When most voters finally take notice of candidates, it is usually the higher-profile ones—the ones in the news and who are running media ads, forcing their candidacies on the voter. Voters pay much less attention to down-ballot races.

Although some voters pay little or no attention to the campaign hype, the ones that do take notice don't begin doing so until very close to Election Day. In order to turn out these voters, candidates must force themselves and their message on the voters within a very narrow time frame.

Down-ballot races are usually considered the redheaded stepchild of political campaigns; they are simple-minded, desperately seeking attention, and always feeling slighted by their higher-profile siblings. But these races have the capability to be more personal, which, if organized and channeled properly, can give them an advantage with respect to voter turnout on Election Day.

So how do local campaigns turn out voters on Election Day? These campaigns must carve out unique ways to garner attention, perhaps by means of knocking on the doors of voters and repeating a consistent message (thus establishing a campaign brand that voters will support) or raising critical funds for disseminating that message through, for instance, direct mail or TV/radio advertising.

THE THREE M'S

In down-ballot races, compared with the higher-profile races on the same ballot, the campaign strategy and tactics can be very different, but the structural formula is the same. Successful down-ballot races must focus on the "three M's"—money, messaging, and management—to distinguish their candidates from the others and thereby put them in the best position to turn out the voters and win.

Money. Down-ballot candidates must raise funds for research and media efforts, get-out-the-vote activities, and staff. They must do this to distinguish their candidacies not only from their opponents, but also from other, high-profile candidates on the ballot.

Messaging. A down-ballot candidate must brand a tested message and never deviate from that message (one that presumably will resonate with voters and motivate them to choose that candidate).

Management. Management simply refers to organizing volunteers and staff to implement a successful grassroots/get-out-the-vote operation that engages voters one at a time and motivates them to vote for that candidate on Election Day.

When movies portray a smiling, idealistic nobody with good intentions who wants to enter politics, it makes the audience feel warm and fuzzy. Hollywood never fails to depict the noble campaign that is different from all the rest.

In reality, candidates and campaigns are not like that. Sure, good people with great intentions do run for office, but campaigns for the most part have to follow a process that puts the candidate in the best position to win. That does not mean an "outside the box" down-ballot candidacy cannot succeed; it can. But just as in a new business venture, it is best to follow the process that offers the best shot at winning. Ninety-nine percent of the time, such campaigns do not follow the Hollywood storyline.

Metaphorically, it is like a football coach putting eight men on the field (instead of eleven) because he thinks that he can "out-coach" the other team with fewer players. Occasionally that coach may eke out a victory against lesser competition, but the majority of the time he will lose. It does not make sense to put one's team at a competitive disadvantage, and candidates who ignore a successful process of getting elected are doomed to fail most of the time.

The process that ultimately gives down-ballot candidates the best shot at boosting voter turnout and winning starts with money. And anyone who says money is not the mother's milk of campaigns in this country has been watching too many movies.

Money

A down-ballot candidate who wants to brand a campaign message through earned media, paid media, and volunteer grassroots efforts can achieve that only by spending money. Excluding those who can afford their own funding, candidates who piously shun fundraising lack common sense, prefer ignorance, and will most likely lose. For down-ballot candidates, raising money is even more critical because a candidate must break through the clutter of messages from their opponents and from all the higher-profile races on the ballot.

How important is money in a down-ballot race? Consider a down-ballot candidate in state running for a legislative House seat who faces the following challenges:

- The opponent has higher name recognition and is raising money to win the race.
- There is a contested state senate race in the same district where a minimum of two candidates are raising money.
- Every statewide constitutional race is on the ballot, including those for treasurer, attorney general, lieutenant governor, and governor. These candidates are all trying to raise millions to fund their campaigns.

How can that down-ballot candidate succeed in raising adequate resources to win? First, any candidate and campaign team should develop a finance plan. For down-ballot races, it should be simple but observe the following guidelines:

1. Pick off the low-hanging fruit first. Compile a list of all family, friends, co-workers, and so on, and ask them for contributions. Identify a target amount to solicit from each individual. This is the easiest money to collect because of the close nature of the relationship.
2. Ask the people on the "low-hanging fruit" list to give you additional names for soliciting funds. Hold these people accountable. Staging fundraising receptions is one option (the rule of thumb is *never* to spend more than 10 percent of the take on the reception itself).
3. Install a finance chairman who will be personally responsible for raising a set amount of funds.
4. Create a finance committee and hold each person responsible for raising a set amount of funds. Check on the committee for progress through regular conference calls.

There are other factors involved in developing a finance plan, and every campaign is different in its approach, especially in down-ballot races. But the above four factors should form the basis of any plan. The bottom line is to produce a candidate who is an enthusiastic fundraiser willing to do what it takes to succeed.

Next, it is critical to follow the rules developed by the fundraising specialist Erin DeLullo Lewis, who gives her down-ballot candidates the following pointers:

- Do not make excuses for the contributors; they will make enough excuses on their own. Just ask for the money.
- *Never stop asking.* Even if someone has given eleven times, keep asking until he or she stops giving.
- "Buy down" the contributor. Ask for top dollar; if that is too much, ask for half of that dollar. If the contributor still says no, then ask for a quarter, and so on.
- Keep the door open. A contributor may not give now, but be sure not to shut out future opportunities.
- Always go back and ask again.

Why do most candidates shun fundraising? Because it is a hard, invasive, and uncomfortable process. People are asked to take out their wallets and hand out money—and in return they get . . . good government. That is not a natural act. It is even harder for down-ballot candidates. But those who accept and meet the challenge will put themselves in a better position to win on Election Day—but only if they continue to follow the correct process, which includes using that money to brand a message that will turn out voters.

Messaging

A voter's attention span is short. Voters have other priorities, such as work, children, sports practices, and church. A voter's attention span is even shorter for down-ballot candidates running for seats that are not considered "sexy." When such candidates talk to voters, they should be able to reel off two or three core campaign issues and hope they resonate with the voters (and continue to resonate until Election Day). That is why media messaging is so important; a candidate must hammer home the same two to three points over and over again, thus branding the campaign with a theme that results in Election Day success. The biggest blunder in messaging strategy is for the candidate to try to be all things to all people and never settle on a consistent campaign theme.

Down-ballot candidates will always struggle against higher-profile campaigns to have their messages heard and remembered. If the candidate spends days on the campaign trail talking about his or her stance on various issues, and then spends money on media—such as direct mail—focusing on different issues, the voter will remember nothing. With their short attention spans, voters need to hear the same ideas from all directions, be it from the campaign trail, the media, the Web site, or elsewhere.

Big media consultants think messaging involves only paid and earned media. But in down-ballot races, it also must include grassroots activities, such as e-mail, public events, phone banks, and door knocking.

The proper process for down-ballot messaging is simple, and it *will* result in more votes on Election Day. To determine their campaign message, down-ballot candidates need to ask themselves the following questions:

- What are my passionate issues and core beliefs?
- How do those issues and beliefs differentiate me from my opponent(s)?

Once those questions are answered, it is time to test which of those core beliefs will have the most impact on the electorate. Voters must discern a consistent message because they will not be reading much about those candidates in the press. The campaign message should be determined with the help of a type of scientific research called a benchmark survey.

A benchmark survey should be conducted to test how voters feel about a candidate's ideas. It should not be about testing the voters' ideas. The biggest mistakes candidates make when conducting a benchmark survey are the following:

1. They pay attention to name recognition, and a low rating can give the perception of a weak campaign.
2. They develop their campaign themes from a survey and not from their core beliefs.

Down-ballot candidates should use benchmark surveys to test their core beliefs, to identify which of their issues resonates most strongly with voters, and to find the most effective way to communicate their ideas on these issues to the electorate. Once those issues are identified, the candidate should settle on two or three issues and never deviate from them. Message branding should not be left to chance; that is why scientific research is so important.

The next step in messaging is to disseminate the message to the voters. For most down-ballot races with limited resources, this can be done through a few channels:

- Earned media
- Traditional paid media (TV, radio, direct mail)
- E-campaign activities
- Grassroots efforts

Honing a consistent message through earned and paid media is incredibly important. Grassroots activities will be covered in the section on management.

The following case study is a unique illustration of how a down-ballot candidate used a niche idea to gain earned media. Once this idea caught the voters' attention, the candidate reinforced it with paid-media efforts. The result of utilizing a consistent message with earned and paid media paid the ultimate dividend on Election Day.

CASE STUDY

Overview. Illegal immigration was bubbling over as a very hot issue in a down-ballot state legislative race. The growing illegal-immigration problem was enraging voters in this district. Candidate A needed to communicate his position to the voters, but the earned-media outlets were focusing exclusively on the high-profile statewide candidates.

Taking Action with a Consistent Message. Candidate A decided to issue a letter requesting a senior state government official to seek federal emergency funding for the growing illegal-immigration problem. The official was outraged by Candidate A's chutzpah, and that outrage garnered major media attention and brought the campaign's message to the media forefront. Candidate A's opponent did not get involved, leaving Candidate A to own the issue. In addition, Candidate A produced direct mail (paid media) targeting voters who were outraged by the illegal-immigration problem.

The Result. The uniqueness of the candidate's request and the angry response by the senior government official led every major newspaper in the state to cover the story. National television networks, including MSNBC and Fox News, also covered the spat. Candidate A exploited this earned-media attention to pound home a major theme of the campaign, which, combined with direct-mail efforts that engaged voters passionate about the issue, resulted in an election victory by a few hundred votes (less than 2.3 percent). Candidate A followed the process of engaging numerous communication angles (through earned and paid media), which created such a multiplier effect that it ultimately led to victory on Election Day.

In addition to earned media and traditional paid media, today's candidates must utilize technology and e-campaign efforts as an avenue for getting voters to the polls. Though Web efforts can get very expensive, it is incredibly important for a candidate to communicate his or her message through a Web site and through e-mail. Candidates must remember that voters are often too busy to study up on the many office seekers they will have to choose among on Election Day. But a down-ballot candidate who employs e-mail and a Web site creates another outlet for communicating the campaign's message as well as a means of soliciting voter input. This additional reinforcement is critical to success in today's political climate.

Creating a consistent message for a down-ballot candidate is vital in breaking through the message clutter of higher-profile campaigns. Testing that message to make sure it is communicated properly and then using creative earned- and paid-media efforts to get the message to voters will help to ensure that they will remember and ultimately vote for the down-ballot candidate on Election Day.

Management

Once a down-ballot candidate has raised enough money to meet budget goals and has established a message through earned and paid media, that candidate must plan and execute a grassroots effort that will complement the message and turn out voters on Election Day. "Management" refers to organizing volunteers and staff to "touch" voters one at a time through effective e-mail, door-to-door visits, and phoning programs. Down-ballot candidates must engage voters one on one to break through the higher-profile races on the ballot. The ultimate goal of any grassroots campaign effort is a successful get-out-the-vote (GOTV) effort on Election Day.

The phrase "get out the vote" has been a part of the political lexicon for a long time. Abraham Lincoln spoke of GOTV efforts in 1840, when he stated:

> Organize the whole state so that every Whig can be brought to the polls. Make a perfect list of all the voters and ascertain with certainty for whom they will vote. Keep a constant watch on the doubtful voters and . . . have them talked to by those in whom they have the most confidence. . . . And on Election Day see that every Whig is brought to the polls.[1]

Unfortunately, in today's down-ballot races, GOTV is usually used as a buzzword and not organized or executed as well as Abe would have liked. This is often the result of a candidate's laziness, political inexperience, or blatant ignorance.

Managing the grassroots efforts to turn out voters is the final key to success for a down-ballot candidate. The candidate and supporters must make sure their activities to engage voters are organized. The key is to identify prospective supporters or voters, target them effectively, and get them to vote on Election Day. This process should be conducted in two phases:

1. Build a list of supporters and undecided voters and the issues they share with the candidate. This is known as voter identification (voter ID).
2. Use that list of issues to persuade voters to move toward and eventually turn out to vote for the candidate on Election Day. This is known as voter persuasion.

These two phases are planned and executed by the candidate's volunteers and staff through the following means:

1. *Door-to-door efforts.* During the voter ID phase a volunteer, a staffer, and the candidate will go door to door and ask voters about the issues they care about most. When the voters' position on the issues aligns with the candidate's platform, their names are recorded and used for voter persuasion. The persuasion process includes organizing the list of supportive and undecided voters and discarding the list of nonsupportive voters developed from the voter ID phase. In the final seventy-two hours before Election Day, the final list is printed and used by the volunteers, staff, and candidate to again knock on the doors of supportive and undecided voters with a persuasive message focusing on:

   a. The issue that voters previously stated they cared about—and how the candidate supports that position.
   b. The importance of remembering to vote on Election Day and of encouraging friends, family, co-workers, others, to do the same.
2. *Phone banking efforts.* Typically, the same process used for door-to-door efforts will be utilized with phone banking.
3. *E-mail.* The process here is a bit different. The candidate and staff should collect e-mail addresses throughout the campaign. Although not as targeted as door-to-door and phone efforts, e-mail initiatives are critically important to the GOTV process. Building e-mail lists and utilizing them to communicate a message is part of the voter persuasion process.

High-profile campaigns have the capacity to perform many more organized GOTV tasks leading up to Election Day, but down-ballot races must remain simple, targeted, and organized. The management of the GOTV organization could make the difference between success and failure.

The following case study involves a down-ballot race in which the challenger was initially given zero chance of winning the primary election. But that candidate established a consistent message and reinforced it through a successful grassroots GOTV operation. The result shocked the political and media establishments.

CASE STUDY: THE LONG-SHOT CANDIDATE

Overview. Candidate A faced overwhelming odds when he challenged a seven-term, entrenched incumbent for a legislative seat. The challenge involved not only age (Candidate A was a 20-something neophyte) and incumbency, but also the fact that both candidates belonged to the same party.

The party held a majority in both chambers of state government. Without fear of reprisal, the incumbent voted and helped pass a huge tax increase for the state. Incensed by the incumbent's actions, Candidate A launched a long-shot primary bid for the seat, claiming that the party stood for lower taxes. Starting at zero in the polls and facing higher-profile races on the ballot, Candidate A realized he had to run a targeted and cost-efficient grassroots campaign to win.

Following the Correct Process. Candidate A first lined up donors and raised enough money to run a credible campaign. Next he conducted a benchmark survey that provided scientific evidence that voters would be outraged if they were to learn that their legislator had voted for the tax increase. Candidate A and a consultant formulated the message and strategy. The campaign activated key coalition groups to contact targeted voters through volunteer mail, door-to-door efforts, phone calls, and public events. Candidate A spent one solid year conducting voter ID by knocking on doors and calling voters in the district. The process included walking through the entire district eight times and knocking on doors, not to mention the staff's work visiting and calling voters (i.e., conducting voter ID and spreading the same message as the candidate). Simultaneously, a second wave was launched to mobilize key constituencies with the use of a tested and consistent message. The grassroots campaign tactics included an e-campaign and targeted direct mail to sway public opinion.

The Result. By Election Day, voter sentiment had shifted, and the 20-something challenger beat the odds and upset the entrenched incumbent. Among the five down-ballot challenger races that year, Candidate A was the only victor, and he garnered an eye-popping 66 percent of the vote (his opponent received 34 percent). It was the country's biggest down-ballot political upset of the year and made national news.

The following outline is from an actual 90-day grassroots management plan and is a great example of how the GOTV process helps turn out voters in lower-profile races.

CASE STUDY: CANDIDATE X FOR STATE SENATE—90-DAY POLITICAL PLAN

This plan focuses on two areas:

1. Targeting and prioritizing precincts for GOTV efforts. The plan breaks precincts up into two tiers, prioritizing the areas most important to win.
2. Identifying the goals for staff and volunteer activities. Due to the fact that X campaign lacks experienced grassroots staff, it is important to do a few things really well, rather than many things poorly. In this case, we need to focus on two things (maybe three if we get organized quickly enough) and do them well, not five or six things.

Those two efforts should be volunteer phone banks and door-to-door efforts. We should not have any other priorities.

If the goal is to ID 8,000 supporters in the next three months, then we will be breaking out a few aspects of the volunteer plan (with the paid plan).

I. Targeting:

Tier 1 Counties and Precincts:

To be determined

Tier 2 Counties and Precincts:

To be determined

Goal for ID'd supporters in order to meet the Election Day vote goal: 8,000.

II. Volunteer Activities:

Staff is responsible for pulling lists and maps for door-to-door targeting.

A. Goals to Accomplish:

- **Door-to-door**
  - Republicans remain top priority, but further analysis of a precinct's voting pattern should be observed. It is also important to target higher-density precincts to maximize volunteer efforts.
  - A tested message will be prepared for all door-to-door efforts. Volunteers will be armed with scripts as they target the homes in door-to-door walking.
  - Due to the size of the district, it is reasonable to assume that the campaign door-to-door (d-t-d) efforts will only focus on Tier 1 precincts (high density), and the volunteer phone efforts will focus on Tier 1 and Tier 2 areas.
- **Phone Banking**
  - Securing locations for phoning is critical for the election. The political operation should immediately begin securing phone locations.
  - A scripted voter ID and persuasion phone message will ask whom the voters support and the issue that they care about the most. We will capture that information in our database for GOTV and mail efforts. We will also give an advocacy message about the candidate and his or her stance on that issue most important to the caller.
  - Detailed phone lists should be provided to all phone volunteers.

B. Month-by-Month Timeline

- **Month 1:**
  - Month 1 must be used for identifying the households to target in Month 2.
  - Precinct maps should be obtained during Month 1 and reproduced for walking packets. This is the responsibility of staff.
  - Packets must be prepared during Month 1 for the phone and door-to-door operation. Packets should include maps, scripts, walking lists, positive news articles, talking points, and instruction sheets (consultant will draft scripts and instruction sheets).
  - Phone banks (ID/persuasion) should start in week 3. D-t-d should start in week 3 as well.
  - Message: Scripts based on survey results, and following the message of direct mail, should be drafted for both walking and phoning.
    - The door-to-door message should consider precinct concerns.
    - The phoning message should be specific to household ID'd concerns.

    - Month 1 should be used for *heavy* recruitment of student volunteers and retired locals. Student volunteers will best be equipped to work the weekdays (in summertime) and handle the door-to-door operation.
- **Month 2**
    - Weekdays
        - ID and persuasion calls to targeted households in Tier 1 and Tier 2 precincts
        - Preparation for weekend door-to-door
    - Weekends
        - Door-to-door activities in Tier 1 and Tier 2 precincts
- **Month 3**
    - GOTV
        - Phone and door-to-door message become GOTV

C. Week-by-Week Timeline

- **Month 1—First Week:**
    - Break down current voter file
    - Recruit volunteers for phones and door-to-door efforts
    - Secure location for phone center
    - Secure maps for walking precincts in Tier I and Tier II precincts
    - Prepare for door-to-door and phone activities
- **Month 1—Second Week:**
    - Break down current voter file
    - Recruit volunteers for phones and door-to-door effort
    - Secure location for phone center
    - Secure maps for walking precincts in Tier I and Tier II precincts
    - Conference call for volunteers—with a VIP
    - Prepare ID/persuasion call scripts for phoners
    - Prepare persuasion scripts for precinct walkers
- **Month 1—Third Week:**
    - Break down current voter file
    - Recruit volunteers for phones and door-to-door efforts
    - Finish securing maps for walking precincts in Tier I and Tier II precincts
    - Weeknights (5 to 8 p.m.)—ID/Persuasion calls
    - Weekends—Door-to-door canvassing in Tier I precincts
- **Month 1—Fourth Week:**
    - Recruit volunteers for phones and doors
    - Weeknights (5 to 8 p.m.)—ID/persuasion calls
    - Weekends—Door-to-door canvassing in Tier I precincts
    - Volunteer appreciation/kickoff party with candidate

- **Month 2—First Week:**
  - Weeknights (5 to 8 p.m.)—ID/persuasion calls
  - Weekends—Door-to-door canvassing in Tier I precincts
  - Recruit volunteers for phones and doors
  - Candidate volunteers attend any festivals deemed necessary
- **Month 2—Second Week:**
  - Weeknights (5 to 8 p.m.)—ID/persuasion calls
  - Weekends—Door-to-door canvassing in Tier I precincts
  - Recruit volunteers for phones and doors
- **Month 2—Third Week:**
  - Weeknights (5 to 8 p.m.)—ID/persuasion calls
  - Weekends—Door-to-door canvassing in Tier I precincts
  - Recruit volunteers for phones and doors
  - Conference call for volunteers with VIP
- **Month 2—Fourth Week:**
  - Weeknights (5 to 8 p.m.)—ID/persuasion calls
  - Weekends—Door-to-door canvassing in Tier I precincts
  - Recruit volunteers for phones and doors
  - Volunteer appreciation/kickoff party with candidate
- **Month 3—First Week:**
  - Weeknights (5 to 8 p.m.)—ID/persuasion calls
  - Weekends—Door-to-door canvassing in Tier I precincts
  - Recruit volunteers for phones and doors
- **Month 3—Second Week:**
  - Weeknights (5 to 8 p.m.)—ID/persuasion calls
  - Weekends—Door-to-door canvassing in Tier I precincts
  - Recruit volunteers for phones and doors
- **Final Two Weeks:**
  - Monday
    - 7 a.m. to 9 a.m.: precinct "targeted" sign waving on major thoroughfares
    - 5 p.m. to 9 p.m.: phone banking—ID, persuasion, and GOTV
  - Tuesday
    - 7 a.m. to 9 a.m.: precinct "targeted" sign waving on major thoroughfares
    - 5 p.m. to 9 p.m.: phone banking—ID, persuasion, and GOTV
  - Wednesday
    - 7 a.m. to 9 a.m.: precinct "targeted" sign waving on major thoroughfares
    - Team A: 5 p.m. to 9 p.m.: phone banking—ID, persuasion, and GOTV
    - Team B: 4 p.m. to 8 p.m.: door-to-door advocacy and GOTV

- Thursday
  - 7 a.m. to 9 a.m.: precinct "targeted" sign waving on major thoroughfares
  - Team A: 5 p.m. to 9 p.m.: phone banking—ID, persuasion, and GOTV
  - Team B: 4 p.m. to 8 p.m.: door-to-door advocacy and GOTV
- Friday
  - 7 a.m. to 9 a.m.: precinct "targeted" sign waving on major thoroughfares
  - Team A: 5 p.m. to 9 p.m.: phone banking—ID, persuasion, and GOTV
  - Team B: 4 p.m. to 8 p.m.: door-to-door advocacy and GOTV
- Saturday
  - 11 a.m. to 8 p.m.: door-to-door advocacy and GOTV
- Sunday
  - 1 p.m. to 8 p.m.: door-to-door advocacy and GOTV

- One Week to Go:
  - Monday
    - 7 a.m. to 9 a.m.: precinct "targeted" sign waving on major thoroughfares
    - Team A: 5 p.m. to 9 p.m.: phone banking—ID, persuasion, and GOTV
    - Team B: 4 p.m. to 8 p.m.: door-to-door advocacy and GOTV
  - Tuesday
    - 7 a.m. to 9 a.m.: precinct "targeted" sign waving on major thoroughfares
    - Team A: 5 p.m. to 9 p.m.: phone banking—ID, persuasion, and GOTV
    - Team B: 4 p.m. to 8 p.m.: door-to-door advocacy and GOTV
  - Wednesday
    - 7 a.m. to 9 a.m.: precinct "targeted" sign waving on major thoroughfares
    - 5 p.m. to 9 p.m.: phone banking—All GOTV
    - 10 a.m. to 12 p.m.: door-to-door canvassing—All GOTV
    - 2 p.m. to 8 p.m.: door-to-door canvassing—All GOTV
    - Victory rally for volunteers
  - Thursday
    - 7 a.m. to 9 a.m.: precinct "targeted" sign waving on major thoroughfares
    - 5 p.m. to 9 p.m.: phone banking—All GOTV
    - 10 a.m. to 12 p.m.: door-to-door canvassing—All GOTV

        - 2 p.m. to 8 p.m.: door-to-door canvassing—All GOTV
    - Friday
        - 7 a.m. to 9 a.m.: precinct "targeted" sign waving on major thoroughfares
        - 5 p.m. to 9 p.m.: phone banking—All GOTV
        - 10 a.m. to 12 p.m.: door-to-door canvassing—All GOTV
        - 2 p.m. to 8 p.m.: door-to-door canvassing—All GOTV
- Final Weekend:
    - Saturday to Monday
        - 11 a.m. to 8 p.m.: phone banking—All GOTV
        - 10 a.m. to 8 p.m.: door-to-door canvassing—All GOTV
- Election Day
        - 9 a.m. to 6:30 p.m.: GOTV door-to-door canvassing and GOTV phone calling
        - 8 p.m.: Victory

CONCLUSION

Down-ballot candidates face many hurdles in turning out the voters on Election Day. Those who follow an organized process have a better shot at overcoming those challenges and winning elections. The process starts with raising money, followed by broadcasting a tested message, and then executing a successful campaign through the proper management of media and GOTV efforts. A down-ballot candidate who follows that plan will consistently turn out more voters than one who does not. This process may not follow a Hollywood script, but it will win elections.

NOTE

1. *Addresses and Letters of Abraham Lincoln*, Circular from the Whig Committee, 1840.

14

Navigating the Maze of Election Law Changes

Campaign Finance Laws and the United States Constitution

Richard L. Hasen

Candidates, parties, political action committees, and others spent over $4.2 billion in connection with elections for federal office in 2004.[1] That amount does not include the substantial sums spent on state and local races. It is no wonder that campaigns are expensive, given the high cost of television and other advertising, the intensely polarized and competitive political environment, and the need to attract the attention of busy (and sometimes uninterested) voters.

Putting aside some public financing of campaigns (discussed later), the bulk of the money spent on elections in the United States comes through private contributions and expenditures. Some see private funding of electoral campaigns as creating at least one of four potential problems:

- *Corruption.* Candidates might be tempted to exchange large donations for a legislative quid pro quo, or at least for preferred access to officeholders.
- *Equality.* There is a tension between an ideal of voter equality (sometimes referred to as the "one person, one vote" principle) and a system that gives the wealthy (who can make more substantial donations) either greater influence over the outcome of the elections or better access to officeholders compared with other voters.
- *Public confidence.* Even if a system of privately financed elections does not lead to actual corruption or inequality, a public perception along those lines could damage voter confidence in the integrity of the political process.
- *Candidate time allotment.* If officeholders must spend a great deal of time raising funds, they will have less time to engage in legislative activities.

Congress, as well as some state and local governments, have enacted various campaign finance laws with the declared objective of addressing some or all of these concerns. Congress may pass laws governing the financing of presidential and congressional races across the country; states and localities may pass laws governing state and local races, such as governor or mayor.

Some opponents of campaign finance regulation reject these concerns as illegitimate or dismiss the idea that campaign finance regulation is an appropriate way to address them. Moreover, opponents argue that these laws in fact are often enacted to protect incumbents from political competition, and in any case the laws violate the First Amendment of the United States Constitution, which protects the right to free speech and association.[2]

There are four major types of campaign finance regulation: contribution limits, spending limits, disclosure rules, and public financing plans. The U.S. Supreme Court's jurisprudence in this area has been exceedingly complex and somewhat contradictory, reflecting changes in the Court's view on how much deference is appropriate to legislative efforts to limit the role of money in politics. This chapter provides only an introduction to these thorny issues.

CONTRIBUTION LIMITS

Contribution limits put a cap on the amount that an individual may give to a candidate, party, or political committee. On the federal level, as of 2007 an individual may give no more than $2,300 (an amount indexed to inflation) per election to a candidate for federal office, such as U.S. senator; no more than $5,000 per calendar year to a political action committee (or PAC), which itself may either contribute (up to $5,000 per election) to a federal candidate or spend the money to support or oppose candidates for federal office; no more than $28,500 per calendar year to a national political party committee; and aggregate limit of $108,200 on federal contributions over a two-year period.[3]

Defenders of contribution limits argue that such laws are necessary to prevent corruption of candidates as well as prevent the "appearance of corruption," which seems to be a concern about voter confidence. (Note, however, that such limits work against an interest in officeholder time allotment, because they require candidates to spend more time raising smaller donations.) In *Buckley v. Valeo*,[4] the United States Supreme Court considered the constitutionality of federal contribution limits imposed in the 1974 amendments to the Federal Election Campaign Act (FECA). In upholding FECA's $1,000 individual contribution limit, the Court established that the amount of campaign contributions could be limited to prevent corruption or the appearance of corruption. The Court declared that limits on the amount of contributions only "marginally" restricted First Amendment rights (because the important First Amendment act involved was the symbolic act of giving, and not the amount of the gift) and such limits therefore were subject to lower constitutional scrutiny.

Since *Buckley*, the Court's approach to the constitutionality of campaign contribution limits has shifted as the Justices have changed over time.[5] Despite *Buckley*'s holding that restrictions on the amount of contributions entail only a marginal restriction on speech, the Court soon thereafter held that limits on contributions to a local ballot measure committee could not be sustained because there was no candidate to corrupt.[6] Two decades after *Buckley*, the Court upheld a $1,075 contribution limit in Missouri state elections against a challenge that the amount was too low for challengers to mount an effective campaign, despite the fact that the $1,000 limit was worth only a fraction of the value of *Buckley*'s $1,000 contribution limit in 1976 dollars.[7] In that case, *Nixon v. Shrink Missouri Government PAC*, the Court expressed such a deferential standard for review of a constitutional challenge to the amount of campaign contributions that it would be hard for any contribution limit to fail constitutional scrutiny as too low. Yet only a few years later, after Chief Justice John Roberts and Justice Samuel Alito replaced Chief Justice William Rehnquist and Justice Sandra Day O'Connor, the Court, in *Randall v. Sorrell*, virtually ignoring but not expressly overturning *Shrink Missouri*, held that Vermont's campaign contribution limits were too low, and that the amounts must be high enough to allow for meaningful political competition.[8]

The future of the constitutionality of campaign contribution limits is uncertain, though things appear to be moving in the direction of deregulation, as advocated by Justice Clarence Thomas in a dissent in the *Shrink Missouri* case: "In my view, the Constitution leaves it entirely up to citizens and candidates to determine who shall speak, the means they will use, and the amount of speech sufficient to inform and persuade."

SPENDING LIMITS

Contribution limits cap the amounts given *to* a candidate, party, or committee. Spending limits put a cap on independent spending supporting or opposing a candidate for office or a ballot measure. (When someone spends money in coordination with a candidate, it is treated like a contribution and subject to contribution limits.)

In *Buckley v. Valeo*, the Court held that strict scrutiny must be applied to the review of spending limits, meaning that the government must come forward with a compelling interest to justify laws limiting spending and that the means must be narrowly tailored to meet that compelling interest. This is a tougher standard of review than the standard the Court set regarding contribution limits. The Court justified the tougher standard for spending limits on the grounds that such limits bar core political speech. Under the 1974 FECA amendments, for example, an individual could not spend more than $1,000 to take out a newspaper ad or engage in other spending urging the election or defeat of a presidential candidate.

Although the Supreme Court in *Buckley* agreed that preventing corruption of candidates constituted a compelling interest justifying campaign finance regulation, it held that the FECA spending limit failed strict scrutiny because it was not narrowly tailored: the Court stated that truly independent expenditures do not raise the same danger of corruption, because a quid pro quo is less attainable if politician and spender cannot communicate about the expenditure.

With the corruption prevention interest having failed to justify a limit upon independent expenditures, the Court considered the alternative argument that spending limits were justified by "the ancillary governmental interest in equalizing the relative ability of individuals and groups to influence the outcome of elections." In one of the most famous (some would say notorious) sentences in *Buckley*, the Court rejected this equality rationale for campaign finance regulation, at least in the context of expenditure limits: "[T]he concept that government may restrict the speech of some elements of our society in order to enhance the relative voice of others is wholly foreign to the First Amendment."

The Court followed *Buckley*'s striking down of spending limits applied to individuals and candidates with a ruling a few years later in *First National Bank of Boston v. Bellotti*[9] striking down limits on spending by corporations in ballot measure elections. There the Court took an expansive view of corporate free speech rights, but left an important footnote suggesting that corporate spending limits in candidate elections might be permissible to prevent corruption of candidates. The Court then held, in *Massachusetts Citizens for Life v. Federal Election Commission (MCFL)*,[10] that nonprofit ideological corporations that do not take corporate or union money cannot be limited in spending their treasury funds on candidate elections; but a few years later the Court, in *Austin v. Michigan Chamber of Commerce*,[11] confirmed that for-profit corporations could be so limited. The Court did not address whether corporate spending limits might be justified to prevent corruption of candidates (as the Court had suggested in *Bellotti*) but held the law was justified to prevent a "different type of corruption": "the corrosive and distorting effects of immense aggregations of wealth that are accumulated with the help of the corporate form and that have little or no correlation to the public's support for the corporation's political ideas." Though the Court called this interest one in preventing "corruption," it really represented an embrace of the equality rationale (at least as to corporations) that the Court had rejected in *Buckley*.

The Court then appeared to backpedal even further from *Bellotti*. In *FEC v. Beaumont*[12] the Court held that even *MCFL* corporations could be barred from making any campaign contributions, adding that "corporate contributions are furthest from the core of political expression, since corporations' First Amendment speech and association interests are derived largely from those of their members, and of the public in receiving information. A ban on direct corporate contributions leaves individual members of corporations free to make their own contributions, and deprives the public of little or no material information."

The matter recently came to a head when Congress passed the Bipartisan Campaign Reform Act of 2002 (BCRA, more commonly known as "McCain-Feingold" after its leading Senate sponsors). BCRA made a number of changes to federal campaign finance law, including the imposition of additional limits on amounts that could be raised by national political parties to support federal candidates (so-called soft money donations). The law also made it harder for corporations (and labor unions) to spend money intended to influence, or at least likely to influence, the outcome of federal elections.

Before BCRA, the United States witnessed a proliferation of "sham issue ads" that went something like "Call Bob Dole and tell him what you think of his lousy plan to gut Medicare."[13] By avoiding words of "express advocacy" such as "Vote for Clinton," the ads could be paid for out of corporate or union treasuries, and no disclosure was required. (Corporations and unions could pay for express advocacy only through PACs, which could be funded with a contribution no greater than $5,000 from any one individual).

BCRA changed the law by specifying that if corporations or unions wanted to run television and radio ads close to Election Day featuring a candidate for federal office, they had to be paid for out of the same PAC funds, and anyone (including individuals) paying for such ads had to disclose where the money came from—regardless of whether the ads contained express advocacy. This is BCRA's "electioneering communications" requirement.

In *McConnell v. FEC*[14] the Supreme Court, by a 5-4 vote, upheld the requirement that corporations and unions pay for electioneering communications from their PACs and not from corporate or union treasuries. The Court reaffirmed *Austin* and extended its holding to unions without explaining why unions, which amass wealth in a much more egalitarian way than corporations, presented the same "distortion" dangers of corporations recognized in *Austin*. The *McConnell* Court said that corporations and unions could exercise their First Amendment rights through other means, such as raising money for a separate PAC that could then spend money on election-related activities and make contributions to candidates.

McConnell hardly settled the matter, however. As the Supreme Court's most recent campaign finance case, *FEC v. Wisconsin Right to Life (WRTL)*,[15] makes clear, the replacement of Justice O'Connor with Justice Alito had a major effect on how the Court viewed the constitutional question. In *WRTL* a nonprofit corporation, Wisconsin Right to Life, took over $300,000 in for-profit corporate money to pay for television ads that were crafted to challenge *McConnell*'s holding. The ads mentioned Wisconsin's two senators—Herb Kohl and Russ Feingold—and urged that they not filibuster judicial nominees. The ads also pointed to WRTL's Web site, where voters could learn that WRTL had taken a position against Feingold's reelection.

WRTL argued in the Supreme Court that its ads were really an attempt at "grassroots lobbying" on the issue of filibusters and that BCRA's limit on funding such ads from corporate treasuries could not constitutionally be applied against it (on the theory that BCRA could target only purely election-related ads). But the Supreme Court went even further than WRTL asked, ruling that the PAC requirement for corporations and unions runs afoul of the First Amendment, except when applied to advertising that "is susceptible of no reasonable interpretation other than as an appeal to vote for or against a specific candidate." Though the precise reach of the case is unclear, *WRTL* appears to allow a great deal of corporate and union spending on election-related advertising. Moreover, the case appears to be the harbinger of more deregulation of campaign financing by the Court, and calls into direct question the vitality of the *Austin* precedent.[16]

DISCLOSURE RULES

Supporters and many opponents of contribution and spending limits advocate campaign finance disclosure rules, requiring campaigns and others to disclose amounts received and spent in relation to political campaigns. Supporters view disclosure as a means to help enforce other campaign finance laws, as well as deter corruption though transparency of political donations, which will allow the press and others to "follow the money." Some opponents of contribution and spending limits view disclosure as a more narrowly tailored means to deter corruption compared with limits.

But other opponents of contribution and spending limits see a First Amendment problem with compelled disclosure, on the grounds that publicity can deter some individuals from contributing (or spending money independently) to support politically unpopular candidates or causes. Others oppose disclosure because they see it as a foot in the door toward further regulation.

As with other constitutional questions surrounding campaign finance, *Buckley v. Valeo* is the starting point for any constitutional analysis.[17] The 1974 FECA amendments imposed various reporting requirements on candidates, political committees, and others, which were challenged as violating the First Amendment. In *Buckley* the Court rejected a First Amendment challenge to a provision of FECA requiring individuals and groups that expressly advocate the election or defeat of candidates for federal office to file reports detailing contributions and expenditures with the Federal Election Commission. The Court upheld the disclosure requirements because they furthered three "sufficiently important" interests: (1) deterring corruption, by allowing interested parties to look for connections between campaign contributors or spenders and candidates who benefit from those contributions or spending; (2) providing information helpful to voters; and (3) aiding in the enforcement of other campaign finance laws, such as contribution limits. The *Buckley* Court stated that it might grant exemptions from disclosure requirements to individuals or groups facing a threat of harassment. The Court indeed recognized such an exception for the Socialist Workers Party in *Brown v. Socialist Workers '74 Campaign Comm. (Ohio).*[18]

In a 1995 case, *McIntyre v. Ohio Elections Commission,*[19] the Supreme Court muddied the constitutional waters by holding that the First Amendment prevented Ohio from enforcing its law requiring disclosure on the face of any document designed to influence voters in an election against a woman distributing unsigned leaflets expressing her opposition to a local referendum. Because the statute concerned ballot measures, it could not be justified as deterring corruption or facilitating enforcement of candidate contribution limits. The *McIntyre* Court held that the informational interest identified in *Buckley* in support of the FECA disclosure requirements was insufficient to justify the Ohio statute.

The contrast between *Buckley* and *McIntyre* raised many questions. Was the right to anonymous speech recognized in *McIntyre* limited to those persons engaging in face-to-face communications, leaving laws requiring disclosure in separately filed reports constitutionally sound? Did it matter that the *McIntyre* plaintiff was a lone pamphleteer using modest personal resources, in which case *McIntyre* left undisturbed laws requiring disclosure in other, larger circumstances? Did the *McIntyre* right to anonymity extend only to ballot measure elections and not to candidate elections?

Among the most important—and urgent—questions not answered was the extent to which Congress and state legislatures could require disclosure of contributions and expenditures that were intended to affect (or were at least likely to affect) elections but that avoided using words of express advocacy. Such "sham issue advocacy" had ballooned significantly in election cycles beginning in 1996 as groups tried to avoid disclosure and other campaign finance requirements.

BCRA extended disclosure requirements to all electioneering communications over a certain dollar threshold in an effort to require more disclosure of election-related spending. In *McConnell* the Supreme Court, in an 8-1 vote, upheld BCRA's new disclosure requirements. Only Justice Thomas dissented, believing the case was controlled by *McIntyre.*

The issue of disclosure of electioneering communications was not presented again to the Court in the *WRTL* case, and it does not appear that a majority of the current Court is prepared to hold core disclosure requirements in candidate elections to be a violation of the First Amendment. Still, *McIntyre* raised a number of questions about the constitutional scope of disclosure, particularly in ballot measure campaigns, and disclosure issues continue to be litigated in lower courts.

PUBLIC FINANCING

Some state and local governments have enacted laws providing for the full or partial public financing of campaigns (funded through general taxpayer revenues or some other mechanism). On the federal level, the 1974 FECA amendments provided for partial public financing for presidential candidates during the primary election stage, with full financing for major party candidates in the general election. In recent years the amount of money available under the federal program has paled in comparison with the amount that candidates can raise through private donations, and it is not clear that major presidential candidates will again use the public financing system, absent some change in the program by Congress. There is no public financing available for congressional campaigns. Some programs on the state and local level appear to be more successful.

In a typical public financing program, a candidate opting into the program must demonstrate some support among the public (such as by collecting signatures or nominal donations) and then pledge not to raise private funds (or not to raise funds over some limit) in exchange for receipt of the public financing.

The idea of coupling public financing with spending limits raises a constitutional question: if it is generally unconstitutional to limit candidate spending, can the receipt of a government benefit (in this case, public financing) be conditioned on giving up the right to spend unlimited sums on a campaign? In *Buckley v. Valeo*, the Supreme Court held that such a system is in fact constitutional, so long as the decision to participate is truly a *voluntary* one. When other campaign finance laws make it very difficult to run for office as a privately funded candidate and essentially force candidates to take public financing, the system is coercive rather than voluntary and therefore unconstitutional. State and local financing programs continue to be challenged on this basis, though not with great success.[20]

CONCLUSION

On the federal level, and in many states and local jurisdictions, campaign finance laws are quite complex. No competent candidate would choose to run for office without receiving constant advice from a campaign lawyer and treasurer. The constitutional issues overlay the complexity of statutory and regulatory law. The Supreme Court's approach to the constitutionality of campaign finance laws has shifted over time, swinging like a pendulum between periods of deference to legislative judgments about the need for regulation and periods of

First Amendment skepticism about such regulation. It appears that we may be moving into a new period of deregulation of campaign financing, accomplished by a new Supreme Court majority more skeptical than earlier Court majorities about the propriety of limiting the amounts and sources of money in politics.

NOTES

1. Kelly D. Patterson, "Spending in the 2004 Election," in *Financing the 2004 Election*, edited by David B. Magleby, Anthony Corrado, and Kelly D. Patterson (Washington, DC: Brookings University Press, 2006), 68, 69.

2. U.S. Const. amend. I ("Congress shall make no law . . . abridging the freedom of speech, or of the press").

3. For a chart showing the 2007–2008 contribution limits, see Federal Election Commission, Contribution Limits Chart, http://www.fec.gov/pages/brochures/contriblimits.shtml.

4. *Buckley v. Valeo*, 424 U.S. 1 (1976).

5. For more details on these cases, see Daniel H. Lowenstein and Richard L. Hasen, *Election Law—Cases and Materials,* 3rd ed. (Durham, NC: Carolina Academic Press, 2004), 717–1024.

6. *Citizens Against Rent Control v. City of Berkeley*, 454 U.S. 290, 299 (1981).

7. *Nixon v. Shrink Missouri Government PAC*, 528 U.S. 377 (2000).

8. *Randall v. Sorrell*, 126 S. Ct. 2479 (2006). For a detailed analysis of the case, see Richard L. Hasen, "The Newer Incoherence: Competition, Social Science and Balancing after *Randall v. Sorrell*," *Ohio State Law Journal* 68 (2006):849.

9. *First National Bank of Boston v. Bellotti*, 435 U.S. 765 (1978).

10. *Federal Election Commission v. Massachusetts Citizens for Life*, 479 U.S. 238 (1986).

11. *Austin v. Michigan Chamber of Commerce*, 494 U.S. 652 (1990).

12. *Federal Election Commission v. Beaumont*, 539 U.S. 146 (2003).

13. The next few paragraphs are drawn from Richard L. Hasen, "Faux Judicial Restraint in Full View," *The Recorder*, June 29, 2007, http://www.law.com/jsp/ca/PubArticleCA.jsp?id=1183021580352.

14. *McConnell v. Federal Election Commission*, 540 U.S. 93 (2003).

15. *Federal Election Commission v. Wisconsin Right to Life*, 127 S. Ct. 2652 (2007).

16. For more on this point, see Richard L. Hasen, "Beyond Incoherence: The Roberts' Court's Deregulatory Turn in *FEC v. Wisconsin Right to Life*," http://papers.ssrn.com/sol3/papers.cfm?abstract_id=1003922. Some of the analysis in this chapter is drawn from this article.

17. The next few paragraphs drawn from Richard L. Hasen, "The Surprisingly Easy Case for Disclosure of Contributions and Expenditures Funding Sham Issue Advocacy," *Election Law Journal* 3(2) (2004):251–257.

18. *Brown v. Socialist Workers '74 Campaign Comm. (Ohio)*, 459 U.S. 87, 88 (1982).

19. *McIntyre v. Ohio Elections Commission*, 514 U.S. 334 (1995).

20. For a post-*Buckley* case considering the voluntariness of Maine's public financing system, see *Daggett v. Commission on Governmental Ethics and Election Practices*, 205 F.3d 445 (1st Cir. 2000).

Part 2

Who Can Vote?

15

Trends in Voter Participation

A Primer on National Electoral Turnout and Comparison of Recent National Participation

Andrew Myers

THE PATH TO TODAY'S ELECTORATE

In any activity, the rules influence the outcome. Turnout among the American electorate is no exception, and since the nation's founding, the playing field has not always been level.

No discussion of American electoral turnout can begin without a discussion of eligibility to vote, a uniquely American story in and of itself. Indeed, as we look back and trace eligibility among the American electorate, it is clear that it has expanded significantly since the country's inception, specifically due to the expansion of suffrage to more groups. When America was founded, only white male property owners, with limited exceptions, were eligible to participate in elections—a strongly patrician orientation to eligibility and one that was present throughout the home countries of many early American immigrants. This arrangement was subject to complications within individual states marked by a myriad of differing property requirements as well.

Not until the enactment of the Fifteenth Amendment to the Constitution did African Americans receive the right to vote, and even then they encountered numerous, often insurmountable obstacles placed in their path to exercising their suffrage by a number of individual states. Remarkably, the debates on suffrage continue today.

For women, the path to suffrage was even longer than for African Americans. While some states did in fact allow women, particularly property owners, the right to vote, it was not until the 1920s and the passage of the

Nineteenth Amendment that women throughout the nation were granted this right.

Further changes resulted in the expansion voting eligibility throughout the turbulent 1960s and 1970s, during which time many young men were drafted to fight in Vietnam yet were ineligible to vote. A movement thus began to lower the voting age from 21 to 18, and in 1971, with the passage of the Twenty-sixth Amendment, 18-year-olds were granted the right to vote.

The electorate has been as broad and encompassing as it is today for roughly only 25 years, with all citizens over the age of 18 having the right to cast a ballot in the United States, with some exceptions for criminals in various states. Despite the lengthy and often difficult path to suffrage that many endured, possessing the right to vote has not meant that all have chosen to exercise this privilege.[1]

GIVEN ELIGIBILITY, WHO VOTES?

A plethora of researchers, statisticians, and others have dedicated a significant amount of research to this simple question: who votes? This question gained significance in the period following John F. Kennedy's election in 1960 through the 1988 election of Ronald Reagan. Over this period of nearly three decades, voter participation showed a marked decline. That decline is of major interest, particularly in connection with some population trends in the United States during the same period.

It is commonly accepted that some of the primary factors predicting likelihood to vote are income, education, and minority status: the higher up one is on the demographic scale, the more likely he or she is to vote. Nonetheless, although the average American income increased, as did the overall education level of the American populace, during the period from 1960 to 1988, voter participation declined. These socioeconomic trends and the decline of voter turnout in spite of them present interesting questions.

A comparison of exit poll data over the past two election cycles and census data from 2000 shows that there are a number of demographic groups who vote in greater proportions than their composition of the overall American population would suggest. As is clear from Table 15.1, whites are far more likely to participate in elections than are minorities—by a margin of 10 percentage points in the last presidential election and by 12 percentage points in the last midterm election. Education, however, provides the clearest distinction, with college-educated voters participating in elections at a percentage nearly double that of their proportion of the U.S. population, according to the 2000 census.

Minnesota, which routinely has one of the highest voter turnout rates in the country, provides ample evidence of these trends. Minnesota's voter turnout rate

Table 15.1
Demographic Population Estimates Compared with Demographic Voter Estimates from Exit Polling

	Census Population Percentage	Percentage Voted in 2004	Percentage Voted in 2006
White	67%	77%	79%
Non-white	33%	23%	21%
College graduate	24%	42%	45%
Non-college educated	76%	58%	55%
Under 65	88%	84%	81%
Seniors	12%	16%	19%
Married	51%	63%	68%
Not married	49%	37%	32%
Women	51%	54%	51%
Men	49%	46%	49%

is attributed to its voters' relative racial homogeneity, its slightly older population, its higher percentage of college graduates, and the high employment rate of its citizens

HOW WE MEASURE VOTER TURNOUT

Most media accounts of voter participation are based on a comparison of the total vote, that is, the total number of people who voted, with the total population of eligible citizens over the age of 18. As Table 15.2 shows, using this calculation, voter participation over the past eight election cycles has been, frankly, abysmal.

Table 15.2
National Voter Turnout by Total Eligible Voting Population

Election	Percentage
1992	54.7%
1994	38.5%
1996	48.1%
1998	39.3%
2000	55.3%
2002	40.5%
2004	60.9%
2006	41.3%

Figure 15.1
Turnout: Registered Voters versus Voting-Age Population

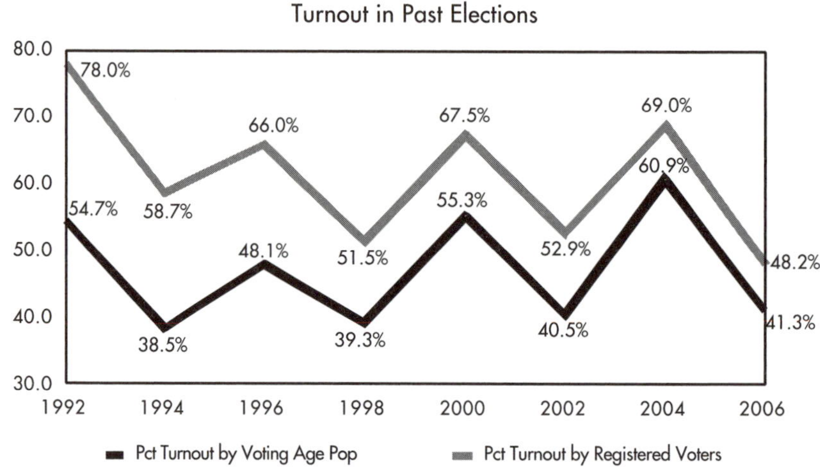

Others, including most political professionals and consultants, prefer to measure turnout against voter registration, meaning that the number of registered voters is divided by the total number who voted in a given election. As will be demonstrated shortly, this method yields markedly different turnout results compared with turnout determined by the voting-age population.

When turnout is measured by those who are registered to vote, no marked decline is evident in presidential election years, and turnout remains relatively stagnant (see Figure 15.1). It is in the non-presidential election years in which turnout has declined most significantly among those who are registered to vote, as continued frustration with Congress has clearly lessened the desire of many to exercise their voting rights.

Indeed, from Table 15.1 it is clear that a voter's race, education, and marital status all have an impact in non-presidential, or midterm, elections. In these lower-turnout elections, white voters, those with a college degree, and those who are married make up a larger portion of the electorate than in presidential election years.

Related to this fact is the simple reality that presidential elections attract the broadest turnout among the American electorate and have done so for many, many years. Most political scientists and even casual observers argue that this trend is in large part driven by the broad media attention surrounding a presidential election.

Another interesting point is that in elections that represent benchmarks of change—notably the midterm 1994 election, where Republicans seized control of Congress, and the midterm 2006 election, where Democrats took it back—turnout nationally did not spike. Rather, participation in these midterm elections was quite similar to that for previous midterms, likely a signal of voter fatigue with continuous highly partisan attacks.

EARLY VOTING

It has been argued that vote-by-mail systems are an easy way to increase voter participation, and in the premier vote-by-mail state, Oregon, where all voting is conducted by mail, turnout has most certainly increased, particularly compared with the nation as a whole (see Table 15.3).

However, the results are mixed on this front when we compare all states that utilize no-excuse vote by mail, which means that anyone can mail in the ballot, even those who are able to go to the polls on Election Day. As Table 15.4 shows, in the 2006 midterm election, just nineteen of the twenty-seven states that allow no-excuse voting by mail had turnout rates that surpassed the national rate; the eight remaining states had turnout equal to or less than the national percentage. Further, only nine states saw an increase in their turnout percentage from 2002 to 2006.

Results are similar for states that allow no-excuse early voting in person, prior to Election Day. About half of the states that allow no-excuse early voting saw greater voter participation rates than the national average in the 2006 midterm election, while the other half saw participation equal to or less than the national rate. Many states are turning toward measures designed to increase voter participation, including allowing voter registration at the polls on Election Day (currently allowed in Idaho, Maine, Minnesota, Montana, New Hampshire, Wisconsin, and Wyoming) as well as removing registration requirements altogether (North Dakota).

Table 15.3
Impact of Vote by Mail on Voter Participation: Oregon versus United States

	2006 Turnout	2004 Turnout	2002 Turnout	2000 Turnout	1998 Turnout	1996 Turnout	1994 Turnout	1992 Turnout
United States	48.2%	69.0%	52.9%	67.5%	51.5%	66.0%	58.7%	78.0%
Oregon	70.2%	85.8%	69.1%	78.9%	56.9%	70.2%	68.4%	82.4%

Table 15.4
Voter Turnout in States That Allow No-Excuse Absentee Voting by Mail

	2006 Turnout	2002 Turnout
North Carolina	34.9%	46.6%
Georgia	41.4%	53.6%
California	44.6%	51.0%
Utah	44.7%	50.8%
Oklahoma	44.8%	60.4%
Florida	46.3%	55.1%
New Jersey	47.8%	51.5%
Arkansas	48.0%	55.3%
United States	**48.2%**	**52.9%**
Iowa	51.0%	56.7%
Nebraska	51.2%	45.3%
Colorado	51.9%	71.6%
Kansas	52.0%	52.7%
New Mexico	52.2%	57.5%
Hawaii	52.7%	69.9%
Ohio	53.2%	47.2%
Maine	55.4%	53.2%
Maryland	57.5%	62.0%
Nevada	59.2%	58.9%
Idaho	60.0%	61.3%
Arizona	60.5%	55.3%
Vermont	60.7%	55.6%
Alaska	60.9%	50.5%
Montana	63.3%	66.1%
Washington	64.6%	56.4%
South Dakota	66.2%	71.6%
Oregon	70.2%	69.1%
Wyoming	74.6%	78.0%

DROP-OFF

Drop-off is an interesting phenomenon that occurs in every election. As voters move down a ballot, a certain percentage "drop off" and simply do not cast votes in lower-level races. Notably, this phenomenon occurs at every level of the ballot, from the top down to the lowest races. An example of drop-off from the presidential contest down to the state legislative level in the 2004 election in Ohio is illustrated in Table 15.5.

What is notable from Table 15.5 is that in both competitive and noncompetitive districts—"competitive" meaning that the political parties were

Table 15.5
Drop-off in the 2004 Election in Ohio

	President	U.S. Senate	Congress	State Legislature
Competitive State House District (HD 25)				
Total votes cast	47,379	44,185	41,436	38,411
Percentage of overall vote	100%	93%	87%	81%
Drop-off margin	—	–7%	–13%	–19%
Non-Competitive State House District (HD 3)				
Total votes cast	51,848	50,580	49,294	47,883
Percentage of overall vote	100%	98%	95%	92%
Drop-off margin	—	–2%	–5%	–8%

actively engaged in the race for the state legislative office—drop-off is particularly notable. In part, this trend could be due to the likely negativity of these contests, where voters are deluged with attacks on the candidates. However, in more rural states such as Iowa, drop-off is significantly lower, regardless of the competitive or non-competitive status of the district, and the percentage of drop-off as voters move down the ballot remains fairly constant (see Table 15.6).

Though there are no known data to substantiate this belief, the difference in drop-off could easily be the result of several factors. First, the Iowa state legislative districts are significantly smaller than those in Ohio. As a result, the legislative elections are likely more personal in nature and the candidates largely enjoy

Table 15.6
Drop-off in the 2004 Election in Iowa

	President	U.S. Senate	Congress	State Legislature
Competitive State House District (HD 18)				
Total votes cast	11,027	10,867	10,843	10,639
Percentage of overall vote	100%	99%	98%	96%
Drop-off margin		–1%	–2%	–4%
Non-Competitive State House District (HD 81)				
Total votes cast	10,180	10,012	9,963	9,799
Percentage of overall vote	100%	98%	98%	96%
Drop-off margin		–2%	–2%	–4%

broader recognition within the community. Second, Iowa voters tend to be older than voters nationally, and it is probably safe to surmise that older voters are more engaged and therefore better informed about the candidates at all levels of government, particularly when one also considers that they are slightly more likely to vote than their younger counterparts.

NOTES

Data compiled from:

- The Election Reform Information Project, www.electionline.org
- The Federal Election Commission, www.fec.gov
- The George Mason University United States Election Project, Elections.gmu.edu.

1. Robert A. Heineman, Steven A. Peterson, and Thomas Houser Rasmussen, *American Government* (New York: McGraw-Hill, 1989), chapter 6.

16

VOTER PARTICIPATION IN THE UNITED STATES VERSUS OTHER DEMOCRACIES

Mark Franklin

Compared with other democracies, voter turnout for elections in the United States is low. Even for presidential elections it is rare for much more than half the voting-age population to participate. At midterm congressional elections turnout is lower still, as it is at state elections, and the proportion of those turning out to vote reaches only single digits in many mayoral or city council elections. Of all elections in the United States, presidential elections witness the highest turnout.

Though turnout at these elections is high compared with turnout in other U.S. elections, it is still quite low in comparative perspective. Other established democracies regularly see voter turnout at national elections reaching 70 or 80 percent, and several enjoy turnout levels above 90 percent at election after election.

Low voter turnout is often considered to be bad for democracy, whether inherently, because it calls the election's legitimacy into question, or because it suggests inegalitarian policies and a lack of representation of certain groups.[1] Above all, commentators see low turnout as calling into question the civic-mindedness of a country's citizens and their commitment to democratic norms and duties. Indeed, falling turnout is often seen as a mark of disengagement if not actual disaffection.[2] Personal research does not support the idea that low voter turnout in the United States is due to "something about citizens" (disaffection, alienation, or lack of civic-mindedness).[3] Such assumptions ignore the fact that within the United States some elections see higher turnout than others, and it is hard to explain how civic-mindedness could vary between different types of elections. In light of the much higher turnout in most other countries, low voter turnout in the United States is much more likely due to "something about elections." As shown in Table 16.1,

Table 16.1
Voter Turnout at Legislative Elections in Twenty-two Countries That Have Conducted Elections Continuously Since 1945

Country	Average Turnout, 1945–1999	Compulsory Voting?	Type of Electoral System **	Executive Requires the Confidence of the Legislature?
Australia	94.6	Yes	Alternative vote	Yes
Belgium	92.6	Yes	PR	Yes
Austria	92.1	Until 1982*	PR	Yes
Italy	90.6	Until 1993	PR until 1993**	Yes
Luxembourg	89.8	Yes	PR	Yes
Iceland	89.5	No	PR	Yes
New Zealand	88.6	No	FPTP until 1996**	Yes
Malta	88.2	No	STV	Yes
Netherlands	87.6	Until 1970	PR	Yes
Sweden	86.1	No	PR	Yes
Denmark	85.6	No	PR	Yes
Germany	85.6	No	Mixed PR/FPTP	Yes
Norway	80.6	No	PR	Yes
Israel	80.4	No	PR	Yes
France	76.7	No	FPTP, runoff	Yes
United Kingdom	76.4	No	FPTP	Yes
Finland	75.9	No	PR	Yes
Canada	74.6	No	FPTP	Yes
Ireland	73.2	No	STV	Yes
Japan	71.3	No	SNTV until 1997**	Yes
Switzerland	56.6	No	PR	No
USA	55.8	No	FPTP	No
European Parliament	55.6	Generally not	Mainly PR	No
All twenty-two countries, 1945–1999 (excluding European Parliament elections)	81.4			

*In presidential elections (until 1992 in certain provinces).

** Change of electoral system to mixed PR/FPTP system. PR = proportional representation, STV = single transferable vote, FPTP = first past the post, SNTV = single non-transferable vote.

Adapted from Mark Franklin, *Voter Turnout and the Dynamics of Electoral Competition in Established Democracies Since 1945* (New York: Cambridge University Press, 2004).

countries with the highest turnout all make voting compulsory. This does not affect the civic-mindedness of the people of those countries, but it does ensure that they vote. If compulsory voting can affect voter turnout levels, then might other aspects about elections, such as the electoral system employed and the relationship between the legislature and the executive, also influence turnout?

Table 16.1 also shows how these two characteristics are distributed across countries. Most of the countries near the top of the table (those with the highest turnout), if they do not employ compulsory voting, do have electoral systems that ensure proportional election outcomes (generally proportional representation systems, though mixed systems and single-transferable-vote systems also ensure proportional outcomes). A proportional election outcome is one in which seats in the legislature are allocated to each political party in proportion to the votes that party receives. Such elections do not suffer from a problem common in U.S. and some other "first past the post" (FPTP) elections in districts where the outcome is a foregone conclusion, whether because the election is uncontested or because the incumbent congressperson is virtually certain of being reelected. In such districts (generally known as "safe" districts in the United States) individual citizens have little incentive to vote because their vote will not change the election outcome (this is often known as the "wasted vote syndrome"). And as the number of safe districts increases, overall turnout goes down (more about this problem later in the chapter). In proportional systems, by contrast, every vote has the chance of contributing to the election of an additional representative of one party or another, so essentially no votes are wasted and there is little opportunity for the wasted vote syndrome to play a part in voter turnout.

A more important consideration affecting turnout is the relationship between the legislature and the executive. Most of the countries listed in Table 16.1 have what are called "parliamentary systems" of government. Normally in such systems the executive is headed by a prime minister, and members of the prime minister's cabinet are all members of the parliament. In other words, there is generally no "separation of powers" in such systems as there is in the United States. Governments are invested by parliament and last only as long as they have the confidence of the parliament. A simple vote of no confidence is enough to dismiss most parliamentary governments—something that would require a complex process of impeachment in the United States. In countries where governments exist only on the sufferance of the parliament, elections to the parliament have considerably greater importance than U.S. congressional elections. In appointing the executive the parliament also determines the policies that the executive will pursue. So elections in parliamentary countries determine not only who governs (just as elections in the United States do), but also what policies the government pursues (something that U.S. elections influence only indirectly). Of course, elections in the United States do involve candidates making policy promises just as they do elsewhere, but there is absolutely no guarantee in the United States that policy promises will be carried out, and no recourse if they are not. In parliamentary systems a government that does not carry out its policy promises stands a good chance of being dismissed, even before the next scheduled national election, by a parliament in which the majority of legislators become anxious about their own reelection prospects if they do not hold the government to its promises.

Whether policy promises can be expected to be kept has been shown to have a strong effect on U.S. turnout by means of an analysis comparing the turnout observed when Congress and the presidency were in the hands of the same political party with the turnout observed under conditions of divided government.[4] Even unified government does not guarantee the carrying out of policy promises, but the chances of this happening under such a government are greater and turnout is correspondingly higher (though still low comparatively). This suggests that eliminating the separation of powers altogether would have a major positive effect on turnout. This argument focuses on the fact that the U.S. political system was designed in such a way as to prevent policies from being carried into law on the basis of a simple majority (the Founding Fathers feared a "tyranny of the majority" if the executive could be controlled by the legislature). Low voter turnout can be said to be the price Americans pay for the use of separated powers as a bulwark against tyranny.[5]

Supportive evidence for the importance to voter turnout of executive responsiveness is provided in Table 16.1 by the data for two other countries where legislatures do not control the policies of executives. One is Switzerland, where after 1963 a few parties joined to form what became known as a "cartel government" on the basis of an agreement between themselves; these parties continue to govern regardless of the outcome of legislative elections, thus cutting the link between legislative elections and the policies of the executive. Before 1963 turnout in Switzerland was as high as in other parliamentary democracies, but after the institution of this cartel arrangement, turnout at Swiss parliamentary elections fell precipitously until it reached levels even lower than turnout at national elections in the United States.[6] Turnout at elections for the European Parliament, also a legislative body with no control over its executive (the EU executive is controlled by the national governments of member states), is equally low.[7]

The strong implication of these comparisons is that low voter turnout in U.S. federal elections, in comparison with the much higher turnout in most other established democracies, is almost certainly due to elections being viewed as less consequential by citizens of the United States compared with citizens elsewhere. Because of the separation of powers, elections often appear to have a limited effect on government policies. Additionally, the high margins of victory in so many congressional races tend to reduce the incentive to vote. This claim is supported by the history of U.S. turnout over the past 200 years.

Turnout in the United States is low not only in comparative perspective but also in historical perspective. Before the end of the nineteenth century turnout in the United States was much higher than in more recent years, averaging about 75 percent between 1845 and 1895. One reason often given for the decline in U.S. turnout during the early twentieth century is the adoption in most states at that time of reforms requiring individuals to register themselves in order to vote.[8] In most countries voter registration is automatic; however, France also has voluntary voter registration, and turnout there is quite similar to turnout in other established democracies. Mitchell and Wlezien argue that earlier studies had greatly overestimated the effects of voter registration laws, and the failure of recent simplifications of registration procedures ("Motor Voter" reforms) points to the same conclusion.[9] Moreover, turnout rose during the middle years of the twentieth century with no corresponding change in registration laws.

An alternative explanation for the historical decline in U.S. turnout was suggested by Walter Dean Burnham, who blamed it on a sectional realignment that followed the election of 1896. The resulting domination of the South and West by the Democrats and the Northeast and upper Midwest by the Republicans was so strong that, within regions, the minority party's capacity to launch competitive races was eliminated.[10] This may well have produced a sense that elections were no longer meaningful contests because the victorious party was predetermined. This is the same reasoning employed earlier in this chapter to explain the difference between proportional and FPTP electoral systems. Indeed, there has been a widespread finding in comparative turnout studies that higher margins of victory bring lower turnout.[11] On this reasoning, the impact on the eligible electorate of the decline in electoral competitiveness in the United States in the early twentieth century was, as Burnham has argued, tantamount to political "desocialization" leading to declining participation.[12] In other words, following the 1894–1896 realignment and continuing nearly until the New Deal reforms, elections apparently lost their significance to a large proportion of the citizenry, who as a result were discouraged from voting. As shown in Figure 16.1, the drop in voter participation began immediately after the election of 1896 and continued until the mid-1920s.

Other work has shown that turnout in House elections is very strongly influenced by the average margin of victory in congressional districts, with a small effect from the closeness of the race nationwide.[13] Turnout in presidential elections is determined in much the same way, though there is evidence of additional effects that come into play over and above the closeness of the race. Still, there is strong evidence that house margins influence presidential-election turnout more than the other way around.[14]

Also as shown in Figure 16.1, turnout moves more or less inversely with changes in the margin of victory in House elections observed since 1840. The relationship is not perfect (there are especially anomalous results during World War II), but

Figure 16.1
Changing Turnout in Presidential-Year Congressional Elections, 1840–1988, Compared with Changes in the Margin of Victory

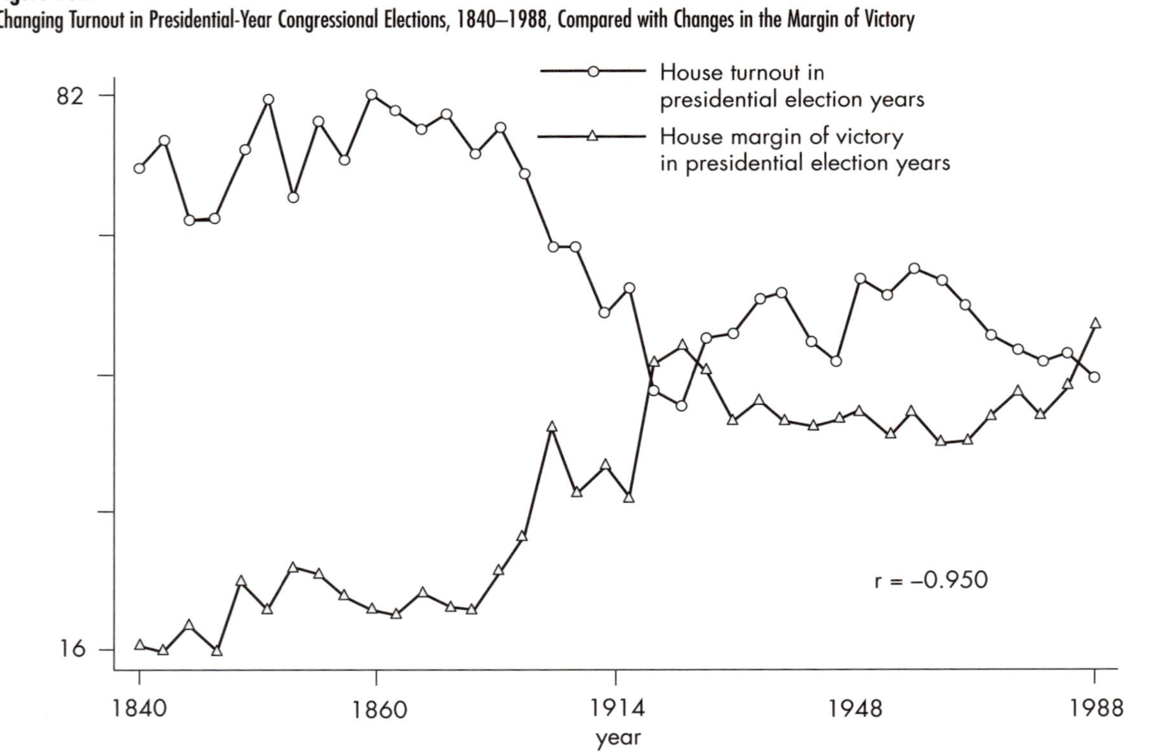

Source: Mark Franklin, *Voter Turnout and the Dynamics of Electoral Competition in Established Democracies Since 1945* (New York: Cambridge University Press, 2004).

the correlation between the two series is exceptionally strong and it is possible to see the marginality of House races as predicting a baseline turnout level from which actual turnout at House elections can drift for a time, but to which it tends to return. Long-term changes in House voter turnout apparently only occur with changes in that baseline.

It is important to note that the pattern of House victory margins does mirror the rise in House voter turnout during the 1930s and its subsequent fall after the 1960s, as well as the more dramatic turnout shift that occurred at the turn of the twentieth century. Since there were no further changes in election laws between 1920 and the 1960s, these findings show margin of victory to provide a better explanation than changes in election laws for the overall direction of House voter turnout since 1840. Increasingly competitive elections during the New Deal era have been explained by Kristi Andersen in terms of a challenge to the status quo in the context of economic crisis, and the more recent phenomenon of the "vanishing marginals" has been explained by Morris Fiorina and by David Mayhew in terms of incumbent legislators' maneuvering to secure reelection.[15] So an explanation for turnout change that focuses on electoral competition (district by district and over the country as a whole) is one that illuminates broad patterns in the evolution of U.S. voter turnout over the course of the twentieth century. It seems that competitive elections increase turnout, whereas non-competitive races (which may result from natural causes, such as realignments, but which in the United States have more recently resulted from the efforts of politicians to insulate themselves from election verdicts) have adverse effects on turnout. Apparently, whether people bother to vote is strongly influenced by whether they live in districts where the race is close enough to make it worth the effort to go to the polls. Congressional races where the outcome is too close to call are rare in modern-day America. During the 2002 midterm congressional elections, out of 435 districts in which House elections were conducted, only about 35 (or 8 percent) of the races were considered truly competitive.[16] The implication is clear that voting in America is discouraged by the lack of electoral competition that is the norm.

The pattern linking electoral competition to electoral behavior district by district seems very clear when one looks at the nationwide trend over time, yet few accounts of U.S. turnout frame the analysis in this way. Most accounts of why people vote focus not on nationwide turnout rates but on the individual decision to vote or not, as revealed by survey data. There is a good reason for this. Deducing the behavior of individuals from aggregate patterns is subject to what is known as the "ecological fallacy"—the faulty assumption that individual and aggregate behavior march in step. Aggregates of individuals do not necessarily behave in the same manner as the individuals of which the aggregates are composed. The most dramatic example of the ecological fallacy is a traffic jam. Viewed from the air, the traffic appears to be moving backward (sometimes at fairly high speed). Yet, of course, no individual vehicle is moving backward. Insofar as any individual car or truck is moving at all, it is moving forward even while the aggregate entity that we call a traffic jam appears to move in the other direction. Turnout is an aggregate concept, so inferring individual behavior from the aggregate pattern could be just as misleading as inferring the behavior of individual vehicles from the behavior of a traffic jam.

Moreover, there are theoretical reasons for doubting the importance of congressional margins of victory in determining individual behavior. This is because the chances are vanishingly small that an individual vote could affect an election outcome in an area as large as a congressional district, even in a very tight race. So, as pointed out by Riker and Ordershook in 1968,[17] unless individual voters are very much misinformed as to the likelihood that their votes will prove decisive, it does not seem plausible that the congressional district margin would influence individual behavior. And when voters have been asked about their perception of the closeness of an election in which they will be asked to participate, this variable has not been found to be at all important in explaining the decision of whether to vote. It is not mentioned by Verba, Schlozman, and Brady in their exhaustive list of reasons for participating in an election given by those they interviewed.[18]

On the basis of survey data, the factors that appear to be important in determining the decision to vote or not are primarily information, civic skills, political interest, and encouragement from others.[19] With the possible exception of the last item, all of these are functions of education, whose direct and indirect effects taken together outweigh all other influences on participation.[20] So education and things associated with education appear to be the linchpins determining political participation at the individual level.

But there is something very strange about this finding. As pointed out by Brody as long ago as 1978, if education is so critical at the individual level, one would expect the huge expansion in higher education that occurred in the United States beginning in the 1960s to have been responsible for an increase in turnout levels nationwide.[21] Yet, as illustrated in Figure 16.1, from the early 1960s onward turnout underwent a major and sustained decline. Again, of course, the expanded provision of education is an aggregate-level phenomenon whereas the importance of education is an individual-level phenomenon. Just as the importance of political competition at the aggregate level could lead us astray in deducing individual-level effects of political competition, so the individual-level effects of education could lead us astray in deducing aggregate effects. Yet at some point the difference between aggregate-level and individual-level findings needs to be reconciled. With traffic jams, reconciliation is easy: the aggregate entity moves backward because its composition changes as more and more vehicles join the tail. Once that is understood there is no longer a paradox. So it must be with electoral participation and turnout. Something about our understanding of either the aggregate entity or the individual-level effects must be mistaken.

There appears to be a misconception regarding the individual-level model used to calculate the effects of other variables on electoral participation. The mistake has been to assume that these effects operate equally on all members of the electorate. The idea that effects may be different on different categories of individuals has been suggested several times in recent scholarship. Gerber, Green, and Schachter have suggested that those with a high propensity to turn out should be analyzed separately from those with a low propensity to turn out.[22] Hilliguys has similarly suggested distinguishing those who are likely to vote from those who are not.[23] But what should be the basis for distinguishing these two groups? The clue is to be found in a 2002 article in the *American Political Science Review* in which Eric Plutzer establishes the manner in which young voters acquire the habit of voting.[24] He points out that sometime during early adulthood most voters make a transition from habitual nonvoting to habitual voting. Though Plutzer does not phrase his account in this way, it seems that many of the effects thought to be so important by Verba and colleagues are important not so much in determining whether individuals will participate in a particular election as in determining whether or not they will acquire the habit of voting. In light of these findings, accurate estimates of the effects of all variables require that we distinguish their effects on young adults from their effects on older individuals.

In fact, there are two separate processes at work, and they have been confounded in most past research. On the one hand there is a process of political learning, relevant to young adults, that determines what sort of behavior can be expected from them in later life. The education variable is one of those that distinguish those who have acquired the habit of voting and those who have not. Another such variable is encouragement, which Verba and his collaborators refer to as recruitment. On the other hand, there are a variety of factors that influence those who have not yet acquired a habit of either voting or not voting. These operate mainly on young adults, and here the character of elections is critical. As shown in *Voter Turnout and the Dynamics of Electoral Competition*, the expected margin of victory and other variables involving the character of a particular election, which have little influence on all voters taken together, have a considerable influence on young adults considered separately.[25]

In particular, features of the electoral context have strong indirect effects on young adults by way of their influence on the way in which elections are perceived. Such variables as the importance of party differences, interest in public affairs, interest in the election, and caring about the outcome take on different values for young adults at the time of more competitive elections, presumably because family and friends make greater efforts at mobilizing them. These findings are most fully established in comparative perspective,[26] but they are also found to apply in the United States when viewed over time; that is, analysis of U.S. survey data collected after presidential elections from 1964 to 2004 show the same need to separate the electorate into two groups based on age and show the same indirect effects of electoral context by way of campaign effects.[27]

One nice feature of the U.S. findings is that they render it unnecessary to take separate account of respondents' ages as an influence on their likelihood to vote. There is no theoretical basis for this variable. It serves as an umbrella concept to stand for things about people that change as they get older.[28] The need to include this variable in conventional models of electoral participation, and the strength of its effects in such models,[29] make it clear that there are things about age differences that those models have not identified. When young adults are taken separately from older adults, the different effects found for young adults (especially the difference relating to recruitment) account for the differences between older and younger voters, making age redundant as a predictor of whether people vote or not.[30] These individual-level findings also validate the aggregate-level findings about the influence of electoral competition on turnout, increasing confidence in the explanation for the difference between nineteenth-century U.S. turnout and twentieth-century U.S. turnout.

That the prevalence of safe districts in U.S. congressional elections is responsible for the low turnout is important in determining the suitability of one of the cures often proposed for non-competitive U.S. congressional elections: term limits. Term limits have been suggested and widely supported as a solution to the problem of unresponsive representatives. By outlawing the acquisition of seniority beyond a limited number of terms, rotation of elected representatives is ensured. But a much better alternative would be to enact a reform that restored competition to house races. This would shorten the number of terms served by the average congressman or congresswoman, because competitive elections would ensure occasional defeats by incumbents. But competitive elections would also raise turnout, something term limits would not do, by raising the frequency of true electoral contests that people would take seriously as providing real opportunities to unseat incumbents. Increasing the number of districts with competitive races would achieve the objectives of the term limits lobby while mitigating the problems of low turnout mentioned at the start of this chapter.

Many suggestions have been made for ways of restoring competitiveness to U.S. House elections. Strict limits on campaign spending together with free television time for candidates (which could be a television station licensing condition, as in other countries) would clearly be a step in the right direction. Relaxing the locality rule so that experienced politicians could challenge each other for the same seats (as they do in other countries and as now happens in certain areas, such as New York City, and occasionally elsewhere after redistricting) would also help. Redistricting itself could be taken out of the hands of state legislatures and/or performed on the basis of simple rules that eliminate collusion to benefit incumbent politicians (independent redistricting commissions are normal in other countries, and one was used in Iowa following the 2000 census). It is not hard to think of reforms that would have the desired effect. Most reforms that would be good for American democracy would also be good for voter turnout. In this sense, low turnout in the United States serves as a warning that the system is in need of reform.[31]

NOTES

1. Ruy Teixeira, *The Disappearing American Voter* (Washington, DC: Brookings Institute, 1992); Frances Piven and Richard Cloward, *Why Americans Still Don't Vote: and Why Politicians Want It That Way* (Boston: Beacon Press, 2000); Thomas Patterson, *The Vanishing Voter: Public Involvement in an Age of Uncertainty* (New York: Knopf, 2002); Martin Wattenberg, "The Decline of Party Mobilisation," in *Parties without Partisans,* edited by Russell Dalton and Martin Wattenberg (New York: Oxford University Press, 2000).

2. Teixeira, *Disappearing American Voter*; Russell Dalton, "Political Support in Advanced Industrial Democracies," in *Parties without Partisans,* edited by Russell Dalton and Martin Wattenberg (New York: Oxford University Press, 2000), 57–77.

3. Mark Franklin, "Electoral Participation," in *Controversies in Voting Behavior,* 4th ed., edited by Richard Niemi and Herbert Weisberg (Washington, DC: CQ Press, 2001); Mark Franklin, *Voter Turnout and the Dynamics of Electoral Competition in Established Democracies Since 1945* (New York: Cambridge University Press, 2004).

4. Mark Franklin and Wolfgang Hirczy de Mino, "Divided Government, Separated Powers, and Turnout in US Presidential Elections," *American Journal of Political Science* 42 (1997): 316–336.

5. Franklin, "Electoral Participation."

6. Franklin, *Voter Turnout,* 92–97; Boris Wernli, *Constraintes Institutionnelles, Influences Contextuelles et Participation aux Elections Federales en Suisse* (Bern: Haupt, 2001), 214–215.

7. Cees van der Eijk and Mark Franklin, *Choosing Europe? The European Electorate and National Politics in the Face of Union* (Ann Arbor: University of Michigan Press, 1996), 328–329.

8. See, for example, Raymond Wolfinger and Steven Rosenstone, *Who Votes?* (New Haven, CT: Yale University Press, 1980).

9. Glen Mitchell and Christopher Wlezien, "The Impact of Legal Constraints on Voter Registration, Turnout, and the Composition of the American Electorate," *Political Behavior* 17 (1995): 179–202; cf. Stephen Knack, "Drivers Wanted: Motor Voter and the Election of 1996," *PS: Political Science and Politics* 32 (1999): 237–243.

10. Walter Dean Burnham, "The Changing Shape of the American Political Universe," *American Political Science Review* 59 (1965): 7–28; Walter Dean Burnham, "Those High Nineteenth Century American Voter Turnout Figures: Fact or Fiction?" *Journal of Interdisciplinary History* 16 (1986): 613–644.

11. See, for example, G. Bingham Powell, Jr., "American Voter Turnout in Comparative Perspective," *American Political Science Review* 80 (1986): 17–43. See also Franklin, "Electoral Participation."

12. Walter Dean Burnham, "Theory and Voting Research: Some Reflections on Converse's 'Change in the American Electorate,'" *American Political Science Review* 68 (1974): 1013; cf. Burnham, "Changing Shape."

13. Franklin, *Voter Turnout,* 109.

14. Franklin, *Voter Turnout,* 110, note 23.

15. Kristi Andersen, *The Creation of a Democratic Majority, 1928–1936* (Chicago: University of Chicago Press, 1979); Morris Fiorina, *Congress: Keystone of the Washington Establishment* (New Haven, CT: Yale University Press, 1989); David Mayhew, "Congressional Elections: The Case of the Vanishing Marginals," *Polity* 6 (1974): 295–317.

16. Franklin, *Voter Turnout,* 218, note 12.

17. William Riker and Peter Ordershook, "A Theory of the Calculus of Voting," *American Political Science Review* 62 (1968): 25–42.

18. Sidney Verba, Kay Schlozman, and Henry Brady, *Voice and Equality: Civic Voluntarism in American Politics* (Cambridge, MA: Harvard University Press, 1995), 22–23.

19. Verba et al., *Voice and Equality,* 441.

20. Verba et al., *Voice and Equality,* 451.

21. Richard A. Brody, "The Puzzle of Political Participation in America," in *The New American Political System,* edited by Anthony King (Washington, DC: American Enterprise Institute, 1978), 287–324.

22. Alan Gerber, Donald Green, and Ron Schachter, "Voting May Be Habit-Forming: Evidence from a Randomized Field Experiment," *American Journal of Political Science* 47 (2003): 561–573.

23. D. Sunshine Hilliguys, "Campaign Elects and the Dynamics of Turnout Intention in Election 2000," *Journal of Politics* 67 (2005): 50–68.

24. Eric Plutzer, "Becoming a Habitual Voter: Intertia, Resources, and Growth in Young Adulthood," *American Political Science Review* 96 (2002): 41–56.

25. Franklin, *Voter Turnout.*

26. Franklin, *Voter Turnout.*

27. Mark Franklin, "You Want to Vote Where Everybody Knows Your Name: Anonymity, Campaign Context, and Turnout Evolution among Young Adults," paper presented at the annual meeting of the American Political Science Association, 2005.

28. Cf. John Strate, Charles Parrish, Charles Elder, and Coit Ford III, "Life Span Civic Development and Voting Participation," *American Political Science Review* 83 (1989): 443–464.

29. Cf. Verba et al., *Voice and Equality,* 624.

30. See Franklin, "You Want to Vote." Using German survey data, from which the recruitment variable is absent, age continues to have a small effect even when the distinction between young adults and older voters has been made. See Franklin, *Voter Turnout,* 159. The link between margin of victory and turnout may arise precisely because of the activities of friends and neighbors in recruiting young voters to vote in races where the outcome is likely to be close (see "You Want to Vote").

31. See Mark Franklin, "Electoral Engineering and Cross-National Turnout Differences: What Role for Compulsory Voting?" *British Journal of Political Science* 29 (1999): 205–216.

17

Why We Vote

Civic Duty and Voter Apathy

Karlo Barrios Marcelo and Mark Hugo Lopez

"I Voted," reads the sticker awarded to Election Day voters at the polls. Prominently displayed on lapels, purses, shirt sleeves, and school bags, but only for those who voted, the sticker acts as a civic medal of honor. The "I Voted" sticker is one in a diverse arsenal of methods available to get-out-the-vote (GOTV) campaigns. In addition to social and cultural means (e.g., stickers) of encouraging voting, laws, public policy, civic education, and technology are used to target voters and nonvoters alike. Nonetheless, citizens, by their active electoral participation, legitimize a representative's tenure, building the foundation of a representative democracy.[1] In fact, voting is so vital to our political system that it was written into the Constitution. The Twelfth, Fourteenth, Fifteenth, Seventeenth, Nineteenth, Twenty-fourth, and Twenty-sixth Amendments all deal directly with the right to vote.[2] And voting is a right, not a requirement, which means that even among the voting-eligible population (VEP), some choose not to vote.

Not everyone votes, and the reasons for this lack of political engagement are many, including institutional barriers to participation and general voter apathy. This is particularly true for young people, who generally are less likely to vote and the most likely be affected by institutional barriers to participation.

WHY VOTE?

Who votes does make a difference, not only for the outcome of an election but also in the campaign process, in the distribution of public services, and, more broadly, in the larger public policy agenda. More personally, electoral participation "can help develop citizens' awareness, knowledge and self-realization."[3] And among nonvoters, young people are often derided as the most apathetic group. This is doubly tragic because not only do the youths' interests go unheard, but voting behavior can become habitual once an eligible voter has had a chance to vote once or twice.[4] Wattenberg (2002) puts the former point more bluntly: "As long as young people have low rates of [electoral] participation . . . then they should expect to be getting relatively little of whatever there is to get from government."[5] Levine (2007) defends young people by attributing part of the blame to campaigns for failing to address the interests of young people. The point remains, however, that age is a strong predictor of voting behavior, as strong as education.[6] Yet Levine and Lopez (2005) note that there are arguments against voting, citing a cost-benefit analysis of voting.[7]

DEFINING NONVOTERS

Before describing nonvoters, one must first have some sense of how to define them. The term "non-voters" encompasses a broad population, but at its core is the simple fact that these people did not vote and may not vote in subsequent elections. There are many ways to slice the nonvoter pie, and many reasons why some citizens may not have voted. Hadley (1978) refers to nonvoters as refrainers, and divides them into six groups based on the main reason for their not voting:

- the Positive Apathetics
- the Bypassed
- the Politically Impotent
- the Physically Disenfranchised
- the Naysayers
- the Cross-pressured

Doppelt and Shearer (1999) classify nonvoters into similar groups: Doers, Unplugged, Irritables, Don't Knows, Alienateds, and Can't Shows. But the groups defined by Hadley and by Doppelt and Shearer focus mainly on the behavioral causes of not voting, and not the structural factors and demographic characteristics associated with nonvoting. Moreover, it is difficult to accurately quantify these groups by using large national surveys, which are the most reliable data sources for quantifying voters and nonvoters.

The path to casting a vote is legislated with qualifications and barriers. For some, only a single barrier, such as registering to vote, is enough to make an eligible voter a nonvoter.[8] Some of these barriers have been removed by the federal government to enfranchise its citizenry, with laws such as the Help America Vote

Act. In the United States, to cast a vote, a potential voter generally must go through a two-step process. First, one must register to vote. The basic qualifications for voter registration are U.S. citizenship and at least 18 years of age on Election Day. Further qualifications, which vary by state, include residency status and non-felon status. Those who meet these qualifications can register to vote (except in North Dakota, where it is necessary to prove only one's residency at the polls). Registration is claimed to ensure accurate vote counts and to function as a check on fraudulent voting, requiring would-be voters to prove their identities. Registration rates, much like voter turnout rates, are lower for young people compared with adults, although 70 percent of young people were registered to vote in the 2004 presidential election, compared with 84 percent of adults. In 2006 the corresponding figures were 51 percent for young people ages 18 to 29 and 72 percent for adults 30 and older.[9]

Second, once registered to vote, one can participate in the electoral process by showing up on Election Day at a designated polling station and casting his or her vote during voting hours. Some states have made this easier to do by extending the hours polling stations are open, and also by allowing voters to cast votes early or by mail. Thus, a likely voter may be snagged in a variety of places, without having to engage directly in the electoral process. For young people, barriers in the registration process and in the process of casting a vote can be enough to make a potential voter into a nonvoter. According to a survey conducted by the Center for Information and Research on Civic Learning and Engagement (CIRCLE) in 2002, 16 percent of young people said it was "very" or "somewhat difficult to register to vote," and 15 percent said it was "very" or "somewhat difficult to actually cast a vote." Though small, these proportions are sufficient to suggest the presence of barriers to young people's participation in the voting process.

We can define three broad populations of nonvoters:

1. Non-naturalized persons: residents without citizenship (immigrants)
2. Nonregistered voters: citizens who are 18 years or older and not registered to vote
3. Registered voters: citizens who are 18 years or older but despite being registered, did not cast a vote

Of the 47 million young American residents (ages 18 to 29) during the last presidential election in 2004, 6 million were non-naturalized persons, 16 million were nonregistered voters, and 25 million were registered voters.

Another way to categorize nonvoters, other than by their voting qualifications, is by their nonvoting behavior:

- Would-never-be-voters
- Boycotting citizens
- Voters who have their voting rights violated
- Citizens who do not vote for other, personal reasons

Unfortunately, we do not have quantifiable data on these populations, but they are nonetheless important. For the purposes of this chapter, general definitions will suffice. Would-never-be-voters are also nonvoters; even though they meet all the basic qualifications to vote, some still choose not to. Indifference and apathy are the usual suspects. Allowing citizens the right the vote, rather than making voting mandatory (as do many nations, such as Cuba, though it is unclear if this is the best way to encourage voting), means that citizens can participate in democracy by boycotting elections. More insidiously, some nonvoters are discouraged or prevented from voting through discriminatory laws and shady campaign tactics. Finally, personal reasons, such as competing time commitments, also prevent citizens from voting.

DEMOGRAPHICS OF NONVOTERS

In the past, nonvoters were more likely to be young, African American, female, and among the least educated.[10] Although it is still true that young people are more likely to be nonvoters than are older citizens (25 percent vs. 54 percent in 2006), their turnout in recent elections has increased at higher rates than for any other age group.[11] And it is not just college students and whites who are showing increases. In 2004 all subgroups of young people increased their voter turnout from the previous presidential election cycle.[12] Specifically, young African Americans' turnout rates are commensurate with those of their white counterparts, and young women have surpassed young men in voter turnout since the early 1980s.[13] On the other hand, the least educated still have extremely low turnout rates.

Comparing subgroups of nonvoters may shed some light on the demographic characteristics of nonvoters. Here two ways are used to identify the characteristics of nonvoters: the demographics of nonvoters (Table 17.1) and of those most likely to be nonvoters (Table 17.2). Table 17.1 displays the breakdown of the young (ages 18 to 29) nonvoting population in the 2004 presidential. As shown, nonvoters were more likely to be male and Latino or Asian, compared with voters.[14] Furthermore, young nonvoters were more likely to be less educated and not currently in school. Finally, young nonvoters are more likely to be living in the South and in rural areas compared with young voters.

VOTER TURNOUT RATES BY SUBGROUP

Table 17.2 displays the voter turnout rates by subgroup, which is more informative as to who is most likely to be a nonvoter. Table 17.2 confirms some notions about nonvoters: they are more likely to be men, racial/ethnic minority

Table 17.1
Demographics of 18- to 29-Year-Old Voters and Nonvoters

	Voters	Nonvoters
Male	45.9%	52.9%
Female	54.1%	47.1%
White	72.4%	63.3%
Black	14.4%	14.1%
Latino	8.7%	15.2%
Asian	2.3%	4.6%
Less than high school diploma	6.4%	20.4%
High school	24.1%	37.2%
Some college	44.9%	32.0%
B.A. or more	24.7%	10.5%
High school student	2.9%	4.9%
College student	28.5%	18.1%
Nonstudent	68.6%	77.0%
Married	28.5%	27.8%
Single	71.6%	72.3%
Northeast	18.2%	18.0%
Midwest	26.1%	21.7%
South	34.1%	38.1%
West	21.6%	22.2%
Urban	29.8%	27.5%
Suburban	40.6%	39.1%
Rural	15.6%	18.6%
Registered	100.0%	21.7%
Not registered	N/A	78.4%

Source: Authors' tabulations from the *Current Population Survey*, November (Voting) Supplement, 2004.

members, less educated, located in a rural area, and living in the South. Because of the under-representation of these subgroups, some have used terms such as "elite democracy" or "participatory distortion" to describe the higher profile of older, more educated citizens in the electoral process.[15]

Young women show higher registration and voter turnout rates than men. The turnout of racial minorities will be especially important in future elections, because the youth population is growing more diverse and minority youth may have different views on policy than their white counterparts.[16] Wolfinger and

Table 17.2
Voter Turnout Rates among 18- to 29-Year-Old Citizens

	2004 (Presidential)	2006 (Midterm)
Female	52.4%	27.1%
Male	45.5%	23.9%
White	52.3%	27.8%
Black	49.5%	24.0%
Latino	35.5%	18.6%
Asian	32.4%	16.5%
Less than high school diploma	23.1%	11.4%
High school	38.4%	17.8%
Some college	57.4%	28.7%
B.A. or more	69.4%	41.0%
Married	49.6%	28.4%
Single	48.7%	24.4%
High school student	36.0%	15.6%
College student	60.2%	27.3%
Nonstudent	46.1%	25.5%
Northeast	49.3%	23.4%
Midwest	53.6%	31.1%
South	46.2%	22.7%
West	48.2%	25.6%
Urban	51.0%	25.5%
Suburban	49.9%	27.3%
Rural	44.7%	25.8%
Registered voter	81.6%	50.2%
National youth turnout	49.0%	25.5%

Source: Authors' tabulations from the *Current Population Survey*, November (Voting) Supplement, 2004 and 2006.

Rosenstone (1980) find that "by any standards, education has a powerful independent influence on turnout."[17] Nie, Junn, and Stehlik-Barry (1996) go so far as to state that the correlation between education and political participation is the "best documented finding in American political behavior research."[18] In 2004 young citizens with no college experience had a voter turnout rate below the national youth average. In fact, as indicated in Table 17.2, young citizens with less than a high school diploma had the lowest voter turnout rate of any group. Furthermore, a substantial proportion (over 40 percent) of nonvoters have no college experience. The South has traditionally been associated with the lowest voter turnout compared with other regions of the country, even as far back as the 1940s.[19]

WHY THEY DON'T VOTE

Despite the relatively low rate compared with older citizens, the youth voter turnout rate jumped 9 percentage points, from 40 percent to 49 percent, between 2000 and 2004. Still, the majority of citizens ages 18 to 29 did not vote in the 2004 presidential election. Prior to the 2000 election, the youth voter turnout rate, no matter how measured, had been declining since 1972, although McDonald and Popkin (2001) argue otherwise.[20] Although young people have lower voter turnout rates relative to other age groups, in the two most recent elections their turnout has surged compared with adults, as shown in Table 17.3. Furthermore, young people are engaged in society in a number of other ways. The 2006 Civic and Political Health of the Nation Report (CPHS) found that young people were more likely to volunteer and to participate in protests than their adult counterparts (Lopez et al. 2006; Lopez and Marcelo 2007).[21] As some young people suggest, voting is just one way to be engaged in a participatory democracy, and it requires some effort, to say the least.[22]

CITIZENS' REASONS NOT TO VOTE

There are many reasons why a citizen may not vote. They include institutional barriers, such as registration to vote, which research has shown can influence voting through election laws and rules, and other factors that limit the ability of young citizens to make it to the polls. Registering to vote is often the first hurdle on the way to voting.[23] In 2004 non-registered young people cited a lack of interest in

Table 17.3
Changes in Voter Turnout Rate for Various Age Groups

Age	2004	2000	Change	2006	2002	Change
18–29	49%	40%	+9 pts.	25%	22%	+3 pts.
30–44	62%	59%	+3 pts.	43%	42%	+1 pt.
45–59	70%	67%	+3 pts.	56%	55%	+1 pt.
60+	71%	70%	+1 pt.	63%	62%	+1 pt.

Source: Authors' tabulations from the *Current Population Survey*, November (Voting) Supplement, 2000–2006.

Table 17.4
Main Reasons 18- to 29-Year-Olds Did Not Vote (Among Registered Voters)

	2006	2004
Too busy, conflicting work or school schedule	35%	27%
Not interested, felt vote wouldn't make a difference	14%	11%
Out of town or away from home	12%	11%
Other	9%	12%
Forgot to vote (or send in absentee ballot)	7%	6%
Registration problems (e.g., didn't receive absentee ballot, not registered in current location)	6%	10%
Didn't like candidates or campaign issues	5%	9%
Illness or disability (own or family member's)	3%	4%
Inconvenient hours or polling place, or lines too long	3%	3%
Transportation problems	2%	2%
Bad weather conditions	0%	0%

Source: Authors' tabulations from the *Current Population Survey*, November (Voting) Supplement, 2004 and 2006.

elections and politics as the number one reason they did not register (38 percent). Adults cited the same reason (39 percent), and this shows that no matter what one's age, lack of interest is the main reason citizens do not register to vote.[24]

Once registered, however, many young people still do not vote. Table 17.4 lists the main reasons that 18- to 29-year-old registered voters did not vote in the two most recent election cycles, the 2006 midterm elections and the 2004 presidential election. Few young citizens cited institutional rules as a reason they did not vote. In 2004, 10 percent of young citizens cited registration problems and only 3 percent cited inconvenient hours or long lines. The plurality of young citizens did not vote in either the 2004 or 2006 election because of other time commitments. Those who felt that their vote wouldn't make a difference offer a convincing argument; however, despite the fact that there is an infinitesimally small probability that one vote would make a difference at the national level, the 2000 presidential election proved that every vote counts in some cases.[25] Voter apathy is difficult to discern from the reasons listed in Table 17.4, but Morin and Dean (2000) report that apathy is on the rise compared with three decades ago. Experts point to a number of causes: the media, lack of strong civic education, uninteresting elections, and politics itself.

Voter registration and extended polling hours are positively correlated with voting.[26] Voter registration complexities and inconvenient polling place hours are only two of the myriad institutional barriers that affect all voters, but they do not affect all voters equally. Young people are more adversely affected by registration rules than adults because of their transience, and research finds that residential mobility affects turnout.[27] Also, college students continue to fight for their right to establish residency in their college towns, and to be eligible to vote where they live.[28]

EFFICACY AND VOTING BEHAVIOR

In 2006 young people were asked how much difference they believed they could make by addressing problems in their community; 48 percent of young people (ages 18 to 29) said they could make "some difference" or a "great difference." These same young people were more likely to be civically engaged. Levine (2007) notes that "political participation also has a strong relationship with 'efficacy,' the sense that one can have an impact or make a difference through politics or civic engagement."[29] People who believe they can make a difference are more likely to vote and be otherwise engaged in civil society. Tables 17.5 and 17.6 examine the "efficacy" of young people as it relates to voting. As Table 17.5 shows, voting and efficacy are strongly positively related when voting is viewed as a responsibility or a way to make a difference: regular voters ages 20 to 29 were least likely to view voting as a choice (22.8 percent); the plurality of regular voters viewed voting as a responsibility (39.3 percent). Nearly 46 percent of young immigrants did not report a view on voting or refused to comment; young immigrants vote at lower rates than their native-born counterparts.[30] Table 17.5 shows that young Democrats (and liberals) are less efficacious than their Republican (and conservative) counterparts.

THE IMPORTANCE OF VOTING

Is voting important? Voting legitimizes a government and helps direct public services and resources. Actively choosing not to vote is a way to send the message that a citizen does not approve of either the political candidates or their policy agendas. Democrats were likely to view voting as extremely or very important compared with Republicans and Independents. Thus, while Republicans were found to be more efficacious, Table 17.6 shows that Democrats are not less cognizant of the importance of voting.

CONCLUSION: ENCOURAGING VOTERS

There are many ways to encourage more youth to engage in electoral politics. First, young people can be reached by get-out-the-vote efforts. Recent research suggests that this can be a very effective way to increase voter turnout among

Table 17.5
Views on Voting among 18- to 29-Year-Olds (2006)

	Responsibility	Make a Difference in the Election's Outcome	Expression of My Choice	Don't Know/ Refused
Male	29.2%	27.2%	34.4%	9.2%
Female	22.1%	31.0%	30.8%	16.1%
White	28.7%	29.3%	35.4%	6.7%
Black	21.3%	39.5%	30.7%	8.4%
Hispanic	16.2%	28.3%	21.2%	34.3%
Asian	27.9%	31.7%	37.9%	2.5%
High school student	27.0%	27.5%	42.0%	3.6%
College student	28.9%	34.6%	34.8%	1.7%
Nonstudent	22.1%	27.7%	33.9%	16.4%
Married	30.9%	28.0%	31.4%	9.7%
Single	24.5%	29.8%	36.5%	9.3%
Northeast	22.3%	35.5%	36.2%	6.0%
Midwest	30.0%	22.6%	38.1%	9.3%
South	26.0%	29.8%	30.0%	14.2%
West	24.1%	29.1%	29.4%	17.4%
Urban	26.4%	29.0%	31.1%	13.5%
Suburban	27.4%	28.1%	33.3%	11.3%
Rural	19.8%	28.2%	33.8%	18.3%
Registered	31.6%	30.7%	32.5%	5.2%
Not registered	16.0%	26.2%	32.9%	24.9%
Democrat (including leaners)	23.5%	31.7%	36.1%	8.6%
Republican (including leaners)	32.3%	35.2%	27.9%	4.7%
Pure Independent	22.7%	17.7%	31.8%	27.8%
Conservative	32.4%	30.2%	29.5%	7.9%
Moderate	26.4%	33.0%	35.2%	5.4%
Liberal	18.9%	25.5%	36.9%	18.7%
U.S.-born to U.S.-born	28.6%	30.0%	35.1%	6.4%
Foreign-born to U.S.-born	22.0%	46.7%	28.8%	2.5%
Foreign-born to foreign-born	14.6%	18.0%	21.4%	45.9%
Regular religious service attendance	32.3%	33.1%	24.3%	10.3%

Table 17.5 *(Continued)*

	Responsibility	Make a Difference in the Election's Outcome	Expression of My Choice	Don't Know/ Refused
Moderate religious service attendance	22.7%	28.8%	37.9%	10.6%
No religious service attendance	21.3%	27.6%	36.1%	15.0%
Regular voter (ages 20+)	39.3%	35.8%	22.8%	2.1%
Non-regular voter (ages 20+)	20.7%	25.3%	34.8%	19.2%

Source: Authors' tabulations from the 2006 Civic and Political Health of the Nation Survey (CIRCLE).

young people.[31] Second, institutional barriers to voting can be reduced to ease the process of registration and hence the likelihood that a young person will vote. Finally, schools, through civic education, can make a difference by improving the civic knowledge and skills of youth.

Get Out the Vote

Practically speaking, get-out-the-vote (GOTV) campaigns, either partisan or nonpartisan, have limited human and financial resources to reach out to citizens and encourage them to vote. Because of the constraints on the reach of GOTV campaigns, political campaigns in particularly target voters based on how many resources it can dedicate to reach each voter. The good news is that likely non-voters (youth, immigrants, and racial/ethnic minorities) can be targeted in a cost-effective way through methods such as door-to-door canvassing, bilingual phone banking, outreach by volunteers representing the racial/ethnic makeup of the targeted voters, and Election Day reminders.[32] Robocalls and direct mail are expensive tactics that are not effective in encouraging young voters, because of their lack of a personal connection.

Ease Voting Rules

The social science research is conclusive in finding that easier voting rules boost voter turnout. Wolfinger and Rosenstone (1980) have argued for easier registration, since it is often the first institutional barrier to voting. Federal laws such as "Motor Voter" and the Help America Vote Act (2002) are positive steps toward realizing a fully registered citizenry. And youth registration rates are on the rise.[33]

Post-registration rules also affect turnout. Wolfinger, Highton, and Mullin (2004) found that "mailing sample ballots and polling place location information to all registrants and offering extended polling hours on Election Day" positively affect turnout of registered voters.[34]

Table 17.6
Importance of Voting among 18- to 25-Year-Olds (2004)

	Extremely Important	Very Important	Somewhat Important	Little Importance	Not Important/ Don't Know
Male	19.7%	35.5%	23.9%	15.3%	5.6%
Female	14.4%	35.9%	29.9%	12.4%	7.5%
White	18.2%	38.5%	23.6%	14.7%	5.2%
Black	14.6%	29.1%	32.4%	17.2%	6.8%
Latino	14.3%	31.9%	27.2%	12.8%	13.8%
Full-time student	21.2%	47.7%	20.0%	8.5%	2.6%
Part-time student	22.0%	23.7%	30.3%	16.1%	7.9%
Nonstudent	15.0%	32.6%	28.9%	15.7%	7.8%
Married	25.9%	35.4%	24.1%	10.3%	4.2%
Single	14.9%	36.2%	28.0%	14.1%	6.8%
Democrat	20.0%	42.3%	25.9%	9.2%	2.7%
Republican	21.8%	39.3%	26.4%	10.9%	1.5%
Independent	10.6%	23.8%	29.0%	20.4%	16.2%
Conservative	20.7%	38.8%	24.0%	12.8%	3.7%
Moderate	12.1%	39.6%	27.5%	13.1%	7.7%
Liberal	18.0%	33.5%	30.2%	14.3%	4.1%
Regular religious service attendance	27.3%	42.3%	19.6%	6.5%	4.3%
Moderate religious service attendance	13.5%	40.5%	28.7%	12.8%	4.6%
No religious service attendance	15.6%	20.9%	29.3%	22.3%	11.9%
Registered	21.2%	41.0%	23.1%	11.2%	3.6%
Not Registered	5.6%	19.8%	37.6%	22.2%	14.9%

Source: Authors' tabulations from the National Youth Survey, 2004 (CIRCLE).

Civic Education

In a study of 805 local party leaders, Shea (2004) found that these leaders thought that "deficient high school civics programs" were at the "root" of the problem of youth disengagement. It is at the high school level that civics programs can have a strong effect.[35] Around age 17, during adolescence, Levine (2007) notes, young people "will be permanently shaped by the way they first experience politics, social issues, and civil society."[36] He further points out that it is very difficult to change the civic identities of adults over 30. But what kind of civic education is most effective? Formal education in civic knowledge and exposure to the electoral process impart two practical lifelong skills that promote positive voting behavior. Learning about how the government works equips students with a basis for understanding the news and making decisions about candidates. One way to increase civic knowledge is to "incorporate discussion of current, local, national, and international issues and events into the classroom, particularly those that young people view as important to their lives."[37] Teaching students about the electoral process, such as how to register to vote or how to use a voting machine, provides hands-on experience that can help them to surmount certain institutional barriers to voting.[38]

NOTES

Authors' Note: We thank Peter Levine and Deborah Both for comments on previous drafts of this document. We also thank Kumar Pratap for excellent research assistance. All errors, in fact or interpretation, are our own. Address correspondence to Mark Hugo Lopez, CIRCLE, School of Public Policy, University of Maryland, 2101 Van Munching Hall, College Park, MD, 20742-1821. E-mail: mhlopez@umd.edu. Phone: 301-405-0183.

1. See Tocqueville ([1840] 1945).

2. Visit the Cornell University Law School Web site for definitions of these amendments: http://www.law.cornell.edu/constitution/constitution.overview.html.

3. See Michael R. Kagay, "The Mystery of Nonvoters and Whether They Matter," *New York Times,* August 27, 2000, p. 4–1.

4. See Eric Pultzer, "Becoming a Habitual Voter: Inertia, Resources and Growth in Young Adulthood," *American Political Science Review* 96(1) (March 2002).

5. See Wattenberg (2002), p. 98.

6 See Pultzer, "Becoming a Habitual Voter."

7. See Anthony Downs, *An Economic Theory of Democracy* (New York: Harper, 1957).

8. See Marcelo (2007).

9. Marcelo (2007).

10. See Wolfinger and Rosenstone (1980). Also see Charles Edward Merriam and Harold Foote Gosnell, *Non-Voting* (Chicago: University of Chicago Press, 1924).

11. See Lopez, Marcelo, and Kirby (2007).

12. See Marcelo, Lopez, Kennedy (2008).

13. See Lopez, Kirby, and Sagoff (2005). Also see Lopez, Marcelo, and Kirby (2007).

14. Racial/ethnic groups are defined in the *Current Population Survey* November Supplements as including those with Hispanic background such as Latino, and individuals who cite a single race or ethnicity and who are non-Hispanic, such as white, African American, and Asian American.

15. See Verba, Schlozman, and Brady (1995), p. 15 and especially Chapter 6. Also see Patterson (2002).

16. See Lopez and Marcelo (2006).

17. See Wolfinger and Rosenstone (1980), p. 25.

18. See Nie, Junn, and Stehlik-Barry (1996).

19. See Connelly and Field (1944), pp. 175–187.

20. See Levine and Lopez (2002). For a full discussion of the different ways voter turnout can be calculated, see Mark Hugo Lopez, Emily Kirby, Jared Sagoff, and Chris Herbst, *The Youth Voter 2004: With a Historical Look at Youth Voting Patterns 1972–2004.* CIRCLE Working Paper 35 (July 2005). All voter turnout estimates presented in this fact sheet are calculated for U.S. citizens only, according to the "Census Citizen Method" described in this document.

21. See Lopez et al. (2006). Also see Lopez and Marcelo (2007).

22. See Kiesa et al. (2007).

23. See Wolfinger, Highton, and Mullin (2004). Also see Fitzgerald (2003).

24. See Marcelo (2007).

25. Wattenberg (2002).

26. See Marcelo (2007) and Wolfinger, Highton, and Mullin (2004).

27. See Highton (2000).

28. See Adler (2007).

29. See Levine (2007), p. 50.

30. See Lopez and Marcelo (2008).

31. See Green and Gerber (2004).

32. See Michelson (2004), Gerber (2004), Green and Gerber (2004), Green (2004), Nickerson (2006), Ramirez (2005), Ramirez and Wong (2006).

33. See Marcelo (2007).

34. See Wolfinger, Highton, and Mullin (2004), p. 13.

35. See Shea (2004), p. 2.

36. See Levine (2007), p. 70.

37. See Carnegie Corporation of New York and CIRCLE (2003), p. 6.

38. Carnegie Corporation of New York and CIRCLE (2003), p. 6.

REFERENCES

Adler, Ben. (2007). "Campus Voting Access Not Making the Grade." Available online at *Politico.com* (accessed October 9, 2007).

Carnegie Corporation of New York, and CIRCLE. (2003). *The Civic Mission of Schools.* Washington, DC: Carnegie Foundation for the Advancement of Teaching, and CIRCLE.

Connelly, Gordon M., and Harry H. Field. (1944). "The Non-Voter—Who He Is, What He Thinks." *Public Opinion Quarterly*, Vol. 8, No. 2, pp. 175–187.

Doppelt, Jack C., and Ellen Shearer. (1999). *Nonvoters: America's No-Shows.* Thousand Oaks, CA: Sage Publications.

Fitzgerald, Mary. (2003, February). *Easier Voting Methods Boost Youth Turnout.* CIRCLE Working Paper 01. www.civicyouth.org

Gerber, Alan S. (2004). "Does Campaign Spending Work? Field Experiments Provide Evidence and Suggest New Theory." *American Behavioral Scientist*, Vol. 47, No. 5, pp. 541–574.

Gimpel, James G., J. Celeste Lay, and Jason E. Schunknect. (2003). *Cultivating Democracy: Civic Environments and Political Socialization in America*. Washington, DC: Brookings Institution Press.

Green, Donald P. (2004). *The Effects of an Election Day Voter Mobilization Campaign Targeting Young Voters*. CIRCLE Working Paper 21. www.civicyouth.org.

Green, Donald P., and Alan S. Gerber. (2004). *Get Out the Vote! How to Increase Voter Turnout*. Washington, DC: Brookings Institution Press.

Hadley, Arthur T. (1978). *The Empty Polling Booth*. Englewood Cliffs, NJ: Prentice-Hall.

Highton, Benjamin. (2000). "Residential Mobility, Community Mobility, and Electoral Participation." *Political Behavior*, Vol. 22, pp. 109–120.

Kiesa, Abby, Alexander P. Orlowski, Peter Levine, Deborah Both, Emily Hoban Kirby, Mark Hugo Lopez, and Karlo Barrios Marcelo. (2007, November). *Millennials Talk Politics: A Study of College Student Political Engagement*. CIRCLE Special Report Series. www.civicyouth.org.

Levine, Peter. (2007). *The Future of Democracy: Developing the Next Generation of American Citizens*. Medford, MA: Tufts University Press.

Levine, Peter, and Mark Hugo Lopez. (2002, September). "Youth Voter Turnout Has Declined, by Any Measure." CIRCLE Fact Sheet. www.civicyouth.org.

———. (2005, September). "What We Should Know about the Effectiveness of Campaigns but Don't." *Annals of the American Academy of Political and Social Science*, Vol. 601, No. 1, pp. 180–191.

Lopez, Mark Hugo, Emily Kirby, and Jared Sagoff. (2005, July). "The Youth Vote 2004." CIRCLE Fact Sheet. www.civicyouth.org.

Lopez, Mark Hugo, Peter Levine, Deborah Both, Abby Kiesa, Emily Kirby, and Karlo Marcelo. (2006, October). *The 2006 Civic and Political Health of the Nation: A Detailed Look at How Youth Participate in Politics and Communities*. Center for Information and Research on Civic Learning and Engagement. www.civicyouth.org.

Lopez, Mark Hugo, and Karlo Barrios Marcelo. (2006, November). "Youth Demographics." CIRCLE Fact Sheet. www.civicyouth.org.

———. (2007, April). "Volunteering among Young People." CIRCLE Fact Sheet. www.civicyouth.org.

———. (Forthcoming April 2008). "The Civic Engagement of Immigrant Youth: New Evidence from the 2006 Civic and Political Health of the Nation Survey." *Applied Developmental Science* (special issue on Immigrant Civic Engagement), Vol. 12, No. 2.

Lopez, Mark Hugo, Karlo Barrios Marcelo, and Emily Hoban Kirby. (2007, June). "Youth Voter Turnout Increases in 2006." CIRCLE Fact Sheet. www.civicyouth.org.

Marcelo, Karlo Barrios. (2007, October). "Registration among Young People." CIRCLE Fact Sheet. www.civicyouth.org.

Marcelo, Karlo Barrios, Mark Hugo Lopez, and Chris Kennedy. (Forthcoming January 2008). *The Youth Vote 2008: A Demographic and Issues Portrait of Young Voters*. CIRCLE and Rock the Vote Special Report. www.civicyouth.org.

McDonald, Michael P., and Samuel L. Popkin. (2001, December). "The Myth of the Vanishing Voter." *American Political Science Review*, Vol. 95, No. 4.

Merriam, Charles Edward, and Harold Foote Gosnell. (1924). *Non-Voting*. Chicago: University of Chicago Press.

Michelson, Melissa. (2004). *Mobilizing the Latino Vote.* CIRCLE Working Paper 10. www.civicyouth.org.

Morin, Richard, and Claudia Deane. (2000, November 4). "As Turnout Falls, Apathy Emerges as Driving Force." *Washington Post*, p. A–1.

Nickerson, David W. (2006). "Volunteer Phone Calls Can Increase Turnout: Evidence from Eight Field Experiments." *American Politics Research*, Vol. 34, pp. 271–292.

Nie, Norman H., Jane Junn, and Kenneth Stehlik-Barry. (1996). *Education and Democratic Citizenship in America.* Chicago: University of Chicago Press.

Niemi, Richard G., and Jane Junn. (1998). *Civic Education: What Makes Students Learn.* New Haven, CT: Yale University Press.

Patterson, Thomas E. (2002). *The Vanishing Voter: Public Involvement in an Age of Uncertainty.* New York: Alfred A. Knopf.

Ramirez, Ricardo. (2005). "Giving Voice to Latino Voters: A Field Experiment on the Effectiveness of a National Nonpartisan Mobilization Effort." (The Science of Voter Mobilization. Special Editors Donald P. Green and Alan S. Gerber.) *Annals of the American Academy of Political and Social Science*, Vol. 601, pp. 66–84.

Ramirez, Ricardo, and Janelle Wong. (2006). "Non-Partisan Latino and Asian-American Contactability and Voter Mobilization." In *Transforming Politics, Transforming America: The Political and Civic Incorporation of Immigrants in the United States.* Taeku Lee, Karthick Ramakrishnan, and Ricardo Ramirez, eds. Charlottesville: University of Virginia Press.

Shea, Daniel M. (2004, April). *Throwing a Better Party: Local Mobilizing Institutions and the Youth Vote.* CIRCLE Working Paper 13. www.civicyouth.org.

Tocqueville, Alexis de. ([1840] 1945). *Democracy in America.* New York: Alfred Knopf.

Verba, Sidney, Kay Lehman Schlozman, and Henry E. Brady. (1995). *Voice and Equality: Civic Voluntarism in American Politics.* Cambridge, MA: Harvard University Press.

Wattenberg, Martin P. (2002). *Where Have All the Voters Gone?* Cambridge, MA: Harvard University Press.

Wolfinger, Raymond E., Benjamin Highton, and Megan Mullin. (2004, June). *How Postregistration Laws Affect the Turnout of Registrants.* CIRCLE Working Paper 15. www.civicyouth.org.

Wolfinger, Raymond E., and Steven J. Rosenstone. (1980). *Who Votes?* New Haven, CT: Yale University Press.

18

The Urban/Rural Divide

Understanding Voter Participation by Location

Kimberly A. Karnes and James G. Gimpel

The election night maps for recent presidential elections have highlighted the contrast between the East Coast and West Coast, in Democratic blue, and much of the Midwest and South, in Republican red. Upon closer inspection, a county-level breakdown of these commonplace maps shows that, in fact, there is a stark division within states, defining a rural/urban rift in political party support. By several definitions of "urban" and "rural," the gap between country and city in support of the Republican candidate has been in the neighborhood of 20 to 25 percentage points.[1]

This well-documented divide between rural and urban residents in regard to party backing is only one of many intriguing partitions in the national electorate. What is less commonly noted in press coverage about contemporary political campaigns, however, is that rural residents continue to exhibit far greater involvement in politics than their city cousins. As we address the differences in participation between urban and rural residents, we are not just referring to casting ballots on Election Day, although voting participation is usually emphasized because it is important and relatively easy to accomplish compared to more demanding forms of involvement, such as volunteering in a campaign or contacting officeholders.

For example, statistics early in the twenty-first century indicate that urban residents are far less inclined to contact an elected official about an issue or grievance than people who live in less populated areas. Activities such as attending community meetings are also less prevalent among residents of large cities.[2] The urban/rural gap in political participation is a long-standing difference in behavior that predates the oft-noted urban and rural differences in party loyalty and vote choice. Most research on the participation gap suggests that its roots lie in the history and sociological characteristics of big cities and small towns.

There is no universally accepted definition of what "rural" means, but it is important to emphasize that rural does not necessarily mean "agrarian." Farmers are often treated as a specific subset within the larger rural population, but only a small fraction of rural residents are actually employed in agricultural pursuits. Here "rural" is understood as encompassing not only farming populations but also residents of small towns (fewer than 10,000 people) that serve as retail and wholesale hubs for surrounding lower-density areas of settlement.

The simple contrast in the social settings between rural and urban residents helps explain historical differences in political participation between the two locales. Because rural areas were overwhelmingly agricultural in the nineteenth century, the life of the farmer and the small-town merchant were quite different from that of an urbanite in the industry-fueled cities.

First of all, the small-town inhabitant was less mobile and was more commonly a property owner rather than a renter. Even without owning property, however, rural residents were likely to remain in the same place for longer periods of time, whereas the city dweller was more frequently both a renter and a regular migrant. Migration and frequent changes of residence are commonly associated with low levels of political participation. This is because moving prevents people from collecting the necessary information about the politics of a location and keeps them from developing a vested interest in a particular place. This vested interest, or attachment to a place, is often linked to participation among stable and affluent populations.

Notably, rural residents were not much more literate than their urban counterparts at the end of the nineteenth century. Data from the *Eleventh Census of the United States* (1900) clearly indicate that the literacy rates of men of voting age living in low-density areas were, at best, only 1 to 2 percent higher than those living in larger cities, and in some states they were *lower* than the literacy rates in cities.

Even so, small towns were rich in the social capital bonds that promote civic engagement of all types, not just voting. Social influences are present in small towns to promote community participation, whereas the anonymity of big-city life undermines the social influence process that contributes to citizen activism.

What rural areas did lack, and what cities possessed, were strong political party organizations, often described as "machines," that could mobilize large numbers of voters on Election Day at low cost, given the density of urban settlement. Although rural areas usually lacked urban party machinery, and their literacy rates were not appreciably higher than those of cities, we find that the turnout rates in the nation's most rural counties ran well ahead of turnout in large urban counties throughout the nineteenth and twentieth centuries.[3] Remarkably, the smaller the population, the higher the turnout, although there are exceptions in the South, where turnout has customarily lagged across the entire region (Figure 18.1).

Figure 18.1
Average Level of Voter Turnout in U.S. Presidential Elections, by County, 1996–2004

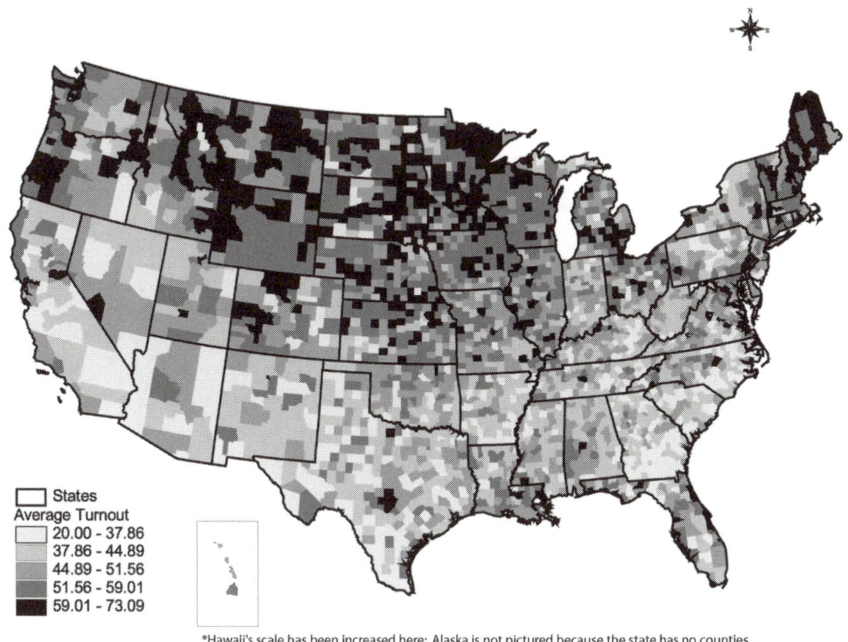

Differences in rural and urban political participation levels are important because turnout shapes election results, determines who wins elective office, and ultimately steers public policy. Many of the individual traits of voters—race, education, income, and political ideology, for example—explain their interest in politics and their levels of political participation. In this manner, much of the participation gap can be boiled down simply to the population composition of cities as compared to small towns. The importance of community social dynamics also looms large; the social capital rural residents derive from their communities accounts for their higher participation levels relative to city folk.

INDIVIDUAL CHARACTERISTICS, CIVIC SKILLS, AND POLITICAL PARTICIPATION

Demographic and socioeconomic characteristics of individual voters—their levels of income and education, their race and ethnicity, their age—are frequently used to explain the differences in political participation between urban and rural residents. By these accounts, rural and urban areas differ politically because of the differing types of people who live at each location.

Perhaps the most notable voter characteristic that separates urban from rural areas at the beginning of the twenty-first century is racial composition. Although there are rural African American populations in the South, throughout most of the country rural areas and small towns are homogeneously white. Similarly, large Latino native and immigrant populations have been drawn to large cities, and only recently have they dispersed in large numbers into less densely populated areas. Because these minority populations remain densely concentrated in big cities, their effect is to depress urban turnout. The absence of minority populations in rural locales serves to increase turnout there, producing the urban/rural participation gap.

The explanations for low political participation among racial and ethnic minorities vary, but most take into account factors closely associated with the unequal status of racial and ethnic groups in American society. Most inner-city minority neighborhoods are mired in poverty, low educational attainment, political cynicism, and civic illiteracy, all of which diminish the likelihood of political engagement. Geographic isolation from the positive example of politically active populations also undermines participation. Without regular exposure to other, civically literate populations within the city, most residents dissociate themselves from politics in general.[4] Having little interaction with the government, or experiencing hostile interactions with government authorities, including law enforcement, produces a sense of low political efficacy that results in alienation of citizens from political leadership.[5]

Lack of interest in political participation is also associated with people who have less formal education and low socioeconomic status, regardless of their race. Education and high socioeconomic status are associated with the acquisition of interpretive and organizational skills necessary for political participation. For example, time is an important resource required for involvement, but not all citizens possess equal amounts of time away from the duties associated with work, family, and school.[6] The advantage of affluence in regard to political participation is clear. Citizens with more money may also have more leisure time to devote to politics, and more resources to obtain political information and build civic skill. Moreover, they may also come into regular contact with other affluent and politically efficacious individuals, both at work and in the neighborhood.[7] In connection with voting, citizens who lack basic knowledge about the political process—how to vote, where to register, when to vote—will almost always fail to engage in more demanding political activities, such as donating to campaigns or contacting their elected officials.[8] Rural populations may participate at higher levels, in part because they have more time to acquire political information and pursue political involvement. The concentration of impoverished populations in large cities also helps us to understand why turnout in big city neighborhoods is so low.

Although wealth is certainly a predictor of political participation, it is not the only important factor. Surprisingly, rural Americans are often as poor, if not poorer, than those who live in cities. Rural residents commonly have lower levels of formal education than residents of major metropolitan areas. Although we can attribute some non-participation to low income and low educational attainment, these factors do not appear to have the same effect in rural areas that they have in cities. In recent times, rural residents are more likely than urban residents to participate in politics, regardless of their education level and socioeconomic standing. That means there could be other reasons for the urban/rural participation gap.

Finally, high levels of migration and youthful populations are productive of low urban turnout levels. Moving residence from one place to another is harmful to turnout because prospective voters must re-register with local officials in order to vote. Although voter registration has been simplified in recent years, this is a barrier potential voters must overcome if they are to begin participating in their new neighborhoods. Young people are also very slow to begin voting after reaching age eligibility; steady participation habits may not emerge until middle age, when an individual has settled down and started a family. In cities with youthful age distributions, voter turnout rates will typically be lower than in small towns, with their much older populations.

SOCIAL CAPITAL AND POPULATION SIZE

Certainly one important explanation for high levels of political participation in rural areas, in spite of low income, is the greater social capital prevailing among small-town populations. In this case, Robert Putnam's definition of social capital applies: "features of social organization, such as networks, norms, and trust, that facilitate coordination and cooperation for mutual benefit."[9] High levels of political engagement stem from a culture within the community that promotes such action as being a benefit to both the individual and her town. Not all rural areas are alike, so we cannot conclude that these norms are present everywhere. On average, however, rural communities are much deeper repositories of social capital than are large cities.

Small size promotes social capital formation. Because rural areas are much smaller, residents are more likely to know their neighbors. With small populations, there are more social pressures to conform to community norms, including the norm to vote regularly. The old adage that in a small town "everybody knows everybody else's business" surely rings true in this situation. Some may participate simply because they know there will be talk at the local diner or beauty shop if they do not. Or perhaps they know that they will be asked by someone if they voted, and they do not want to lie. As a consequence, civic responsibilities are felt more acutely in rural areas than in cities. Moreover, citizens in a crowded city may reason that there are many *other* people outside of their personal networks who are willing to participate in politics and run the affairs of the community. In rural areas, however, there is less of a sense that these legions of willing others exist. Instead, citizens conclude that they must step up, or no one else will.

Participation-enabling social capital in small towns is strengthened and maintained through religious observance. Rural Americans are more religious than urbanites, largely because of the stability of small town populations that keeps church traditions alive. Although there are often durable ties to churches in urban areas, particularly among African Americans, most evidence points to a weakening of religious belief and observance among more migratory, urban populations.

In terms of job satisfaction, sociological surveys of rural residents have shown that they are more content with their jobs than are urban residents and, consequently, report being happier about life in general.[10] A more positive outlook about their jobs may, as a result, spur rural residents to be more active outside of the job. When life is more satisfying, residents want to invest in keeping it that way, and political participation may be one avenue for residents to maintain their high quality of life.

At the same time, low-income rural residents do not seem to develop cynicism or negative attitudes about government to the same degree that poor urban residents do. Rural poverty, in this sense, may be easier to cope with than urban poverty, perhaps because there are nonmonetary sources of exchange in the countryside that do not exist in the city. A prevailing sense of economic equality among rural residents reduces distrust and mitigates the class resentment poor residents express when they experience urban poverty. The gaping disparity between rich and poor is not nearly as evident or as wide in small towns as it is across the landscape of metropolitan America.

Finally, economics plays a critical role in the increased political participation among rural citizens because of the number of residents who are home owners or small business entrepreneurs—which gives them a sense of having a stake in the process that is not present among a city's renters and laborers. Rural stakeholders will want their investments to be protected, hoping that their property and capital will be secure, however meager those possessions might be.[11]

Despite the conventional wisdom, rural residents are not more likely to be patriotic than those living in other areas. Recent survey research indicates that there is no stronger statistical connection between rural residents and feelings of patriotism than there is for residents of any other location. Quite often, theories about patriotism and being a "good American" are applied to rural voters to explain their high level of political activity. There is a persuasive argument, however, that an acute sense of individual responsibility in rural social settings best explains the political participation patterns that are exhibited in election results. This sense of responsibility stems from an individualist ethic that is deeply ingrained in American political culture, but rural residents experience greater exposure to social enforcement of this ethic than city dwellers do.[12]

In summary, the influence of community norms in rural America makes political participation there a more integral part of life than it is in large cities. Currently, there does not appear to be anything like the same type of social capital production in major metropolitan areas that occurs in the nation's small towns—but that does not mean that cities are destined always to have low political participation levels. Perhaps one of the most important lessons to take from a thoughtful study of the participation gap is to examine the ways in which rural communities create and sustain participation-enabling social networks.

To be sure, mobilization by political organizations will remain more important in cities than in rural areas. Urban populations can be organized and contacted through canvassing efforts at much lower cost than people in sparsely settled locations can. It is important to emphasize, however, that turnout levels generated by party contacting efforts are significantly different from turnout that finds its source mainly in the motivation of individual voters.

CONCLUSION

Political parties posture to garner support from rural or urban electorates, choosing issues that activate voters who might otherwise stay home. Recently, political parties have adopted campaign strategies that play to rural or urban cultural differences. In part, these strategies are designed to persuade voters to favor one side rather than the other, but they are also intended to activate voters who might otherwise stay home. The premise that urban and rural populations are motivated to vote because of different factors is itself worth further investigation going forward.

What does the future hold for the gap in political participation between urban and rural voters? Despite efforts at increased mobilization by political parties in recent presidential and down-ballot elections, there appears to have been very little dramatic and sustained change in the voting participation of Americans. The gulf between urban and rural participation levels appears likely to continue into the indefinite future. In fact, it is likely to grow wider as more people move around, and as the population becomes more divided by the choices people make about where to live.

Rural populations continue to shrink. As the rural population ages, we see decreases both as a result of mortality and from the migration of younger populations out of rural areas, usually in search of better job opportunities. As more Americans move to major metropolitan areas, rural areas will continue to lose political influence. Rural locales will decline even further in their importance to statewide election results. Despite this decline in importance and the possible impact it will have on how much candidates pay attention to rural voters, there is no reason to expect their participation levels to diminish. Rural residents are likely to remain highly active, in spite of their electoral marginality. Cities, for their part—especially those with large minority and poor populations—will continue to be underrepresented at the polls in most elections. Historical patterns are sticky; they do not change course suddenly, or at the whims of wishful thinkers. That does not mean, however, that efforts to build political confidence among long-standing non-participants should be abandoned. We believe that careful study of long-neglected rural areas would prove helpful toward that end.

NOTES

1. There are numerous definitions of "rural" used in political science and sociological research. In this instance "rural" is defined as inhabitants of nonmetro counties with less than 10,000 people. Rural residents are compared with urban residents, who reside in counties with more than a million people.

2. See Eric J. Oliver, "City Size and Civic Involvement in Metropolitan America," *American Political Science Review* 94 (2000): 361–373. See also Robert Dahl and Edward Tufte, *Size and Democracy* (Palo Alto, CA: Stanford University Press, 1973); Robert Dahl, "The City in the Future of Democracy," *American Political Science Review* 61 (1967): 956–970.

3. We wish to thank Peter Nardulli at the University of Illinois, Urbana-Champaign, and David Darmofal at the University of South Carolina for generously sharing their impressive collection of nineteenth- and twentieth-century data on county-level political participation in presidential elections.

4. Cathy Cohen and Michael C. Dawson, "Neighborhood Poverty and African American Politics," *American Political Science Review* 87 (1993): 286–302.

5. Richard D. Shingles, "Black Consciousness and Political Participation: The Missing Link," *American Political Science Review* 75 (1981): 76–91.

6. Raymond E. Wolfinger and Steven J. Rosenstone, "The Effect of Registration Laws on Voter Turnout," *American Political Science Review* 72 (1978): 22–45.

7. Sidney Verba and Norman Nie, *Participation in America* (Chicago: University of Chicago Press, 1972).

8. Eric J. Oliver, "City Size and Civic Involvement in Metropolitan America," *American Political Science Review* 94 (2000): 361–373. There is also some evidence, however, that urban minority residents will participate more when the political atmosphere is right—for example, when there is minority leadership in the city. See also Lawrence Bobo and Franklin D. Gilliam, "Race, Sociopolitical Participation, and Black Empowerment," *American Political Science Review* 84 (1990): 377–393.

9. Robert Putnam, "Social Capital and Public Affairs," *Bulletin of the American Academy of Arts and Sciences* 47 (1994): 5–19.

10. Renee Drury and Luther Tweeten, "Have Farmers Lost Their Uniqueness?" *Review of Agricultural Economics* 19 (1997): 58–90. See also Oscar B. Martinson and E. A. Wilkening, "Rural-Urban Differences in Job Satisfaction: Further Evidence," *Academy of Management Journal* 27 (1984): 199–206.

11. James G. Gimpel and Kimberly A. Karnes, "The Rural Side of the Urban-Rural Gap," *PS: Political Science and Politics* 39 (2006):467–472.

12. Verba and Nie, *Participation in America.* See also David Knoke and Constance Henry, "Political Structure of Rural America," *Annals of the American Academy of Political and Social Science* 429 (1977): 51–62.

19

Mobilizing the Registered

Tactics for Improving Voter Turnout

Melissa R. Michelson, Lisa García Bedolla, and Donald P. Green

Many observers have noted with dismay the low rates of political participation in American elections. Participation rates are particularly low among racial and ethnic minority groups: blacks, Asians, and Latinos.[1] During the past decade, starting with Gerber and Green, an increasing number of scholars have turned to field research with these populations in order to determine how best to increase turnout among low-propensity groups, either independently or in cooperation with community organizations.[2]

The James Irvine Foundation's California Votes Initiative (CVI), a multi-year effort to increase voting rates among infrequent voters—particularly those in low-income and ethnic communities—in California's San Joaquin Valley and targeted areas in Southern California, conducted experiments on get-out-the-vote (GOTV) efforts. These are not the first experiments to look at how best to mobilize racial and ethnic minorities. Studies have shown that direct mail and commercial phone banks increased turnout among African Americans only minimally, if at all, whereas door-to-door canvassing resulted in large and statistically significant impacts on voter turnout.[3] Experiments focused on Asian American voters using live telephone calls and postcards have found, as with other populations, that phone banking increases turnout, whereas direct mail is relatively ineffective.[4] Field experiments with Latinos are somewhat more common and have found that door-to-door canvassing and live phone banks are effective methods of increasing participation, whereas indirect methods such as robocalls (prerecorded phone messages) and direct mail are not.[5]

Field experiments in recent years made great strides in terms of developing a list of best practices for mobilizing low-propensity voters. Experiments indicate that door-to-door canvassing is the most powerful method of turning out voters; that phone calls from volunteer phone banks can also significantly increase turnout; and that mailers, robocalls, and other indirect methods tend to be ineffective. Previous experiments also suggest that the quality of a canvassing or phone banking campaign—the sincerity and commitment of those who make contact with voters—is crucial to its success.

But many questions remain. What are the most effective and efficient tactics for mobilizing voters in minority communities? In the interest of mobilizing low-propensity voters on a large scale at minimum cost, are there ways of making impersonal tactics—such as mail and robotic phone calls—more effective? Does the message matter? Does it help to use residents of the targeted community, or can volunteers and/or paid canvassers be dropped into a neighborhood and still be as effective? Is canvassing more effective when done immediately prior to Election Day? Do multiple contacts increase turnout significantly, or is a single personal visit sufficient?

In the weeks prior to the June 2006 primary elections, the November 2006 midterm elections, and the Los Angeles municipal elections of March 2007, a number of community organizations in California worked together to increase turnout among low-propensity voters, particularly people of color. Generally campaigns using direct-contact tactics such as live phone calls or door-to-door canvassing—where only some citizens assigned to the treatment group are actually contacted.[6]

This chapter describes the campaigns of several community organizations participating in the California Votes Initiative. An overview of the experiments is presented in Table 19.1. The diverse array of experiments conducted by the eight organizations over three election campaigns provides a treasure trove of information about what does and does not work to get low-propensity voters to the polls. As Table 19.1 indicates, the groups targeted low-propensity voters in the African American, Latino, and Asian American communities of Central and Southern California. Tactics used included door-to-door canvassing, live calls, robocalls, postcards, mailings containing voter guides, and leaflets. Many of these mobilization tactics proved ineffective, but the most effective campaigns profoundly influenced the voting rates among those targeted.

DOOR-TO-DOOR CAMPAIGNS

Although some of the campaigns were not successful, some were remarkably so. One effort, conducted by the Center for Community Action and Environmental Justice (CCAEJ) in Riverside County for the June 2006 election, resulted in a 33.6 percent increase in turnout among those contacted.[7] Others fell more closely within the expected range of 7 to 12 percentage points. More interesting is how the differences in the way the campaigns were conducted seem to be related to those various outcomes.

Table 19.1
Road Map to the CVI Experiments

	June 2006 Experiments	November 2006 Experiments	March 2007 Experiments
APALC	Live phone banking and mailers in English and relevant language to six Asian national-origin groups in Los Angeles County	Similar campaign, but with nine Asian national-origin groups and an embedded message effect experiment	
CCAEJ	Door-to-door in Mira Loma/Glen Avon community of Riverside County, with pledge cards and Election Day door hangers	Door-to-door in Riverside and San Bernardino counties, with pledge cards, election weekend follow-ups with polling place information flyers, and Election Day door hangers	
CARECEN	Door-to-door and live phone banking of Latino voters in Pico Union/Westlake community of Los Angeles, starting several months before the election	Door-to-door and live phone banking in same community, with voter pledge cards mailed back to voters with polling place information and election weekend follow-up contacts (both door-to-door and by telephone)	
NALEO	Live and robocalls to Latino voters in Fresno, Los Angeles, Orange, Riverside, and San Bernardino counties.	Live and robocalls to same community, with robocalls used to screen numbers for live phone banking	Live and robocalls to Latino voters in the city of Los Angeles, with robocalls used to screen numbers for live phone banking
OCAPICA	n/a	Live phone banking and mailers in English and relevant language to three Asian national-origin groups in Orange County	
PICO	Variety of small-sample efforts throughout the state, including two live phone banking efforts, but focusing on indirect efforts such as mailers, leaflets, and robocalls	Variety of small-sample outreach efforts throughout the state, with more of an effort on personal tactics (door-to-door and live phone banking), as well as the use of multiple contacts	
SVREP	n/a	Door-to-door, live phone banking, and mailers to Latino voters in five communities in Los Angeles, with a focus on telephone calls, and reminder calls to those expressing an intention to vote in initial contacts	
SCOPE	Door-to-door in South Central Los Angeles	Door-to-door in South Central Los Angeles, with some voters targeted for second contact.	

The record-breaking June 2006 CCAEJ campaign had many of the standard components of a successful effort. The group is well established in the community, with 25 years of action on behalf of environmental justice and a number of established volunteers. Canvassers were all residents of the targeted precincts. In addition, volunteers went out starting at 5 a.m. on Election Day to distribute door hangers at the residences of all successfully contacted registered voters, resulting in a number of secondary face-to-face contacts.

Other successful CVI campaigns share these important characteristics: they were conducted by local organizations with a strong community reputation and they were staffed by local volunteers. There is also evidence that some sort of personal follow-up contact with committed voters, either face to face or by telephone, contributes to the success of a door-to-door mobilization. When CCAEJ tried to mirror its earlier success with a larger effort for the November 2006 election, effectiveness dropped to a still-respectable 6.9 percent.[8] When the group moved out of the base community and used some canvassers not from the targeted precincts, it was still able to mobilize voters—but not with the same impact.

Mobilization efforts by other groups provide similar lessons. The campaigns by Strategic Concepts in Organizing and Policy Education (SCOPE) for the June 2006 and November 2006 elections, including both African American and Latino registered voters in South Los Angeles, were situated in a neighborhood in which the group has a long history and strong presence. Not all canvassers were from the targeted neighborhoods, and their effectiveness varied based on how close they were to their home turf. For June 2006, the difference in effectiveness between home-turf and non-home-turf canvassers was suggestive, but not statistically significant: 12.1 percentage points[9] for local canvassers and –0.2 percentage points[10] for nonlocal canvassers. This finding was investigated further in the experiment for the November 2006 election. In November, not only did the effectiveness of canvassers increase markedly when they worked in their home turf (defined by ZIP code), but their effectiveness actually increased as they approached their own neighborhoods and declined as they moved farther away. Overall, the use of home-turf canvassers increased turnout by 7 percentage points,[11] whereas non-home-turf canvassers had an effect of only 3.7 percentage points.[12]

The Pacific Institute for Community Organization (PICO) in Sacramento, Colusa, Fullerton, and Bakersfield conducted well-executed, door-to-door canvassing on a smaller scale for the November 2006 election. PICO is a statewide network of nineteen faith-based community organizations that has been active since 1995. It has conducted civic engagement campaigns in the past, typically focused on local ballot initiatives concerning education and affordable housing. Their voter mobilization efforts in 2006 focused on minority communities in areas near their member congregations, particularly Latino communities. Overall, they had an effect of 4.0 percentage points on contacted voters, but the effect varied considerably by location: 19.8 percentage points[13] in Sacramento, 7.6 percentage points[14] in Colusa,

–5.4 percentage points[15] in Fullerton, and 17.2 percentage points[16] in Bakersfield. Because of the small size of these experiments, the standard errors are relatively large, so it is not certain what the actual effects of these campaigns were. However, three of the four had results of the expected magnitude, and the experiment in Fullerton experienced some difficulties caused by language barriers between canvassers and contacted registered voters. By contrast, all of the Sacramento volunteers were bilingual, and the Colusa volunteers were not only bilingual but tended to be English language learners who had recently completed the group's citizenship classes. These site-specific variations may have impacted the success of the various campaigns.

Another group that conducted door-to-door CVI campaigns in June and November 2006 was less successful. The Central American Resource Center (CARECEN) has been active for twenty-four years in the Pico Union/Westlake community of Los Angeles, including prior GOTV activity. Canvassers were from the local community, and most (forty-one of forty-three) were Latino. The June effort, which included a mix of door-to-door contacts and live phone banking directed at Latino-surname voters in the target area, began several months before the election. In fact, fully 48 percent of those targeted for door-to-door visits were contacted before May 1, and 72 percent were contacted more than three weeks prior to Election Day. The impact on those contacted was only 0.9 percentage points.[17] This was clearly a disappointment, and is likely due to the timing of the outreach effort. For November 2006, CARECEN shifted its strategy to focus on repeated contacts for a smaller treatment group, and a shorter period of time in the field, starting during the last week of September. The organization made follow-up calls starting from the third week of October. Although their door-to-door contact rate increased significantly (from 43.9 percent to 52.8 percent), their effect on turnout did not, unfortunately—the treatment-on-treated effect was only 3.4 percentage points.[18]

One possible reason that CARECEN was not more successful is that their message, even when timed closer to the election, was diluted by the group's focus on informing voters about other services provided by the organization, including legal services and education. Another possibility is that the targeted voters, many of whom are what might be considered "habitual nonvoters," were too set in their ways. Looking only at targeted voters who had participated at least once prior to November 2006, the treatment-on-treated effect increases to a more than respectable 15.7 percentage points (with a standard error of 5.6).[19] This mirrors similar effects found for another Latino door-to-door effort and fits with conventional wisdom regarding the difficulty of turning out habitual nonvoters.[20]

PHONE BANKING CAMPAIGNS

In general, robotic (recorded) phone calls have been found to have no effect on turnout, and low-quality live phone banking can also fail to have much of an impact. However, a high-quality live phone banking campaign is generally expected to raise turnout by 3 to 5 percentage points. The campaign conducted by the Southwest Voter Registration Education Project (SVREP) for the November 2006 election achieved much better results, increasing turnout by a staggering 9.1 percentage points[21] among the targeted Latino population. This is the strongest effect ever noted for a large live phone banking effort (SVREP contacted 5,730 individuals by phone).

The campaign by SVREP included many factors crucial to a successful phone bank. As with successful door-to-door campaigns, SVREP's strong presence in the community and the fact that it has worked for more than thirty years to mobilize Latino voters across the Southwest were keys to success. The campaign was limited to five heavily (averaging 48 percent) Latino districts in Los Angeles, and approximately half of the targeted voters were age 25 or younger. Phone banking began three weeks prior to the election, and all canvassers were bilingual in English and Spanish. During an initial contact, if a registered voter indicated an intention to vote, he or she was called and reminded of that commitment in a second call placed the day before the election. This tactic previously had been found to be highly effective when targeting young voters.[22]

Two CVI groups that had never before engaged in voter mobilization activities conducted very successful multilingual phone banks targeting Asian American voters of a number of different national origins. However, both groups have a strong community presence resulting from many years of advocacy on behalf of Asian Pacific Islanders. The Asian Pacific American Legal Center (APALC), founded in 1983, has long worked in Southern California to advance Asian Pacific American civil rights, provide legal services and education, and work for a more equitable society. For the June 2006 election, they conducted a phone bank in English and six Asian languages (targeting South Asians, Chinese, Filipinos, Japanese, Koreans, and Vietnamese). In Los Angeles County, bilingual interviewers worked for three weeks prior to the election to target Asian voters identified by place of birth and surname. With the exception of Vietnamese Americans, turnout was significantly higher in all of the treatment groups, with treatment-on-treated effects ranging from a low of 1.5 percentage points[23] for Korean Americans to a high of 6.9 percentage points[24] for Filipino Americans, and an overall effect of 2.5 percentage points.[25]

For the November 2006 election, APALC expanded its efforts to include Cambodian registered voters, and it included an embedded experiment for most groups that varied the delivered mobilization message. While some voters received a standard "voting empowers our community" message, others received an alternative message specific to their ethnic group, based on results from focus groups conducted by APALC in the weeks before the campaign. There is substantial variance in the effect for the various national-origin groups, but the overall effort had a treatment-on-treated effect of 3.7 percentage points.[26] There was no measurable difference between the scripts.

The other CVI group, the Orange County Asian Pacific Islander Community Alliance (OCAPICA), conducted a similar campaign for the November 2006 election, based in its home turf of Orange County. OCAPICA has worked for over a decade to improve opportunities and outcomes for low-income Asian and Pacific Islanders in Orange County, although as with APALC, this campaign was its first foray into voter mobilization. In the weeks prior to the election, the group contacted registered voters of Chinese, Korean, and Vietnamese origin, assigning the language of the outreach effort based on nativity and age (foreign-born voters age 35 and younger and all U.S.-born voters were contacted in English; foreign-born voters older than 35 were contacted in other languages). Again, the effectiveness of the campaign varied by national-origin group and by the language of the contact, but pooling the results together generates a treatment-on-treated effect of 4.2 percentage points.[27] For those contacted in English, the effect increases to 9.9 percentage points;[28] for those contacted in another language, there is no measurable effect.

PICO also conducted a number of phone banking campaigns for the June and November 2006 elections. Two affiliated organizations in Stockton, California, conducted phone banks for June. One was associated with a positive effect on turnout and the other had a negative impact, but both sample sizes were too small to allow firm conclusions about their effectiveness.[29] PICO affiliates conducted a much larger number of phone bank campaigns for the November 2006 election, including efforts in Stockton, Colusa, Arbuckle, Williams, Los Angeles, San Bernardino, and Bakersfield. Again the results vary widely, with treatment-on-treated effects ranging from as high as 19.4 percentage points[30] for one group in Los Angeles and 15.2 percentage points[31] in Arbuckle, to negative effects in other locations. The pooled effect was –0.8 percentage points,[32] illustrating that the small size of these campaigns makes their results subject to a great deal of statistical uncertainty. However, there are aspects of the more successful campaigns that suggest why they were more effective. In Arbuckle, in an effort mostly conducted by native Spanish speakers reaching out to other native Spanish speakers, many of the canvassers were recent graduates of PICO's citizenship classes. In the more successful site in Los Angeles, unlike other campaigns conducted by other church affiliates in the city, the phone banking was conducted the night before the election by bilingual youths. Other campaigns were conducted on Sunday and used older canvassers. Future experiments are needed to investigate whether these differences are in fact responsible for the different effects realized by PICO's affiliates.

Other phone banking campaigns conducted by CVI groups were less effective. Results from CARECEN's mobilization efforts, as noted earlier, were inconclusive due to the small size of their experiments, although their results were of the expected magnitude. The pooled treatment-on-treated effect was 3.3 percentage points, but with a standard error of 4.7 percentage points.

The National Association of Latino Elected and Appointed Officials (NALEO) conducted phone banking campaigns for the June 2006, November

2006, and March 2007 elections. NALEO has worked since 1981 on increasing the political empowerment of Latinos in California and nationwide, including numerous live and recorded phone banking campaigns. For the June 2006 election, the group targeted low-propensity Latino voters in the counties of Fresno, Los Angeles, Orange, Riverside, and San Bernardino. The pooled effect was only 2.1 percentage points, but with a relatively large standard error (2.4), which makes it difficult to generate more precise estimates. This is due in part to a low contact rate, ranging from 9.2 percent in Fresno County to 12.4 percent in Los Angeles.

Hoping to improve on these results, NALEO began its fall campaign with a round of robocalls designed to encourage voter engagement, but more important, to screen its list for nonworking numbers. The contact rate for the live phone bank increased to 27 percent, suggesting that a preliminary round of robocalls is an effective and inexpensive means by which to improve the efficiency of a live phone bank. However, the live phone bank was still not particularly effective. Pooled across the five precincts, the effort had a treatment-on-treated effect of only 0.7 percentage points.[33] Considering only young voters (age 18 to 24), however, this figure increases to 4.4 percentage points.[34]

One of the hypotheses coming out of the November 2006 analysis was that perhaps the scripts being used by NALEO were making the mobilizing conversation less effective than it could be. NALEO's phone banking campaign for the Los Angeles municipal election in March 2007 included two randomly assigned scripts designed to test this hypothesis. One relatively short script, mirroring the one used in the group's previous campaigns, reminded voters of the upcoming election and encouraged participation. The second script was more information-dense, aiming also to educate voters about the candidates and issues on the ballot. This third CVI experiment by NALEO unexpectedly proved more successful. Contact rates were significantly higher—45.3 percent for the informational message group and 41 percent for the basic message group. Unfortunately, these significantly different contact rates preclude a direct comparison of the effectiveness of the different messages. Even if inconclusive, however, the data suggest that the longer, more informative scripts worked better in mobilizing targeted voters. Turnout in the control group was 17.3 percent, compared to 19.9 percent for those targeted to receive the informational message and 18.9 percent for those targeted to receive the basic message.

INDIRECT TACTICS

Although a variety of CVI groups incorporated indirect tactics into their mobilization campaigns for June and November 2006, overall these methods proved ineffective at moving voters to the polls. This mirrors previous findings from GOTV experiments on other populations, and is not particularly surprising. What *is* somewhat surprising is that even those indirect efforts that were designed to be more effective—and more personal—were still unable to increase turnout significantly.

For example, in June 2006 the statewide network of nineteen faith-based community organizations known as PICO engaged in a number of indirect methods that produced either disappointing or ambiguous results. One affiliate conducted a number of robotic phone call campaigns that delivered a message from what would presumably be a trusted source: the pastor of the local church. These robocalls produced conflicting results; on average, results from the two sites that used this tactic suggest that such calls do not increase turnout. This finding is consistent with a long list of experimental studies on the mobilizing effects of robotic phone calls.[35] Other affiliates worked to personalize their mailings and leaflets with handwritten notes or homegrown voter guides for local races. The handwritten notes also produced disappointing results, but the small size of the treatment group in this study (223 people) means that the finding is subject to a great deal of statistical uncertainty; this tactic requires further study. Some affiliates also sent out leaflets and postcards that provided useful information about polling place location and local candidates. A meta-analysis of the postcard experiments shows that the standard postcard increased turnout by 0.9 percentage points and the postcard with polling place information increased turnout by 2.0 percentage points, but these results are not statistically significant. The overall findings from all of these indirect interventions lead to the conclusion that indirect methods, even when personalized or from a trusted source, are not effective in mobilizing individuals to vote.

One interesting and unexpected result from June 2006 concerns leafleting. In Orange County, there were no surprises: leaflets with information about recipients' polling place locations raised turnout by 1.1 percentage points, an effect that is almost identical in magnitude to those found in past published work on similar interventions. On the Saturday before Election Day, however, Long Beach canvassers distributed voter guides that summarized local candidates' positions on four leading issues expressed in a PICO-sponsored candidate forum. Here, the effect was immense—a 9.2-percentage-point[36] increase in turnout. The unexpected success of this type of leafleting prompted follow-up experiments in November 2006.

For November 2006, most PICO affiliates chose to move to personal outreach efforts, but some campaigns still included mailers, leaflets, and robocalls. Robocalls from local pastors had an average effect of 0.4 percentage points,[37] and postcards had a negative effect of –1.8 percentage points.[38] In contrast to the June 2006 results, but consistent with other experiments of this kind, neither of the November leafleting experiments raised turnout.

Mailers were also used in the multilingual outreach efforts of APALC and OCAPICA, aimed at increasing turnout among Asian Pacific Islander Americans. Prior to the June 2006 primary election, APALC sent bilingual mailers to about 11,000 registered voters. The same get-out-the-vote message was used for all ethnic groups: "voting empowers our communities and is easy." Mailers also included general information about the races and measures on the ballot, the voter's polling place, and the right of voters who do not list a party identification or select Independent to request partisan ballots. Translation was provided by the relevant partner organizations, and the photos were changed for each version of the mailer to be appropriate to each national-origin group. The mailers failed to influence turnout among any of the groups, with an overall effect of 0.09 percentage points. For the November 2006 campaign, APALC sent out 10,900 mailers, this time using English and translated Easy Voter Guides. They sent translated versions to Chinese, Korean, and Vietnamese voters who were foreign-born and over 35 years old, and other targeted voters received English versions of the guides. As was the case with PICO, the mailers were ineffective at increasing turnout, with a pooled treatment-on-treated effect of 0.7 percentage points. This was despite the fact that the voter guides used as mailers constituted a high-quality source of election information. Although they may have been useful in educating those who did turn out to vote, they did not have a significant impact on turnout.

OCAPICA's mailing effort mirrored that of APALC, as its phone banking campaign had. Translated guides were sent to Chinese, Korean, and Vietnamese voters who were foreign-born and over 35 years old, and English guides went to other targeted voters. Overall, the effect of OCAPICA's mail campaign was weakly negative and statistically insignificant. The overall conclusion is that both the homegrown mailers used by APALC in June and the Easy Voter Guides used by APALC and OCAPICA in November were ineffective as methods of turning out low-propensity voters.

JUDGING EFFECTIVENESS

Door-to-door campaigns are the most effective method for increasing voter turnout. Several CVI groups conducted door-to-door efforts in the weeks and months prior to the June 2006 election. Based on their results, a larger number of groups elected to conduct such efforts in connection with future elections. Although some campaigns were not effective, the majority of the door-to-door mobilization efforts resulted in significant increases in participation among the low-propensity groups targeted. There is also considerable value in the use of local canvassers (from either the same precinct or the same ZIP code as targeted voters). Live phone banking is also a proven and powerful method of turning out voters. Although phone banking usually has a smaller effect than door-to-door canvassing, it can be cost-effective and much easier, which sometimes makes it a better choice—particularly if the targeted voters are dispersed geographically. Various groups using live phone banking for the elections of June 2006, November 2006, and March 2007 were able to move substantial numbers of low-propensity voters to the polls, in some cases at rates exceeding those of door-to-door effects from other campaigns. Such efforts are particularly successful when follow-up calls are made to self-identified likely voters. Finally, a number of groups conducted experiments using indirect methods such as postcards, Easy Voter Guides, leaflets, and robocalls. With a few exceptions, these tactics were found to be ineffective at increasing turnout, even when efforts are made to make the mailings or robocalls more personal or from a trustworthy source.

CONCLUSION

In keeping with prior experimental findings, direct personal appeals tend to work best, but success with this tactic was far from universal. CCAEJ seems to illustrate the dilemma of deploying high-quality personal appeals. After a spectacularly successful canvassing campaign in its first outing in June, CCAEJ expanded its purview in November—ultimately proving unable to cover the ambitious geographic area that it sought to canvass—and its results were less spectacular, though certainly respectable. CARECEN and PICO had more modest success with door-to-door canvassing. The low power of these canvassing experiments may have generated subpar estimates simply by chance; nevertheless, it is interesting that SCOPE, an organization with extensive canvassing experience, had the most consistent success with this tactic. Further investigation is needed in order to discern why different campaigns seem to produce such divergent results, even when targeting voters with similar ethnic and socioeconomic profiles.

A similar mystery concerns phone banking. Several groups had modest success using this tactic, but SVREP's phone banking campaign proved to be several times more effective than those of the other groups. One possibility is that certain voters are especially responsive to phone calls. It is noteworthy that larger effects were observed among NALEO's younger targets and that fully half of SVREP's respondents were age 18 to 25. Another possibility is that treatment effects vary as a function of the way in which targets were called. Whereas other groups aimed to make only a single contact with targeted voters, SVREP made a special point of re-contacting those who initially reported an intention to vote. A determination as to whether this nuance is incidental or crucial awaits further testing.

Less uncertainty attends the question of whether impersonal tactics work. Robocalls failed to generate an appreciable increase in turnout. In itself, this finding is not surprising, because no robocall experiments to date have detected positive effects. What is telling is the fact that one can scarcely imagine a more trusted source than one's local pastor, and the fact that even robotic calls using the pastor's voice do little to increase turnout rules out the hypothesis that these calls will work if recorded by credible sources. The effects of contact by mail are somewhat more elusive. Postcards from local churches had an unexpectedly negative effect on turnout, which may well be attributable to sampling variability. Mail in the form of Easy Voter Guides had a weak positive effect, on the order of less than 1 percentage point. That result is perhaps slightly better than the average nonpartisan mailing, but is nonetheless disappointing to those who hypothesize that voters will cast ballots if furnished with high-quality information. Leaflets were also disappointing, especially in light of the June 2006 results that had unexpectedly shown this tactic to be promising.

It appears that mobilizing voters in low-propensity ethnic communities requires some type of live conversation, whether in person or on the phone. The features required to make this conversation successful remain somewhat mysterious. It is reasonable to suspect that the quality and focus of the conversation determine its effect size, and that the relationship of the canvassers to the community matters. However, experimental researchers have only just begun to conceptualize and measure the dimensions of quality, and rarely have aspects of quality been randomly manipulated within the context of a single outreach campaign.[39] The next steps in this line of research are, first, to observe more closely the mobilization process in each group in order to develop testable propositions about best practices and, second, to craft a new line of experimental studies that can pinpoint which particular aspects of mobilization campaigns are most essential to success.

NOTES

This research was funded by a grant from the James Irvine Foundation as part of its California Votes Initiative, a multi-year effort to increase voting rates among infrequent voters—particularly those in low-income and ethnic communities—in California's San Joaquin Valley and targeted areas in Southern California. The Initiative also aims to discern effective approaches by which to increase voter turnout and share those lessons with the civic engagement field. For more information about the Initiative, see http://www.irvine.org/evaluation/program/cvi.shtml. The James Irvine Foundation bears no responsibility for the content of this report. We also gratefully acknowledge the assistance of Jedediah Alfaro-Smith, Jackie Filla, Jennifer Hernández, Michael Jackson, Margaret McConnell, Ricardo Ramírez, and Betsy Sinclair.

1. Carole J. Uhlaner, Bruce E. Cain, and D. Roderick Kiewiet, "Political Participation of Ethnic Minorities in the 1980s," *Political Behavior* 11(3) (September 1989): 195–231; Sidney Verba, Kay Lehman Schlozman, and Henry Brady, *Voice and Equality: Civic Voluntarism in American Politics* (Cambridge, MA: Harvard University Press, 1995);

Jane Junn, "Participation in Liberal Democracy: The Political Assimilation of Immigrants and Ethnic Minorities in the United States," *American Behavioral Scientist* 42(9): 1417–1438; S. Karthick Ramakrishnan and Mark Baldassare, *The Ties That Bind: Changing Demographics and Civic Engagement in California* (San Francisco: Public Policy Institute of California, 2004).

2. Alan S. Gerber and Donald P. Green, "The Effects of Canvassing, Direct Mail, and Telephone Contact on Voter Turnout: A Field Experiment," *American Political Science Review* 94(3) (2000): 653–663.

3. Donald P. Green, "Mobilizing African Americans Using Direct Mail and Commercial Phone Banks: A Field Experiment," *Political Research Quarterly* 57(2) (2004b): 245–255; Donald P. Green and Melissa R. Michelson, "ACORN Experiments in Minority Voter Mobilization," in *"The People Shall Rule": ACORN, Community Organizing, and the Struggle for Economic Justice,* edited by Robert Fisher (Philadelphia: Temple University Press, 2007).

4. Although it did not result in large turnout gains, Wong's experiment showed the feasibility of using surnames to sort Asian registered voters into national-origin subgroups for language-specific targeting.

5. Richard E. Matland and Gregg R. Murray, "Increasing Voter Turnout in the Latino Community: A Field Experiment on the Effects of Canvassing and Direct Mail," paper presented at the 2005 annual meeting of the Midwest Political Science Association, Chicago, April 7–10; Melissa R. Michelson, "Getting Out the Latino Vote: How Door-to-Door Canvassing Influences Voter Turnout in Rural Central California," *Political Behavior* 25(3) (September 2003): 247–263; Melissa R. Michelson, "Mobilizing the Latino Youth Vote: Some Experimental Results," *Social Science Quarterly* 87(5) (December 2006): 1188–1206; Melissa R Michelson, "Mobilizing Latino Voters for a Ballot Proposition," *Latino(a) Research Review* 6(1–2) (2006–2007): 33–49; Ricardo Ramírez, "Giving Voice to Latino Voters: A Field Experiment on the Effectiveness of a National Nonpartisan Mobilization Effort," *Annals of Political and Social Science* 601 (September 2005): 66–84.

6. "Contact" is defined as the canvassers actually speaking with the targeted voter personally and delivering the intended mobilization message. It does not include messages left on answering machines or with other members of the household (either by telephone or in person). Comparing turnout among those actually contacted with turnout among those not contacted (both those in the control group and the portion of the treatment group not contacted) misestimates the effect of the GOTV effort, because some individuals are simply easier to contact and are potentially more likely to turn out to vote. In other words, it was not simply random chance that some voters in the treatment were contacted and others were not. See Kevin Arceneaux, Alan S. Gerber, and Donald P. Green, "Comparing Experimental and Matching Methods Using a Large-Scale Voter Mobilization Experiment, *Political Analysis* 14 (2006): 1–36).

7. Standard error (s.e.) = 11.7

8. s.e. = 4.1

9. s.e. = 7.2

10. s.e. = 3.7

11. s.e. = 2.8

12. s.e. = 2.7
13. s.e .= 13.6
14. s.e. = 4.0
15. s.e. = 5.0
16. s.e. = 10.6
17. s.e. = 2.7
18. s.e. = 2.9
19. Only 35.9 percent of individuals in CARECEN's target pool had voted in at least one prior election.
20. Michelson, "Mobilizing Latino Voters."
21. s.e. = 3.2
22. The campaign also included an initial mailing and a very limited door-to-door campaign, but given other findings on the minimal impact of direct mail and the limited scope of the door-to-door effort, it seems appropriate to treat this field experiment as a phone banking effort. The effect of the phone calls remains undiminished when data from precincts where no canvassing occurred are analyzed. See also Donald P. Green, *The Effects of an Election Day Voter Mobilization Campaign Targeting Young Voters* (2004), CIRCLE Working Paper 21.
23. s.e. = 2.4
24. s.e .= 4.8
25. s.e .= 1.5
26. s.e .= 1.4
27. s.e. = 2.3
28. s.e. = 4.4
29. It should be noted that any given experiment's results are subject to sampling fluctuation. Thus it is not unusual to encounter negative results in reviewing several dozen experiments. Such findings can be expected as a matter of chance. Therefore, the negative effect reported here is interpreted to mean that intervention simply had no positive effect on turnout.
30. s.e = 16.1
31. s.e. = 9.3
32. s.e. = 2.3
33. s.e. = 1.5
34. s.e. = 3.0
35. Donald P. Green and Alan S. Gerber, *Get Out the Vote: How to Increase Voter Turnout* (Washington, DC: Brookings Institution Press, 2004).
36. s.e. = 3.5
37. s.e. = 0.8
38. s.e. = 0.7
39. David W. Nickerson, "Quality Is Job One: Professional and Volunteer Voter Mobilization Calls," *American Journal of Political Science* 51(2) (April 2007): 269–282.

20

Educating the Public about Elections

The Role of Civic Education in Politics

Richard K. Scher

The questions go back to pre-Platonic times: How do states turn ordinary people, especially new generations of young people, into supportive, contributing citizens? Are the tasks required to do this in modern democracies, such as the United States, different from those in states that rely on authoritarianism or state-sponsored terror? There are numerous variations on these questions: How does a conquering nation gain the allegiance of the vanquished? If a government is overthrown in a coup, how do the new rulers convince the citizens that they are the rightful and legitimate power holders?

There are and have been numerous ways of answering these questions: executions and the jailing of dissidents have proved to be popular and effective ways to secure needed goals. Exiling and mass resettlements are another. Spying, secret police, and terror against residents have often been used to keep populations under control, if not to buy affection and respect. After ridding the country of historically undesirable individuals and groups—"The first thing we do, let's kill all the lawyers" in Shakespeare's memorable line—regimes generally rewrite textbooks in order to justify who they are and what they have done, and to convince citizens that they are the good guys, not the bad ones.

The list, of course, is endless—as endless as the need for states to take steps to ensure the allegiance, or at least the quiescence, of people living within their borders. Since its colonial period, the United States has faced the same question as other states: how to secure the support of people and make the nascent democracy work? Indeed, how to create "Americans"? For the most part, the

United States has relied on education and public schools to answer these questions—it's called civic education. But of course there have been some tragic exceptions. Partitioning and segregating Indian tribes and quarantining Japanese descendants during World War II are two examples in which the nation chose not to educate groups into becoming contributing citizens/Americans, but rather to keep them apart from the population as a whole, on the grounds that they could not be trusted.

When the nation was young and relatively homogeneous, civic education—that is, those bits of knowledge about the polity and the skills for living in it that all citizens needed to possess—was a comparatively easy task: youth and immigrants had to be socialized into the dominant Anglo-Saxon culture and value system. But by the late nineteenth century, as the nation's population became heterogeneous from tidal waves of immigrants washing up on American shores, the task had become much more daunting, and controversial. Were Anglo-Saxon values the only ones suitable for Americans? Could not civic education recognize that it was possible to become "Americanized" but still leave room for cultural, religious, national, and ethnic diversity?

These crucial questions remain just as pertinent today as they were a hundred years and more ago. Americans continue to debate, and be seriously divided on, the purpose and content of civic education. Indeed, questions of what constitutes appropriate civic education have merged with much larger current political questions, such as those concerning the culture wars that divide the nation and the impact of ongoing—especially Hispanic—immigration on "mainstream" American values and culture. As of this writing, it is not at all clear how the controversies over civic education will be resolved.

A LOOK BACKWARD

Schools in Puritan New England would not have recognized a curriculum called "civic education." All schooling—for those few who could take advantage of it—was designed to promote allegiance to the state, and also to promote the glories of God. Indeed, Puritan schools did not make any sort of church/state distinction; learning one's civic responsibilities was the same as learning to fear and worship the Almighty.

Following ratification of the Constitution in 1789, schools continued to intermingle civic and religious education. The famous *New England Primer,*[1] designed to teach children to read, combined these two educational purposes in such verses as "In Adam's fall/We sinned all," and "The idle fool/Is whipt at school." It also contained such hortatory civic/religious sentiments as "The Children's Promise": "I will fear God and honor the King. I will honor my Father and Mother. I will obey Superiors."

The famous McGuffey Reader series, used by hundreds of thousands of young students in American schools throughout the nineteenth and early twentieth centuries, continued to combine civic and at least quasi-religious themes in its offerings. An examination of one of the readers documents the emphasis on patriotic and heroic themes, and on the students' emulation and development of personal qualities and virtues that can only be described as mainstream Protestant.[2]

Important early public intellectuals also weighed in on the crucial significance of civic education. Thomas Jefferson, in his *Notes on the State of Virginia* (1781–1782) and later in the "Rockfish Gap Report" (1818), argued that a failure to educate students in history and civics would endanger what was still a very fragile American democracy. Horace Mann, the so-called father of the common school, emphasized that an increasingly diverse population required a curriculum that would not only "Americanize" foreigners, but would also entice, encourage, and cajole them to abandon their native ways in favor of American (that is to say, Anglo-Saxon/Protestant–dominated) culture.[3]

Indeed, Mann put his finger on the key problem of American civic education, even as the nineteenth century gave way to the twentieth and the onset of World War I. As the population became more heterogeneous and Catholics grew into a major religious and political force in the nation, they and other groups began to question the idea that the Protestant ethic should be the driving force behind what children learned as they became Americanized. Could not Catholics become "American" even if they were educated in their own schools? Did other groups have to abandon all traces of their national, ethnic, and religious heritages in order to be accepted as Americans?

To some extent World War I and the "Red scare" of the twenties put these questions on hold, but they did not go away. To a great degree they were overwhelmed by the arrival of so-called progressive education from Europe, vigorously endorsed by the prestigious philosopher and educator John Dewey. Progressive education was many things, and its promoters often pushed it far beyond what Europeanists and Dewey envisioned. As far as civic education was concerned, progressives recognized the diversity of the population and the individuality of the child. In their view, civic education meant fostering children's democratic social skills, not teaching them an ideologically driven American "creed."

Conservatives were horrified, appalled, and furious. Progressives were accused of turning civic education into mush, of not establishing "standards" to which all Americans must adhere. But the progressives countered that the conservatives were little more than elitists who wanted to destroy the rich fabric of diversity that marked American culture and to transform it into a version dominated by traditional Protestant values and ideals.

THE CONTEMPORARY DEBATE

By the 1970s progressive education was on the wane, but it was replaced by a new war cry for those who argued that civic education must be based on, and celebrate, the extraordinary texture of America's heterogeneous population: multiculturalism. It underscored and reemphasized that the goal of civic education was not to create a single type of American (based fundamentally on Protestant values) but to recognize and welcome a vast array of Americans who realized their identity as much through their racial/ethnic/national/religious heritage as by the name "American." It was the dawn of the hyphenated American. It was the final nail in the coffin of the American melting pot—or so many people thought.

Almost as soon as "multiculturalism" entered the American academic and journalistic vocabulary, it ran into a political brick wall. As the Carter administration waned into oblivion, and the Reaganites stormed the nation from California and the Christian Right moved to take over the Republican Party, it became clear that America had taken a sharp right-wing turn. It was also clear that the rapidly changing political temperature of the country would have profound implications for public schools,[4] and for civic education; the conservative counterreformation aimed at rooting out the last vestiges of progressive education began in earnest. This revolution had both secular and religious roots.

TRADITIONAL VERITIES

The clash over what civic education would become began in modest ways in the first Reagan administration, but picked up speed when the president appointed William Bennett as secretary of the Department of Education in 1985. Bennett, a major public intellectual and advocate of conservative causes, had been an opponent of multiculturalism in America since his days as head of the National Endowment for the Humanities.

Although he was a Catholic, Bennett's views of civic education were actually a throwback to *The New England Primer* and McGuffey Readers. He was convinced that multiculturalism was not simply intellectually bankrupt; it was a powerful negative force in the nation. Its seeming emphasis on differences rather than commonalities could, in Bennett's view, ultimately cause irrevocable rifts in American public life and political culture.

But Bennett did not stop there. He wrote that there were basic values, even truths, that all Americans needed to learn and possess, and the schools needed to place them at the top of their curricular priorities. Bennett felt that progressivism and the emphasis on multiculturalism had caused the powerful tradition founded on these basic values in America to get lost. Needless to say, these values and truths were very much rooted in the Anglo-Saxon, Protestant ethic tradition of America. Bennett later spelled them out in a book entitled *The Book of Virtues: A Treasury of Great Moral Stories* (1993), as well as in other writings.

Bennett was just the tip of a much larger iceberg. When the Reagan and Bush administrations discovered that they could not rid the nation of the Department of Education by administrative fiat, as they had hoped, they instead sought to transform it by packing it with arch-conservatives dedicated to changing the way public education operated, substituting neoliberal, market- and factory-based models of schooling for the traditional, public-enterprise model so long in play. They hoped either to create alternatives to the public schools or, preferably, to abolish them altogether.

The implications for civic education were profound. With such activist conservatives as Chester Finn and Diane Ravitch directing traffic in the Department of Education, progressive and multicultural approaches to civic education were attacked root and branch. Both Finn and Ravitch, and their allies, had previously written (and did so subsequently) that the heritage of progressive reform and its modern, multicultural manifestation had undermined "standards." The schools needed to "return" to their traditional roles of seriously teaching "content" and Americanizing the diverse population that attended them.

The fact that many groups of racial, nationalistic, religious, and ethnic minorities, as well as outspoken academics and journalists, howled loudly during the Reagan/Bush attack on extant civic education curricula bothered the Washingtonians not a bit. Even the criticism that what they were doing smacked of the "r" word fell on deaf ears. The conservative Republicans, who held all the reins of power, seemed determined to roll back the clock on civic education, forcing an Anglo-Saxon/Protestant–based model on all students, no matter who they were.

RELIGIOUS CURRENTS

But the Bennett/Finn/Ravitch axis of civic education was by no means the only one confronting multiculturalism. The Christian Right and its social conservative allies became another powerful force attacking civic education. This political avalanche could be felt at all levels, from the White House and Congress through state education boards and departments to local school districts. The Christian Right, mobilizing its many organizations and working through the Republican Party, in some cases took over state systems (Kansas, Texas), or at the local level dominated or powerfully influenced (or intimidated) boards of education and administrators.

The impact of the religious conservatives on school curricula is well known. They were not content with a band-aid approach, but rather wanted entire school learning programs to reflect their fundamentalist Protestant, Bible-based view of education. The fact that schools might serve non-Christians, or even non-fundamentalist Christians, was inconsequential to them. It was no longer enough for the schools to Americanize students; they had to Christianize them as well, according to a very narrow model.

The Christian Right attack went beyond civic education. Biology was a major target, as religious groups fought to have creationism supplant evolution in classes, sometimes successfully. But the major victory of the Religious Right in curriculum came not in science but in the establishment of "character education" programs. These were first started during the Clinton years, but were warmly embraced by the subsequent Bush administration. They are based on the idea that all citizens need to exhibit certain functional character traits (one hears the echoes of Bill Bennett's *Book of Virtues*), or the polity begins to collapse. Although it is never explicitly stated, the traits of character that are most desired parallel those of *The New England Primer* and McGuffey Readers, and are based in traditional Anglo-Saxon/fundamentalist Protestantism. The Department of Education has awarded millions of dollars in grants for schools establishing and maintaining such character education programs.[5]

WHITHER CIVIC EDUCATION?

The argument over what constitutes civic education in contemporary America rages, enveloped by the larger culture wars currently being fought. For the past twenty years or so, conservative forces have been winning. Although some commentators argue that the power of the Christian Right in American (and school) politics is diminishing, a daily examination of newspaper headlines suggests that this may be wishful thinking on their part. The conservative advocates of Protestant verities seem to be as strong as ever, finding a comfortable niche in the halls of Washington power and in many state capitals as well, as the curricular emphasis on traditional Americanism and character education suggests.

Moreover, because of major political struggles over America's immigration problems, the issue of "what to do about all these new people" has again reared its head, sometimes in ugly ways. In the present instance, the target is the vast Hispanic immigrant population, legal and otherwise, and its potential impact on dominant American culture. The traditionalists have recently been reinforced by a barrage from the eminent American scholar Samuel Huntington, whose salvos of gloom and doom over the Hispanic influx[6] have met with cries of approval from crowds of American nativists.

Multiculturalism is certainly not dead, but it would have to be said that it is fighting a rear-guard action. Other than advocates from a variety of ethnic, national, racial, and religious groups (by no means all of them), a thin stratum of academics and journalists, and whatever is left of the American progressive movement from the 1960s and 1970s, multiculturalism has few friends these days. To be honest, it has not always helped itself. Stupidities such as the Oakland School Board's decision to replace standard English with Ebonics in 1996–1997 pulled the rug right out from under many multiculturalists. Only in limited ways, in some local school districts, has multiculturalism managed to survive.

There are centrists—communitarians,[7] pluralists,[8] and some others—who are seeking a middle ground between the Scylla of right-wing Americanizer-hardliners and the Charybdis of multiculturalists. The importance of these efforts should not be minimized. It may be possible to carve out a viable approach to civic education between the opposing intransigents.

But it is more likely that as long as the argument proceeds in the same way it has since post-colonial times—that is, how do the schools create productive, contributing Americans—nothing will change, and the dreary, unproductive controversy will continue.

Suppose, however, that the terms of the debate over civic education shifted, and we began to view it in a totally different manner. This might push the discussion into more productive realms. To do so, we must recognize the validity of the following two propositions:

- Present-day civic education programs are ineffective. There is no convincing evidence that they produce individuals who are knowledgeable about the requirements of citizenship or are motivated to become productive, contributing citizens.[9]
- From the start, the logic that the purpose of civic education is to produce a product—an "American"—has been fatally flawed. In early colonial and post-colonial homogeneous America, this might have been possible. But even by Horace Mann's time it was apparent that the idea of creating a "one size fits all" type of American citizen was not going to work, given the diversity of our population and the consequent political interests and pressures arising from it.

Thus it is long past time to start over, to rethink what American civic education is supposed to be.

For example, assuredly a better approach would be to have students examine and understand the underlying values, structures, and dynamics of what makes America what it is. They would study such matters as competitiveness and rugged individualism; corporations and the aggregation of capital; the nexus between government and the corporate economy; the distribution of political power; the glorification of markets and the private sector; persistent political and economic inequalities; institutional prejudices and racism; the adulation of athletes, TV/movie/rock stars, and other icons of popular culture; the persistence of the drug culture; and others.

Many will argue that these themes are inappropriate for young children and will not help them become contributing citizens. Why? Instead of civic education consisting of flag waving and a one-sided, distorted view of our history and political culture, why not realistically introduce even young children to the basic values and dynamics of what makes America tick? They certainly will find out soon enough anyway, and what better place to start than in K-12 schools taught by competent instructors? Some students will be convinced, with the aid of parents and churches, that the American system is *sans peur.* Others—probably most—will be unsure. Still others will ask further questions, and will cast a critical eye.

Seen in this way, the arguments of Americanizers, multiculturalists, communitarians, pluralists, and others become irrelevant. Instead of continuing the same sterile arguments about what constitutes "an American," civic education will encourage students to critically consider what energizes the nation, and to evaluate alternative views of what it might and could be. Is not that the real goal of civic education?

NOTES

1. Timothy Shannon, *History 341: Colonial America Homepage,* http://public.gettysburg.edu/~tshannon/his341/colonialamer.htm (Gettysburg College, accessed July 20, 2007).

2. William Holmes McGuffey, *McGuffey's Fifth Eclectic Reader*, http://www.gutenberg.org/catalog/world/readfile?fk_files=169182 (Project Guttenberg, accessed July 16, 2007).

3. See James W. Ceasar and Patrick J. McGuinn, "Civic Education Reconsidered—School Report, Part 3," *The Public Interest* (Fall 1998), http://findarticles.com/p/articles/mi_m0377/is_n133/ai_21186008/pg_1 (accessed July 16, 2007). See also Jeffrey Mirel, "The Decline of Civic Education," *Daedalus* (Summer 2002), http://findarticles.com/p/articles/mi_qa3671/is_200207/ai_n9121411 (accessed July 17, 2007).

4. Michael Apple, *Educating the "Right" Way* (London: Routledge, 2001).

5. See, for example, *Character Plus—School, Home, Community* (a project of Cooperating School Districts), http://characterplus.org/ (accessed July 19, 2007); *New PCEP 2007 Grant Awards* (U.S. Department of Education, Character Education and Civic Engagement Technical Assistance Center), http://www.cetac.org/ (accessed July 19, 2007).

6. Samuel P. Huntington, "The Hispanic Challenge," *Foreign Policy* (March/April 2004), http://www.foreignpolicy.com (accessed June 8, 2007).

7. The Center for Civic Education, based in Los Angeles, is one such example. See its Web site at http://www.civiced.org/ (accessed July 16, 2007). See also Margaret Stimmann Branson, "The Role of Civic Education," a forthcoming Education Policy Task Force position paper from the Communitarian Network, Center for Civic Education (September 1998), http://www.civiced.org/papers/articles_role.html (accessed July 20, 2007); and Margaret Branson, "Critical Issues in Civic Education," speech to We the People. . .State and Local Coordinators, Center for Civic Education in Washington, DC (June 24–27, 2000), http://www.civiced.org/papers/articles_mb_june00.html (accessed July 19, 2007).

8. See Ceasar and McGuinn, "Civic Education Reconsidered," for an example of a pluralist approach to civic education.

9. See, for example, James B. Murphy, "Tug of War," *Education Next* (4) (2003), http://www.hoover.org/publications/ednext/3346656.html. See also Marshall Croddy, *Have We Forgotten Civic Education?* http://www.susanohanian.org/show_commentary.php?id=408 (accessed July 19, 2007).

21

The Elderly and Voting

The Group's Impact on Elections

Kellyanne Conway and Shelley West

Senior citizens (Americans age 65 or older) are reliable voters who make up the most likely age group to participate in elections. They vote the strongest because they have voted the longest, and they deeply believe in the role of government. As stakeholders in massive government entitlement programs such as social security and Medicare, seniors receive information and mobilization for political participation from a number of organizations that claim to represent the cohort and its concerns. Among the best known are the American Association of Retired Persons (AARP), which boasts a nationwide membership of 38 million and an annual budget of nearly $1 billion, the 60 Plus Association, and USA Next.

But to connect with seniors politically, one must first appreciate and understand them culturally. Today's average seniors are healthier and wealthier than those of generations past. They have witnessed (or participated in) wars abroad and cultural wars at home, economic depression, disease, and natural disasters—yet their present quality of life and expected longevity are at an all-time high.

Life expectancy at 65 has grown the most for white females, who have witnessed a 36 percent increase in the number of anticipated remaining years at that juncture, from 11.5 to 16.3 during the twentieth century. Among white males, life expectancy at 65 has increased by 29 percent. Like whites, black females have seen a greater extension of years than their male counterparts (34 percent increase vs. 28 percent increase).[1]

With improved (and extended) physical and financial health come more choices, more freedoms, and a reprioritization in the "Golden Years" of the often-overlooked pleasures in life—typically pushed aside during the working and parenting decades—to the top of the to-do list. These changes in means, attitude, lifestyle, and simple demography have attracted notice by corporate and consumer America. Those in the political and public policy arenas must play catch-up to understand the dynamism of contemporary seniors.

AT HOME

Because women tend to outlive men, the percentage of women over 65 who are married is much smaller than for men of the same age (42 percent compared to 72 percent, respectively). Conversely, 43 percent of women age 65 and older are widowed, compared to only 14 percent of senior men.[2] In 2000, only 4.5 percent of the 65-plus populace lived in nursing homes, and an additional 5 percent lived in retirement communities.[3] Where and with whom seniors live affects everything—from their state of mind and financial stability to their mobility and degree of connection with the outside world. In turn, their living arrangements undoubtedly affect the prism through which they view politics and government.

IN THE WORKFORCE

In the past, older men—if they were fortunate enough to reach age 65—were more likely to have stayed in the workforce than men of the same age today. In 1950, 46 percent of men age 65 and older were employed, compared to only 19 percent in 2003. Only 11 percent of women age 65 and older were working in 1950, and a similar 10 percent held jobs in 2003.[4] Better financial planning has resulted in a greater proportion of seniors being able to opt out of the traditional, full-time employment situation. Still, a growing number of seniors are now choosing to remain employed at some level simply to stay active or to pursue a new job or career (including owning their own businesses), which they were previously unable to do for reasons of family, geography, or finances.

According to a recent study commissioned by the AARP, 23 percent of Americans expect to stop working at age 65, and another 16 percent said they would clock out at 70. A small, but notable, 7 percent said they planned never to cease employment.[5]

LOOKING FORWARD

The domestic elderly population will grow dramatically in the next 25 years, as 80 million Baby Boomers (those born between 1946 and 1964) come into the age category and become eligible to receive all of the trappings of senior status that the United States affords. Taking into account the declining fertility and birth rates of women across the country, the demographic profile of the country can expect to undergo a dramatic transformation in the upcoming years. Currently, for example, Americans age 65 and older account for approximately 12 percent of the population, but in 2030 they are expected to constitute 20 percent of the total population.[6]

VOTING BEHAVIOR

Since the U.S. Census Bureau began to collect voter turnout data in 1964, the percentage of Americans age 65 and older who vote in presidential elections has ranged from a low of 51 percent in the Watergate era (1974) to 70 percent in what was a three-way contest for president in 1992. In the most recent presidential election (2004), 68.9 percent of the elderly voted.

The increased power seniors exercise in the voting booth has more to do with their sheer growth as a population than a noticeable bump in participation rates. The number of Americans over the age of 65 doubled over that same 40-year period, from 17 million in 1964 to 34 million in 2004.[7]

A greater proportion of younger women than younger men tend to vote, but the reverse is true among older voters. In 2004, 72 percent of men age 65 and older voted, compared to 67 percent of women in the same age group. Since data collection began, the gender gap in voter turnout has always been present, as Table 21.1 demonstrates. As is true for any age group, turnout falls during non-presidential elections.

However, the "hard number" turnout between men and women of this mature age is a different story. Table 21.2 indicates that a greater *proportion* of men over the age of 65 voted compared to their female counterparts, but a greater *number* of women voted than men. The fact that women outlive men by about six years partly accounts for this difference.

Race also reveals some noteworthy differences among the sexes in the elderly population, a trend that promises to persist over the next couple of decades as

Table 21.1
Life Expectancy (in Years) at Age 65

	1900	2000	Percent Increase
White males	11.5	16.3	29%
White females	12.2	19.2	36%
Black males	10.4	14.5	28%
Black females	11.4	17.4	34%

Source: National Center for Health Statistics.

Table 21.2
Voter Turnout, 1964–2004

Year	Percentage of Men 65+ Who Voted	Percentage of Women 65+ Who Voted
2004	71.9	66.7
2002	65.4	57.7
2000	71.4	64.8
1998	64.6	55.8
1996	70.9	64.1
1994	66.5	57.6
1992	74.5	67.0
1990	66.0	56.3
1988	73.3	65.6
1986	66.8	56.7
1984	71.9	64.8
1982	65.3	56.2
1980	70.4	61.3
1978	62.6	51.3
1976	68.3	58.0
1974	58.7	46.2
1972	70.7	58.4
1970	65.4	50.8
1968	73.1	73.3
1966	64.2	49.8
1964	73.7	60.4

the United States evolves into a majority minority nation and as the sheer number of seniors overall explodes. Refer to Table 21.3 and the following list:

- Among whites, women account for 57 percent of all U.S. residents age 65 and older.
- Within the African American population, women compose 62 percent of the 65-and-older cohort and 67 percent of those age 75 and older.
- In the Hispanic community, women make up 61 percent of those age 65 and older and 58 percent of those age 75 and older.
- Asian American women account for 56 percent of the 65-and-older group and 59 percent of those 75 and older.[8]

POLITICAL IDENTIFICATION

In a post-election survey of *actual* voters conducted by the polling company™, inc./WomanTrend on election night 2006, seniors were more likely than younger

Table 21.3
2004 Election Behavior

	Percentage of Men Who Voted	Percentage of Women Who Voted	Number of Men Who Voted (in thousands)	Number of Women Who Voted (in thousands)	Net Women Voting (in thousands)
Whites 65–74	73.9	71.0	5,403	6,017	+614
Whites 75+	72.8	65.6	4,147	5,814	+1,667
Blacks 65–74	68.2	64.9	499	644	+145
Blacks 75+	62.4	60.2	242	480	+238
Hispanics 65–74	46.6	46.9	258	353	+95
Hispanics 75+	47.3	42.8	170	208	+38
Asian Americans 65–74	44.8	42.7	124	138	+14
Asian Americans 75+	34.1	42.7	61	83	+22

Source: U.S. Census Bureau.

Americans to pledge allegiance to Democrats and a bit less apt to declare themselves Independents. Thirteen percent of the 65-and-older cohort claimed to be Independents in a self-identification question, compared to 17 percent of those age 18 to 64. Among seniors, 37 percent said they were Republicans and 47 percent declared themselves Democrats, whereas 38 percent of 18- to 64-year-olds called themselves Republicans and 42 percent aligned with the Democrats.

Although the plurality of seniors claimed to be Democrats, in a separate question asking them to identify their political, social, and economic views, twice as many identified themselves as "conservative" (45 percent) than as "liberal" (21 percent). The overall percentage of seniors who say they are conservative is a bit higher than it is among all voters younger than them (42 percent for the younger voters), but what is most compelling is the fact that 24 percent of seniors consider themselves to be "*very* conservative," compared to only 17 percent of the younger general population. At the other end of the ideological spectrum, only 6 percent of seniors identified themselves as "very liberal."

POLITICAL IMPLICATIONS

A look at the electoral map and the most recent results at the ballot box illustrate the tremendous political currency possessed by senior voters across America. Notably, the ten states with the *greatest number* of senior voters (California, Florida, New York, Texas, Pennsylvania, Ohio, Illinois, Michigan, New Jersey, and North Carolina) command 256 electoral votes, but the ten states with the *greatest proportion* of senior voters (Florida, Pennsylvania, West Virginia, Iowa, North Dakota, Rhode Island, Maine, South Dakota, Arkansas, and Connecticut) have only 87 electoral votes. Six states from the first group (a total of 160 electoral votes) went to Senator John Kerry in the 2004 presidential election, and four states (with a total of 96 electoral votes) favored President George Bush. In the second group of states, the fortunes were flipped: six states (51 electoral votes) went to Bush, and four states (36 electoral votes) went to Kerry.

In 2000, Vice President Al Gore (D) won the senior vote by a slight margin, claiming 50 percent versus Governor George W. Bush's 47 percent. But four years later, in the first presidential election after 9/11, the incumbent, Bush, improved his take among seniors to 52 percent. Among the various age categories, Bush performed best among the 60-and-older crowd, winning 54 percent of the cohort (up from 47 percent in 2000). He captured only 45 percent of 18- to 29-year-old vote, 29 percent of 30- to 44-year-olds, and 30 percent of 45- to 59-year-olds.[9] That said, in congressional voting in the same election (2004), seniors said they were more inclined to vote for the Democratic candidate than for the Republican (49 percent vs. 43 percent).[10]

In 2006, Republican candidates did not fare as well as Bush had only two years earlier. Although the president captured the senior vote, the 65-and-older crowd evenly split their votes between Republicans and Democrats in races for the House of Representatives (49 percent for the GOP and 49 percent for the Dems). When the age category is expanded to those age 60 and older, the Democrats won older voters 50 percent to 48 percent.[11]

ON THE ISSUES

It is commonly assumed that social security and Medicare are the two most important issues for senior citizens, but when seniors are invited to speak for themselves, the numbers prove otherwise. Whereas senior voters make up approximately 16 percent of the electorate, only 4 percent of respondents (of all ages) in a September 2007 poll said that social security was one of the top two issues for the government to address; 2 percent said "Medicare" and only 1 percent said "programs for the elderly (not Medicare or social security)." On the other hand, 29 percent of Americans in this survey said that the war was one of their top two issues, and 16 percent said healthcare (excluding Medicare).[12]

As Table 21.4 demonstrates, senior voters placed "Iraq" first on the list of issues in both the 2004 and 2006 elections, and at percentages much higher than voters overall. Most amazingly, the number of seniors saying "the situation in Iraq" was the most important issue to them in deciding how and for whom to

Table 21.4
The Important Voting Issues

In deciding on whom to vote for in the election, which of the following issues was most important to you?

2004		2006		
18–64	65+	18–64	65+	
16%	22%	20%	30%	The situation in Iraq
24%	21%	19%	14%	The war on terror/terrorism
18%	13%	13%	8%	Jobs/the economy
16%	12%	10%	7%	Morality/family values
6%	9%	7%	8%	Healthcare/Medicare/prescription drugs
3%	*	5%	2%	Education
n/a	n/a	5%	5%	Immigration
3%	3%	4%	4%	Taxes
n/a	n/a	3%	5%	Abortion
2%	3%	2%	3%	Environment

Source: the polling company™, inc./WomanTrend 2004 and 2006 post-election surveys.

vote grew by 8 percentage points from 2004 to 2006, while during the same two years the number of seniors placing primacy on "the war on terror" dropped from 21 percent in 2004 to 14 percent in 2006. These figures alone could explain the success of Democrats in 2006. Although seniors were early supporters of Bush's invasion of Afghanistan and even the occupation of Iraq, many have migrated to the opposition over the past couple of years. As one senior in a focus group put it, "I lived through three wars, and I don't intend to die while the fourth is going on."

SOCIAL SECURITY AND MEDICARE

Even though seniors do not necessarily place Medicare, healthcare, and social security at the top of their issue matrices, presidential candidates are jockeying for notice by explaining their positions on these issues to seniors. Most Democratic candidates for president of the United States have promised to maintain and expand healthcare as an expansion of entitlement programs, whereas most major Republican candidates have opted to frame the issue in terms of preservation of the current system and its promises to current beneficiaries, with an eye toward allowing greater personal investment options to younger Americans.

For all the talk about "young versus old" and "red versus blue," there is remarkable agreement among Americans on the fate of a social security system left unchanged. Fully 86 percent of registered voters and 87 percent of senior voters believe that it is *very important* that the "president and Congress address the issue of social security in the next few years."[13] Majorities of all demographic, psychographic, and political groups agreed that the executive and legislative branches must quit ignoring this issue and start leading.[14]

SOCIAL AND MORAL ISSUES

Conventional wisdom maintains that as people age they become more conservative, and the data regarding political and ideological self-identification support this notion. Aging appears to lend itself to a certain level of comfort with and adherence to the status quo. The conventional political lexicon that appeals to many Americans is less attractive to seniors. They are not as favorably disposed toward "change," "choices," and "options" as their younger counterparts; many of them live on fixed incomes and/or have established personal habits and daily routines that benefit them, and they have already made—and incorporated—the tough life choices.

This characterization of seniors is reflected in their attitudes toward several controversial issues whose traditional underpinnings are under siege. Seniors are the most likely age group in America to strongly oppose same-sex marriage, gay and lesbian adoption, and allowing homosexuals to serve openly in the military. Table 21.5 compares responses to a March 2006 nationwide survey conducted by the Pew Research Center for People and the Press.

Seniors collectively have changed their minds a bit on these issues over time, however. Fifty-eight percent of those age 65 and older opposed gay marriage in 2004, 75 percent opposed gay and lesbian adoption in 1999, and 50 percent did not favor gays serving openly in the military in a 1994 survey.

On the issue of abortion, Table 21.6 demonstrates that seniors are much more "pro-life" than 18- to 64-year-olds. A plurality of seniors (33 percent) identify

Table 21.5
Seniors Are More Reluctant to Change What Has Been the "Norm"

	Percent Strongly Opposing Gay Marriage	Percent Opposing Gay & Lesbian Adoption	Percent Opposing Gays Serving Openly in the Military
All	28	48	32
18–29	25	38	23
30–49	26	46	30
50–64	30	49	35
65+	33	62	39

Table 21.6
Abortion and Voting

Which of the following statements most closely describes your own position on the issue of abortion?

18–64	65+	
50%	**63%**	**Total pro-life (net)**
13%	18%	Abortions should be prohibited in all circumstances.
14%	12%	Abortions should be legal only to save the life of the mother.
23%	33%	Abortions should only be legal only in cases of rape or incest, or to save the life of the mother.
45%	**30%**	**Total pro-choice (net)**
24%	12%	Abortions should be legal for any reason, but not after the first three months of pregnancy.
8%	3%	Abortions should be legal for any reason, but not after the first six months of pregnancy.
13%	15%	Abortions should be allowed at any time during a woman's pregnancy, and for any reason.

Source: the polling company™, inc./WomanTrend 2006 post-election survey of 800 actual voters nationwide.

with the position that "abortions should be legal only in cases of rape or incest, or to save the life of the mother," compared to 23 percent of 18- to 34-year-olds. In addition, fully 85 percent banning abortions after three months, compared to 74 percent of their younger peers.

IN THE KNOW

Seniors are more likely than younger Americans to follow current events, and they are also able to articulate a higher awareness of world events. In the Pew Research Center's most recent News IQ Survey taken in August 2007, the 65-and-older crowd outperformed younger Americans. The average number of correct answers to a twelve-question quiz among Americans 65 and older was 7.6, compared to 5.5 among 18- to 29-year-olds, 7.1 among 30- to 49-year-olds, and 7.4 for those age 50 to 64. Some of the questions included identifying the sponsor of a recent online debate (YouTube) and Republican candidate Mitt Romney's religion (Mormonism).

In a more in-depth study conducted by Pew, Americans were asked to identify certain figures in the news and in politics (see Table 21.7). With the exception of California Governor Arnold Schwarzenegger, who is best known

Table 21.7
Names in the News

Now I would like to ask you about some people who have been in the news recently. Not everyone will have heard of them. If you don't know who someone is, just tell me and I'll move on. Can you tell me who ____________ is? (Percentage values indicate the number answering correctly.)

	All	65+		All	65+
Hillary Clinton	93%	92%	Barack Obama	61%	68%
Harry Reid	15%	25%	Arnold Schwarzenegger	93%	85%
Nancy Pelosi	49%	61%	Robert Gates	21%	30%
Condoleeza Rice	65%	74%	I. Lewis "Scooter" Libby	29%	40%

for his pre-political career as an actor, seniors were notably more likely than the average respondent to be familiar with a varied list of contemporary political personalities.

Moreover, seniors receive their news and information differently than their younger peers. The top source of political and campaign information for all age groups is still television. Sixty-nine percent of all Americans turned on the TV for most of their news about the 2006 campaign—twice the number who cited newspapers (34 percent) and four times the number who mentioned radio (17 percent) or the Internet (15 percent).[15]

The reliance on television, newspapers, and radio is apt to be much higher among seniors because they are less likely to use the Internet. According to the most recently available figures from the Pew Internet and American Life Project, just 32 percent of seniors were online in March 2007, compared to 65 percent of those age 50 to 64 and 85 percent of 18- to 49-year-olds. Consequently, candidate Web sites and social-networking pages, blogs, online RSS news feeds, and the like have very little impact on the 65-and-older population. They have to be reached "the old-fashioned way."

FUTURE OUTLOOK

As the upcoming generation of retirees, junior seniors (age 50 to 64) will be politically unlike the elders of that age group who preceded them.

Junior seniors are adults age 50 to 64—most of them classified as Baby Boomers—who are on the cusp of their "Golden Years." Many of them are members of the "sandwich generation," caring simultaneously for aging parents and for children who are still living at home. They expect entitlements and eternity as they seek solutions and sophistication. Consider the following facts about junior seniors:

Facts and Figures

- In 2004 a slim majority of these junior seniors, who were then age 45 to 60, voted to reelect President Bush over challenger Senator John Kerry (51 percent to 48 percent), but in 2006 they strongly favored Democratic candidates for the U.S. House.
- Sixty-six percent of women age 50 to 64 are online, compared to 63 percent of men in that group.
- *"I Don't."* Currently, 60 percent of women age 40 to 69 are single.
- *Divorce Court.* Sixty-six percent of all divorces are initiated by women, and that number is even higher among women in their 50s and 60s.
- The number of women age 50 to 64 giving birth is at its highest point ever in the United States—and growing.

The combination of all these factors provides junior senior women with unique perspectives on multiple political issues, including—but not limited to—healthcare and Medicare, social security and retirement, public education, crime, and neighborhood safety.

The purchasing power of junior seniors is tremendous, estimated to total $2 trillion annually. They have a considerable amount of disposable income that goes toward a variety of expenditures, such as home remodeling, travel, and personal luxuries. Additionally, members of this age cohort are expected to inherit large sums of money over the next decade and are growing increasingly conscious of the fiscal challenges of inheriting, saving, and spending money in retirement. They tend to be more socially liberal than their 65-and-older counterparts, having experienced the 1960s as teenagers and young 20-somethings.

CONCLUSION

Having witnessed some of the government's greatest benefits programs and expansions—President Roosevelt's New Deal, President Johnson's War on Poverty, and most recently the $409 billion prescription drug program signed into law by President George W. Bush—members of the 65-and-older legion see government not only as capable of, but as responsible for addressing some of their needs. This "Greatest Generation" does not take the American Dream lightly; it has observed women and minorities becoming able to take new roles in society and being afforded more rights and opportunities to achieve that dream. American seniors have seen international hostilities turn into amicable relationships; science and technology convert impossible fantasies into medical realities; and improvements to health, safety, and the general quality of life truly turn the Golden Years into a desirable framework for living, rather than for simply surviving or "winding down."

Over the next two decades, the number of Americans expecting to receive government support in the form of social security and Medicare will skyrocket while the number of Americans financing the programs simultaneously decreases—an issue familiar to lawmakers and candidates alike. Long referred to as the "third rail of politics," social security reform may be evolving into the *reverse* third rail, meaning that it is the *failure* rather than the *attempt* to address it that risks political currency and votes.

The consistent and high turnout levels of the 65-and-over population can lead politicians to count on seniors to go to the polls, but not necessarily to vote a straight party ticket or exclusively in response to the so-called senior issues. Although the majority of seniors identify with one of the two major political parties, recent elections demonstrate that these voters are politically "up for grabs," since both Republicans and Democrats have been successful in capturing the cohort. The political and ideological inclinations of seniors tend, for the most part, to align with those of the rest of the population, but seniors often hold more conservative opinions on social and moral issues than do younger Americans.

It will be interesting to watch what happens not only in 2008, but also in 2012, when the first batch of the 80 million Baby Boomers officially become members of the senior population. Aging will certainly take on a new face, and both older and younger politicians will have to respond appropriately.

NOTES

1. U.S. Census Bureau, *65+ in the United States, 2005*, p. 35.
2. U.S. Census Bureau, *Current Population Survey* (2004).
3. U.S. Department of Health and Human Services, *A Profile of Older Americans: 2005*.
4. U.S. Census Bureau, "*65+*," p. 2.
5. AARP Bulletin Poll on Workers 50+: Executive Summary (September 2007).
6. U.S. Census Bureau, "*65+*," p. 1.
7. U.S. Census Bureau, *Current Population Survey* (November 2004 and earlier), http://www.census.gov/population/socdemo/voting/cps2004/tab02-1.xls.
8. U.S. Census Bureau, *Current Population Survey* (November 2004), Table 2.
9. CNN 2004 exit polls.
10. the polling company™, inc./WomanTrend 2004 Post-Election Survey.
11. CNN 2006 exit polls.
12. Harris Interactive September 2007 poll.
13. American Solutions August 2007 poll (1,000 registered voters).
14. American Solutions August 2007 poll (1,000 registered voters).
15. Pew Internet and American Life Project, *Election 2006 Online* (January 2007).

22

The Elusive Young Voter

How to Break into the Group

Heather Smith and Kat Barr

In the 2004 elections, 4.3 million more 18- to 29-year-old voters cast ballots than in 2000. Under-30 voter turnout jumped 9 percentage points, from 40 percent in 2000 to 49 percent in 2004, the largest young voter turnout increase seen since 18- to 20-year-olds first entered the electorate in 1972.[1] Indeed, more 18- to 29-year-olds voted in 2004 than did voters 65 and over.[2]

In the 2006 midterm elections, young voters again surged at the polls. By a conservative estimate, young voter turnout increased by 1.2 million from 2002 levels; more likely, turnout increased by as much as 2 million, from 8 to 10 million.[3]

The recent phenomenon of a growing turnout among young voters is slowly beginning to penetrate nearly thirty years of conventional wisdom that young adults don't register, don't vote, and don't care. Today's young adults—the Millennial Generation[4]—are huge in number, increasingly active in politics, and ready to make their voices heard. Politicians and parties who have for so long ignored young voters are slowly realizing that if they expect to win in 2008 and beyond, they need to court and win this electorate.

To understand the importance of today's active youth vote—and the political parties' renewed interest—it is necessary to understand the rise and fall of the youth vote over the past thirty years and the reasons behind it, as well as to understand the face of young America today and what campaigns can and should do to win their votes.

THE YOUTH VOTE HISTORY: 1960–2000

"Old Enough to Fight, Old Enough to Vote"

The story of today's youth vote begins in the late 1960s, at the peak of the Vietnam War and an energized youth movement active in civil rights, free speech, and peace protests. In 1969, U.S. troop levels peaked at 543,000 and casualties surpassed 33,600. The average age of troops killed in Vietnam was 23, and by the war's end 25,493 troops under the age of 21 had died[5]—most of whom did not have the right to vote because the amendment wasn't passed until 1973.

Young adults and supportive elected officials, under the banner of "Old enough to fight, old enough to vote," fought for and won passage of the Twenty-sixth Amendment to the U.S. Constitution, which lowered the voting age in federal elections from 21 to 18. On March 10, 1971, the U.S. Senate unanimously approved the amendment, followed by House passage on March 23. The states ratified the Twenty-sixth Amendment over the next 100 days—faster than for any other amendment in U.S. history—and in 1972, 18- to 20-year-olds voted in their first federal elections.

In the 1972 elections, 55.4 percent of 18- to 29-year-olds voted,[6] a rate unsurpassed since. A look at the next thirty years gives one a sense of why.

A Crisis of Confidence

The 1970s were a blow to Americans' confidence in government. Watergate, the energy crisis, "stagflation," lackluster leadership, and the Iran hostage crisis deflated Americans, hitting their pocketbooks and psyches equally hard. As President Jimmy Carter put it in his famous 1979 "malaise" speech, "'We are confronted with a moral and a spiritual crisis.' . . . It is a crisis of confidence. It is a crisis that strikes at the very heart and soul and spirit of our national will. . . . The erosion of our confidence in the future is threatening to destroy the social and the political fabric of America."

The American public's level of trust in the federal government bottomed out in 1980. In 1964, 78 percent of adults reported that they trusted the government "just about all of" or "most of" the time; by 1972 that was down to 54 percent, and in 1980 it reached a low of 26 percent.[7]

For a young adult poised to register or vote for the first time, this national mood was disheartening. As noted in a 2003 study, among young adults (ages 18 to 25), "the confidence that government officials listen to 'people like me' has eroded over the past half-century, [although this age group] used to be more confident in the government than their elders."[8] Numerous academic studies have shown that the act of voting is a habit that develops over time: once a person begins voting, he or she is likely to continue to do so on a regular basis. But voting for the first time is a new, unfamiliar act that takes an impetus. Living in a time of distrust in government has helped to deter young adults from casting that first ballot.

Declining Civic Education

Americans are not born with an inherent understanding of what it means to be an active citizen. From basic facts, such as how and where to register to vote, to more complex concepts—understanding political issues, a citizen's role in democracy, and the functions of government institutions—citizenship needs to be taught and learned. Recognizing this, the U.S. government established public schools in the nineteenth century with an explicit directive toward civic education as part of their mission.[9] In fact, forty state constitutions mention the importance of civic literacy among citizens; thirteen of these constitutions state that the central purpose of their educational system is to promote good citizenship, democracy, and free government.[10] And until recently, public schools did play an important civic education role.

Unfortunately, the breadth and depth of civic education in schools has been on the decline since the 1960s. Today, most high school students take just one government course, compared to an average of three in the 1960s and earlier.[11] Elementary school students also receive less civic education: from 1988 to 1998, the number of fourth-graders who had daily social studies lessons declined by 49 percent.[12] Further, while an emphasis on the rights and duties of citizens was previously a major component of civics courses, today's courses often present "government" as a more distant entity, with little discussion of a citizen's practical role in democracy.[13]

In the 1990s, a re-energized civic education and "service learning" movement made progress toward re-instilling civic lessons in schools. The result is visible in young adults' growing levels of volunteerism—UCLA's 2005 study of college freshmen found that 83 percent had volunteered at least occasionally during their high school senior year, the highest level recorded since the question was first asked in 1984[14]—and is likely correlated with recent increases in young voter turnout.

A Mobile Generation

Over the past forty years, Americans in general and young adults in particular have become more mobile and global. Unfortunately, it is an established fact that moving has a negative impact on an individual's turnout as a voter. Today's young adults are more likely than any previous generation to attend college, to move away from home, and to move frequently. Although higher education levels are correlated with higher rates of electoral participation, the corresponding mobility significantly impedes voter turnout. For a person who has recently moved, the act of entering an unfamiliar community, the upheaval caused by moving, the need to re-register to vote, the time and cost of obtaining new identification required to register and vote in many states, and other factors all play a role in lower voter turnout.

Today, 30.3 percent of 20- to 24-year-olds move annually, three times more frequently than adults of all ages.[15] A recent five-state analysis found that voters (of all ages) who moved six months before the 2004 election turned out at rates 20 to 34 percentage points lower than voters who had not moved.[16] The negative impact of moving on voter turnout, combined with young adults' growing mobility, is a major factor behind young adults' lower levels of electoral participation.

The Cycle of Mutual Neglect

All of the foregoing factors affected turnout across the population, but they hit the youth cohort disproportionately hard. Young adults' diminishing electoral involvement triggered a cycle of mutual neglect that perpetuated this turnout decrease. Although senior citizens, union members, and other key constituencies are awash in attention during campaign season, young voters are seldom the focus of campaign messages or the recipients of mobilization efforts. And when politicians don't pay attention to young voters, young voters become even less inclined to pay attention to them, and less inclined to vote. Campaigns, of course, are unlikely to invest resources in an unpredictable electorate; instead, they operate under the conventional wisdom that young voters are not worth their time or outreach—because they don't vote. Over time, as young voter turnout continued to decline and the political elite wrote off the youth vote, the cycle worsened.

A NEW GENERATION OF YOUNG VOTERS: 2004–PRESENT

Pay Attention to Us

During the 2004 election cycle, under the new banner of "make them pay attention to us," a new generation of young people entered the electorate and began to crack the cycle of mutual neglect. On November 2, 2004—spurred by an unprecedented investment in mobilization efforts from nonpartisan organizations and a highly competitive election—young voters turned out big. More than 20 million 18- to 29-year-olds voted, a 4.3 million vote increase over 2000 and the largest increase in young voter turnout since 1972.

Of the approximately $4 billion spent in the 2004 election cycle, an estimated $40 million of nonpartisan money was targeted toward young voters—a mere fraction of the total dollars spent, but the most ever targeted toward young people. The largest youth-specific nonpartisan efforts included the Student PIRGs' New Voters Project, Declare Yourself, Hip Hop Summit Action Network, MTV, Rock the Vote, and World Wresting Entertainment's Smackdown Your Vote.

A key difference in 2004, compared to previous youth outreach efforts, was that time-tested grassroots strategies—door knocking, clipboarding, volunteer phone calls, events—played a larger role. As reported in a front-page *New York Times* story in 2004: "After failing to increase turnout with rock-star pleas and celebrity robovoice phone nags, the people involved in the major youth vote drives say they have found success with an old-fashioned strategy—ground troops."[17]

Groups such as the New Voters Project, working with political scientists Donald Green and Alan Gerber of Yale University and David Nickerson of Notre Dame, had in previous years run randomized field experiments to test the exact impact of many of the grassroots tactics. These experiments, which tested outreach techniques by applying treatment to one group of voters while holding another group as a control, proved, for example, that live phone calls encouraging young registered voters to go to the polls raise the probability of turnout by roughly 5 percentage points, whereas face-to-face canvassing increases turnout among those contacted by an average of 8.5 percentage points.[18]

With these experimental results and years of field experience, nonpartisan organizations increased young voter registration in 2004. The New Voters Project, the largest grassroots program, registered 524,000 18- to 30-year-olds in twenty-one states and made more than 530,000 personalized get-out-the-vote contacts in the weeks leading up to the election. Rock the Vote, combining Internet outreach and celebrity star power, registered more than 1 million young adults online.

The political parties also began to pay more attention to what, as the 2004 election approached, was clearly an energized youth electorate. Both the Republican National Committee (RNC) and the Democratic National Committee (DNC) launched youth outreach efforts. The RNC, as part of its effort to register 3 million new voters, brought its registration bus, "Reggie the Rig," to college campuses nationwide. The Bush-Cheney campaign began its youth outreach eight months earlier than in 2000 and signed up more than 40,000 young campaign volunteers through the national Students for Bush organization.

The DNC also registered students as part of registration drives across the country. John Kerry's campaign spent a week on a college campus tour, announcing a youth policy platform called Compact with the Next Generation. Kerry also appeared on an MTV special as part of the Choose or Lose campaign. *USA Today* reported that the DNC made its first ad buy targeting voters under 30, which ran during *Saturday Night Live* and *The Daily Show*.

The Millennial Generation Goes to the Polls

On Election Day 2004, young voters proved that politicians should indeed pay attention to them. On November 2, 20.1 million 18- to 29-year-olds went to the polls, an unprecedented 9-point jump in turnout (from 40 percent to 49 percent). More 18- to 29-year-olds voted in 2004 than did voters over 65 years of age.

Turnout was higher among voters of all ages in 2004 than in 2000—but young voters drove that turnout increase. Whereas overall turnout rose by 4 percentage points, 18- to 29-year-olds' turnout rose 9 points and 18- to 24-year-olds' turnout grew by 11 points, nearly three times the overall electorate's increase.[19]

Turnout increased among all segments of the youth population—from college students to low-income working youth—but certain groups led the way. Turnout by women under 30 jumped 10 points over 2000 levels, and participation by 18- to 24-year-old African Americans jumped 11 points. By comparison, young adults with no college education increased their turnout by 7 points, whereas 18- to 29-year-old Hispanics' turnout grew by 6 points.

Young voters not only surged to the polls in 2004, they broke with tradition. Although young voters had voted for the winner in every presidential election since 1972,[20] in 2004 the 18- to 29-year-old vote went strongly for Democrat John Kerry over Republican George W. Bush, the winner. Young voters were the only age cohort besides voters over 75 to cast the majority of their votes for the Democratic candidate.

Given the significant increase in young voter turnout, it is clear that resources spent on the youth vote saw a return on investment. Consensus among academics and practitioners concludes that this increase in young voter participation was caused by two primary factors. First, this is a new, engaged generation of young people entering the electorate. They are paying attention to the elections, watching the news, and talking to their friends and families about politics at much higher rates.[21] They entered the electorate at a time of war and came of age during the September 11 terrorist attacks. And they, more than any other age group, have a high level of trust in government and see voting less as a duty and more as a way to influence the government.[22]

Second, young voters turned out because they were asked to do so. Unprecedented outreach efforts contacted millions of young adults, who responded by registering and voting in record-breaking numbers. Clearly, young adults today are engaged, paying attention, and eager to get involved and have a say in our democracy when organizations and campaigns reach out to them.

Millennial Momentum

Many in the media and political establishment questioned—reasonably—whether young voters' turnout in 2004 indicated a significant change, or whether it was simply a blip on the radar screen, as the bump in youth turnout was in 1992.

In 2005 and 2006, young voters answered that question with two more resounding showings at the polls, proving that 2004 was in fact the beginning of a trend of increased youth electoral participation.

- In 2005, young voter turnout grew by 19 percent and 15 percent, respectively, in student precincts targeted by mobilization efforts during the New Jersey and

Virginia gubernatorial elections,[23] even while turnout among voters of all ages went down in both states.[24]

- In 2006, turnout among 18- to 29-year-olds increased by approximately 2 million over 2002 levels.[25] Young voters increased their share of the electorate as well, growing from 10 percent of votes cast in 2002 to 12 percent in 2006.[26]

Not only did young adults turn out big in 2006, they made the difference in several close races. The margin of victory in three U.S. Senate races was less than the young voters' turnout increase from 2002 to 2006.

- *Montana:* Jon Tester defeated Conrad Burns by 3,562 votes (youth turnout up by 39,106 votes).
- *Virginia:* Jim Webb defeated George Allen by 9,329 votes (youth turnout up by 110,453 votes).
- *Missouri:* Claire McCaskill defeated Jim Talent by 48,314 votes (youth turnout up by 108,269 votes).

Several U.S. House races and state house seats tell the same story. Clearly, young voters made a significant impact in the 2006 elections.

According to the National Election Poll exit polls, 60 percent of 18- to 29-year-olds voted for Democratic congressional candidates and 38 percent voted for Republicans, the largest Democratic margin of any age group.[27] Although official figures are not yet available from the U.S. Census Bureau for demographic subgroups, polling by Young Voter Strategies indicates that Democrats' strongest support came from African American youth, single young women, and young Hispanics, whereas Republicans were supported by married young adults and Evangelical youth.[28]

As in 2004, experts agree that major youth-focused outreach efforts—combined with this new, engaged generation and high-profile, competitive races—played a significant role in turning out the youth vote. In 2006, nonpartisan groups ran the largest youth registration campaign ever seen in a midterm election. Fifteen organizations, in partnership with Young Voter Strategies, registered more than 542,000 18- to 30-year-olds, reaching nearly every state in the country. These organizations—including the New Voters Project; Project Vote; Women's Voices. Women Vote.; the Center for Civic Participation; Rock the Vote; Black Youth Vote!; and Building Blocks, Building Votes—reached a diverse array of youth cohorts through methods targeted to each unique community. Groups used door-to-door canvassing, direct mail, campus organizing, faith-based outreach, and social networking Web sites to reach young women, college students, urban youth, religious youth, young professionals, African Americans, Latinos, and others.

In addition, the political parties built upon their nascent 2004 interest in young voters with a handful of strategic outreach campaigns. For example, in

Montana, Senator Jon Tester's successful campaign ran a statewide youth effort that integrated events, canvassing, campus organizing, and online social networking to turn out young adults; and in Connecticut, the Democratic Party ran a top-tier campus organizing project that ultimately won the election for Representative Joe Courtney in the Second District.[29] In California, Republican Arnold Schwarzenegger and the statewide GOP mobilized the College Republicans and registered voters with a bus tour, while in Florida, Governor Charlie Crist's campaign registered new voters at events and engaged young Republicans via online social networking.[30] In addition, issues that resonated strongly with young voters, including the Iraq war and college affordability, played a major role in campaigns across the country.

With turnout increases in 2004, 2005, and 2006, the Millennial Generation has clearly arrived. Political parties can no longer afford to neglect young voters. With their sheer numbers, growing voter turnout, and the upcoming election's competitive landscape, young adults have begun to conquer the barriers to participation and are a group to watch in 2008.

2008: THE YEAR OF THE YOUTH?

The year 2008 could be positioned as "the year of the youth" as the result of a confluence of factors: young voter turnout momentum; growing interest from political parties in the younger electorate; high-stakes, high-profile races; and the sheer size of this generation.

Momentum

Voting is habit-forming. An individual who votes in one election is more likely to vote again—and again, and again, and again. Substantial academic literature supports this notion.[31] Notre Dame political science professor David Nickerson states, "One of the most robust empirical regularities discovered in political science is that past voting behavior is a good predictor of future voting behavior."[32]

In 2004, 4.3 million more 18- to 29-year-olds voted than in 2000; in 2006, as many as 2 million more voted than in 2002. Put simply, millions more young adults became voters in the past two elections—and are therefore much more likely to vote in 2008.

Looking to the 2008 elections, young voters are likely to turn out in increased numbers yet again. With nearly 42 million 18- to 29-year-old citizens in the United States,[33] increasing turnout means an ever-expanding impact on elections. Young voters turned out in numbers that helped make or break several U.S. House and statewide races in 2004 and 2006, and 2008 could be the year the youth vote makes its impact felt on the presidential election.

A Huge, Engaged Generation

The Millennial Generation is large—very large—and in the new reality of close elections, they are a bloc that will play an important role in deciding elections in the next decade. Numbering 75 million in 2006,[34] the Millennial Generation is approaching the current size of the Baby Boom generation. By 2015, potential Millennial voters ages 18 to 38 will represent one-third of the U.S. electorate, and the recent turnout of voting-age Millennials shows that they are paying attention and engaged in politics. On the heels of Generation X, which never got its political legs, the new Millennial Generation is re-engaged.

The Millennials' post-2006 political attention is continuing to build. A 2007 Pew Research Center study found that 77 percent of 18- to 29-year-olds say they are interested in local politics, up 28 points from 49 percent in 1999—the highest increase of any age group surveyed. The 2007 survey also found that 85 percent of 18- to 29-year-olds report that they are "interested in keeping up with national affairs," a 14-point increase from 71 percent in 1999 and nearly the same level of interest as adults of all ages (89 percent).

Campaign Interest

Voters' partisan loyalty forms during the youth vote years and then stays remarkably stable after the age of 30.[35] Academic research has shown, for instance, that of individuals who recall their first presidential vote, two-thirds still identify with the party for which they first voted.[36] Looking to 2008, both political parties are beginning to recognize that now is the time to court this big, growing, and increasingly active electorate.

Tracking the rise and fall of America's political parties reveals a remarkable trend: those who win the youth vote are, a generation later, the party in power. As noted by Norman J. Ornstein in 1986: "All the research done on the dramatic Democratic realignment of the 1930s shows that the key was young voters, coming of age as the Depression hit, influenced deeply by the contrast between Hoover and Roosevelt . . . those young voters became lifelong Democrats. . . . The oldest segment of today's population, those who came of age during the golden years for the Republicans (the Roaring Twenties), remain staunchly Republican today."[37]

Picking up where Ornstein left off, the trend continues. Republicans won the youth vote hands down in 1984[38] and again in 1988;[39] even in 1986, when Democrats won every age group in the U.S. House vote, young adults (18 to 29) were more Republican-leaning than any other age group.[40] Those young voters are now the middle-aged core of the Republican Party. Twenty years later, those "youth" are in their 40s and still sharply Republican, compared to other age cohorts.[41] This group of voters played a significant role in the Republican revolution of the early 1990s, when Republicans secured—and kept, until 2006—a stronghold in Congress.

Looking to 2008, with young voters' increasing electoral presence and what is becoming a strong Democratic leaning, both political parties are beginning to pay serious attention to courting the youth vote. Democrats see an opportunity to target and secure an entire generation of base voters that could put them in a powerful position for decades. Republicans, on the other hand, understand well that they cannot afford to be 22 points down with an entire age cohort if they want to regain the presidency and Congress.

Candidates for the presidency and the national political parties are beginning to pay attention to the 2008 youth vote. Student rallies drawing thousands for Barack Obama are already making headlines, part of a phenomenon driven by online networking sites such as Facebook and MySpace. Strategist Karl Rove, a former College Republican and conservative youth leader, has his eye on the 2008 youth vote. According to a Politico.com interview: "Rove, a master of the minutiae of political demographics, has singled out four voter groups that he thinks the Republican Party needs to focus on . . . [one of which is] Younger Voters." All major Republican and Democratic presidential contenders, as of April 2007, are geared up to hire full-time youth outreach directors, and at least two, the John Edwards and Barack Obama campaigns, already have done so. If the partisan community treats young people as voters rather than just volunteers, there will be a significant increase in turnout in 2008. If campaigns use familiar media to communicate in an authentic way about issues that are relevant—and then really target young people through registration, persuasion, and get-out-the-vote efforts—the young people will respond. Research shows that campaigns contacting youth voters in 2004 produced a 9.4 percent increase in turnout among youth.[42]

Nonpartisan Outreach

We saw in 2004, 2005, and 2006 that nonpartisan organizations' outreach to young voters can have a major impact in engaging new young voters. Nonpartisan organizations—including major 2004 and 2006 players such as Young Voter Strategies, Rock the Vote, the New Voters Project, Project Vote, and Women's Voices. Women Vote.—are gearing up for major 2008 campaigns. They plan to register more young voters than ever before, engage them, and collect cell phone and e-mail information for follow-up around the elections.

Election Laws

In 2007, several states considered legislation that would help expand young voters' access to and involvement in elections, including pre-registration for 16- and 17-year-olds, Election Day registration, and automatic re-registration for voters who move.

In Minnesota and Michigan, secretaries of state Mark Ritchie and Terri Lynn Land proposed that any citizen be automatically registered to vote when obtaining a driver's license—including 16- and 17-year-olds, who would be "pre-registered." When the preregistered driver turned 18, the minimum voting age, the state would add that person to the voting rolls and send a registration card to his or her address. The Minnesota plan proposed a second change that would impact young adults. It would automatically update a registered voter's address whenever the voter moves and files a change-of-address form through the U.S. Postal Service. At present, a voter must re-register with each move. Considering the mobility rates of young adults, streamlining this process could play a significant role in increasing young voter registration and turnout.

Similar ideas were debated in Maryland and Connecticut. Maryland State Senator Jamin Raskin (D) introduced a bill that would allow 16-year-olds to pre-register to vote and would encourage voter registration drives at Maryland high schools. Connecticut Secretary of State Susan Bysiewicz is pushing for 17-year-olds to be allowed to vote in primaries if they will be 18 by the time of the general election.

In addition, several states in 2007 considered Election Day registration (EDR). Seven states currently employ EDR, which allows any eligible voters to register at the polls on Election Day.[43] Research shows that EDR can significantly increase voter turnout, particularly among young adults. Young voter turnout results in Montana in 2006 show the potential of EDR. In 2002, 18- to 29-year-olds made up 8 percent of the Montana electorate, but after implementation of EDR in 2006, they were 17 percent of the electorate. Looking at initial estimates of turnout, 18- to 29-year-olds increased their vote total from 39,106 in 2002 to more than 69,000 in 2006.[44] EDR, in combination with outreach efforts and the excitement of a high-profile Senate race, certainly had an impact on the Montana youth vote.

If Election Day registration, pre-registration, automatic re-registration, and other youth-friendly laws are passed, young voter turnout could increase substantially in affected states.

The New American Electorate

The Millennial Generation is the new face of politics. Open to outreach, mobile and educated, diverse, engaged, and Internet-savvy, today's young adults are the present and future of politics.

As the 2008 election approaches, campaign strategists must integrate voter outreach into their plans for November. Based on years of field experience and randomized field experiments, we know what works. There are some basic tactics that campaigns should keep in mind.

1. *Person-to-person contact* has the strongest impact on the likelihood that a young person will register and vote. As noted earlier, experiments by professors Don Green

and Alan Gerber showed a 5 percent increase in turnout resulting from phone calls and an 8 percent increase in turnout following a conversation at the door. Campaign strategists should use these assumptions to incorporate youth into their field plans. If you ask them, they will vote.

2. Ask everyone contacted if they will *volunteer*. Young people today bring tremendous energy, creativity, and leadership to causes they care about. Also, developing volunteer networks allows for inexpensive peer-to-peer contacts.
3. Provide *voter registration*. Many young voters move around. Registration efforts can help with the collection of updated contact information, including cell phone numbers and e-mail addresses.
4. Utilize *online social networking sites*. Facebook and MySpace are where young adults spend their time online, and campaigns can use these sites creatively to energize and recruit volunteers, announce events, and make candidates prominent. However, Internet outreach does not imply the exclusion of field outreach. These sites can be used to *build voter target lists*, identify supportive voters based on their profiles, generate phone banks with posted phone numbers, and translate the reach and speed of the Internet into offline voter and volunteer activity.
5. Go to *college campuses*. It is rare to find one place where so many potential voters from any demographic congregate as young people do on college campuses. Speak to classes and student organizations, spend time at a table, and walk the dorms and dense student neighborhoods. Here's a tip: don't just do a photo shoot and leave; engage students in genuine dialogue.
6. When trying to reach young people *off campus*, think about *how* they live. Site-based canvassing at bars, clubs, concerts, gas stations, laundromats, community centers, festivals, and churches allows for high contact rates among critical groups of young voters.
7. Rather than emphasizing a new *issue platform*, talk about how a candidate's policies will relate to younger people's lives. For example, regarding the Iraq war, explain how the candidate's position will affect the young person's brothers and best friends (rather than their sons and daughters). In regard to pocketbook issues, let young voters know the candidate's stance on healthcare costs and college affordability.

The Millennial Generation proved in 2006 that it has arrived. What happens in 2008 and beyond depends on all of the aforementioned factors—most important, how the political parties and campaigns effectively implement youth outreach strategies and turn out their young voters. If candidates and campaigns talk to and with young voters about important issues, come to their college campuses, knock on their doors at home, call them on the phone, register them to vote, and organize this constituency well, young voters will again turn out big in 2008. Young voters in 2006 had a make-or-break impact on several statewide and local races, and in 2008 this huge and active electorate is poised to have a major impact on one of the most high-stakes presidential elections in history.

NOTES

1. Center for Information and Research on Civic Learning and Engagement (CIRCLE) tabulations of the U.S. Census Bureau *Current Population Survey* (CPS), November 2004 supplement.

2. CIRCLE tabulations of the U.S. Census Bureau CPS, November 2004 supplement.

3. CIRCLE tabulations of the National Election Pool 2006 exit poll.

4. The Millennial Generation, born 1977 to 1997, numbers 75 million. Currently, voting-eligible Millennials number 42 million.

5. National Archives, Combat Area Casualties, current files.

6. CIRCLE tabulations of the U.S. Census Bureau CPS, November 1972 supplement.

7. American National Election Survey, 1964 to 1980, http://sda.berkeley.edu/cgi-bin/hsda?harcsda+nes2000c (accessed April 5, 2007).

8. CIRCLE and the Carnegie Corporation, "The Civic Mission of Schools," p. 12.

9. CIRCLE and the Carnegie Corporation, "The Civic Mission of Schools," p. 11.

10. CIRCLE and the Carnegie Corporation, "The Civic Mission of Schools," p. 11.

11. CIRCLE and the Carnegie Corporation, "The Civic Mission of Schools," p. 15.

12. CIRCLE and the Carnegie Corporation, "The Civic Mission of Schools," p. 15.

13. CIRCLE and the Carnegie Corporation, "The Civic Mission of Schools," p. 14.

14. UCLA Higher Education Research Institute, "The American Freshman, National Norms for Fall 2005."

15. The U.S. Census Bureau CPS, 2005 Annual Social & Economic Supplement.

16. Polimetrix analysis of Iowa, Minnesota, Florida, Missouri, and Ohio state voter files, 2006.

17. Timothy Egan, "The 2004 Campaign: Young Voters; Vote Drives Gain Avid Attention of Youth in '04," *New York Times*, September 15, 2004.

18. Donald Green and Alan Gerber, *Get Out the Vote*, http://www.yale.edu/vote/.

19. U.S. Census Bureau CPS, November 2004 supplement.

20. In 2000, young voters split 48 to 46 percent in favor of Al Gore, who lost the election but won the popular vote.

21. See Polling Report, "Young Voter Strategies," November 2006.

22. See polling from Harvard University's Institute of Politics (2006) and from Young Voter Strategies (2006).

23. CIRCLE analysis of raw precinct data, November 2005.

24. In New Jersey, turnout in 2001 was 49.2 percent for all ages; in 2005, turnout was 48.5 percent (*source:* New Jersey Division of Elections, Office of the Attorney General). In Virginia, turnout in 2001 was 46.4 percent for all ages; in 2005, turnout was 44.96 percent for all ages (*source:* Virginia State Board of Elections).

25. This is a comparison of 2002 and 2006 turnout estimates based on national exit polls. The 2006 turnout is an estimation calculated by CIRCLE from the National Election Pool exit polls.

26. 2002 data: CIRCLE tabulation of the U.S. Census Bureau CPS, November 2002 supplement. 2006 data: National Election Pool exit poll.

27. National Election Pool exit polls, 2006. The second-highest Democratic margin came from 30- to 44-year-olds, who voted 53 percent Democratic and 45 percent Republican.

28. Young Voter Battleground Poll, Young Voter Strategies, November 2006 (conducted by Celinda Lake of Lake Research Partners and Ed Goeas of the Tarrance Group).

29. Ray Hackett, "Congressman Lauds Voting to Ellis Tech Youths," *Norwich Bulletin*, February 21, 2007.

30. For more information, see "Young Voter Mobilization Tactics II: Young Voter Strategies," May 2007.

31. A. Campbell, P. Converse, W. Miller, and D. Stokes, *The American Voter* (Survey Research Center, University of Michigan, 1964); A. Gerber, D. Green, and R. Schachar, "Voting May Be Habit-Forming," *American Journal of Political Science* 47(3) (2003): 540–550; D. Green and R. Schachar, *Habit Formation and Political Behaviour: Evidence of Consuetude in Voter Turnout* (Cambridge University Press, 2000), 561–573; David Nickerson, "Just How Addictive Is Voting, and Why?" Yale University, working draft (October 28, 2004).

32. Nickerson, "Just How Addictive Is Voting,."

33. U.S. Census Bureau.

34. This figure is for the entire Millennial Generation, born 1977 to 1997, and therefore includes many Millennials not yet of voting age.

35. D. Green and B. Palmquist, "How Stable is Party Identification?," *Political Behavior* 16(4) (December 1994): 437–466; M. K. Jennings and L. Stoke, "The Persistence of the Past," paper presented at Midwest Political Science Association Convention, Chicago (April 1999).

36. Campbell et al., *The American Voter.*

37. Norman Ornstein, "The Curse of the Six-Year Itch," *Atlantic Monthly* (March 1986), www.theatlantic.com/politics/polibig/ornstein.htm.

38. Fifty-nine percent of 18- to 29-year-olds voted for Reagan, versus 40 percent for Mondale (www.nytimes.com/images/2000/12/20/politics/elections/nwr_portrait_ age.html).

39. Fifty-two percent of 18- to 29-year-olds voted for Bush, versus 47 percent for Dukakis (www.nytimes.com/images/2000/12/20/politics/elections/nwr_portrait_age. html).

40. CBS News/ New York Times, National Election Day exit poll, 1986: 18- to 29-year-olds voted 48.4 percent for Democrats and 46.0 percent for Republicans.

41. In 2004, 30- to 44-year-olds voted 53 percent to 46 percent in favor of George W. Bush, more Republican-leaning than any age group except those 60 years and over (54 percent to 46 percent Bush over Kerry). *Source:* National Election Pool exit poll, 2004.

42. Richard Niemi and Michael Hanmer, "Voter Registration and Turnout Among College Students," paper prepared for the Annual Meeting of the American Political Science Association, Philadelphia (August 31–September 3, 2006), 22.

43. One of the seven, Montana, currently allows EDR only at certain locations, not at polling places.

44. The 2002 vote total for 18- to 29-year-olds is from CIRCLE tabulations of the U.S. Census Bureau CPS, November 2004 supplement. The 2006 vote total is a YVS tabulation derived from the National Election Pool's Montana exit poll and the Secretary of State's official vote total.

23

The Typecast Voters

Security Moms, Seniors, and the Young

Celinda Lake, Thaddeus Windt, and Daniel Gotoff

On November 8, 2000, Americans woke up and found themselves in a situation unprecedented in the previous century. The day after Election Day, the American people did not know who had been elected as the next president of the United States. The 2000 presidential election campaign ushered in what many commentators called "Red State/Blue State" America. This is shorthand to describe the intense partisan polarization and even political divisions that exist on the national level. The twenty-first century has shown that neither major political party at the national level is able yet to produce a commanding majority, and that the country is closely divided.

There are two additional events that have helped produce the tectonic shift in the contemporary political landscape. Prior to September 11, 2001, it was far from clear how successful a president George W. Bush would turn out to be. His job approval ratings were mired in the low 50s, despite successes in passing tax cuts and education reform titled "No Child Left Behind." In the wake of the terrorist attacks on that day and throughout the remainder of his first term, Bush enjoyed very high marks on the dimension of leadership and keeping America safe. In the midterm elections of 2002, the Republicans defied history by picking up two Senate seats and six seats in the House by emphasizing national security. And in 2004, despite a weak economy and the general sense that the country was headed off on the wrong track, Bush was able to ride the dimensions of strong leadership and protecting America to reelection victory. One of the major themes thus far in the twenty-first century is the reemergence of national security as a major issue, which had dissipated with the ending of the Cold War. In the two election cycles immediately after the attacks of September 11, security was a source of strength for the Republican Party. In 2006 it did not play a major role, but watch for Republicans to try and elevate the issue again in 2008.

The other major event that impacted U.S. politics in recent years was Bush's decision to go to war in Iraq. The United States' war in Iraq began on March 20, 2003. In the run-up to the war, the Republican Party was very successful in leveraging the war as an issue of national security in the 2002 midterm elections. Supporting the war on terrorism and a strong military (34 percent) was the number 1 reason voters supported the Republican candidates for Congress.[1] In the fall of 2002, President Bush had made the case for war by presenting it as part of a broader campaign against terrorism. At that time, fully 50 percent of Americans believed there was enough evidence to link Iraq to terrorism. Forty-five percent did not think there was enough evidence.[2]

By 2006 the war in Iraq had become a major disadvantage for the Republican Party. Right before the elections, 54 percent of voters felt the war in Iraq was not worth fighting, and 44 percent strongly believed it was unnecessary.[3] Voters also reported that the war in Iraq (29 percent) was the most important reason for voting against Republican candidates for Congress.[4] In the 2006 midterm elections, the Democrats were able to capitalize on the issues of Iraq and corruption in Congress, winning back the majority in Congress by picking up thirty seats in the House and six seats in the Senate. The lack of progress in Iraq and the economy had produced a climate for change. Voters fired the Republicans, but did not particularly hire the Democrats. How voters in the mood for change sort out the two parties and evaluate the potential independent candidates will depend on a number of key blocs of voters.

This chapter will examine these key blocs of twenty-first-century swing voters to see how they have historically swung their support between the two parties, with an eye toward the 2008 presidential race.

YOUNGER VOTERS

Younger voters (18–29 years of age) form a bloc that has gone from splitting their support almost evenly between the two parties' presidential candidates to becoming a solid base of support for the Democrats. In 2000, 48 percent of these younger voters cast their ballots for Al Gore. Forty-six percent voted for then-Governor Bush.[5] These voters had grown up during the peace and prosperity of the Clinton years. However, candidate George W. Bush presented a different image than the national Republican Party had in the 1990s by stressing compassionate conservatism and the importance of a federal role in education.

By 2004 younger voters were voting solidly Democratic. Senator John Kerry won 54 percent among this group, a 6-point increase from four years previously.

Forty-five percent voted for Bush.[6] A major reason for the increase in support for the Democratic presidential candidate was the unpopularity of the war in Iraq among younger voters. The war was the most important reason (37 percent) that young voters voted against Bush. At the time, however, younger voters had a divided view as to whether or not the war in Iraq had made the United States safer. Thirty-eight percent thought it made us less secure and 36 percent thought it made America more secure.[7] Younger voters also strongly responded to the declining economy, with record numbers of people stuck in low-paying jobs, in deep debt, and returning home to live with their parents.

In 2006 younger voters were even more supportive of Democratic candidates and were critical to the Democratic takeover of the House and Senate. Younger voters went for the Democratic candidates for Congress by a 15-point margin (50 percent Democrat, 35 percent Republican). Younger voters also continue to have a better impression of the Democratic Party as a whole (51 percent favorable, 37 percent unfavorable) than they do of the Republicans (37 percent favorable, 51 percent unfavorable).[8] Younger voters were also engaged and energized in the midterm elections in record numbers. In 2002, 22 percent of young voters turned out to cast 8.9 million votes. In 2006, 25 percent of young voters (10.8 million) showed up at the polls to vote on Election Day.[9]

In the 2006 midterm elections, Iraq was again the most influential issue (43 percent) in considering whom to vote for. Right behind it were health care (37 percent considered it most important), homeland security and terrorism (36 percent), and creating jobs (36 percent).[10] Looking at the broader issue agenda for the new Congress, younger voters are most concerned about education and the cost of college (15 percent), followed by jobs and the economy (13 percent), Iraq (12 percent), immigration (11 percent), and healthcare and prescription drugs (10 percent).[11] Because younger voters are just starting their careers with entry-level jobs, it comes as no surprise that pocketbook concerns are very important to them. Younger voters worry about rising gas prices, jobs that do not offer quality benefits, affordability of staples such as milk and meat, and healthcare costs that are too high for them to afford. Younger blue-collar voters worry that their lack of a degree is hindering their ability to get work that pays well. College students worry about college affordability and paying down their debts.

One common mistake politicians make when targeting younger voters is that they consider younger voters synonymous with college students. The truth is that both blue-collar and college-educated young voters see politicians as not speaking to their issues, and progressives win among younger voters by targeting both groups. Also, because older voters have higher rates of turnout, politicians tend to gravitate more to their issues. A University of Michigan study has shown that if people vote for a particular party in three consecutive elections, eight out of ten will remain committed to that party for life. The 2008 election is an opportunity for Democrats and progressives to change the future of politics.

Younger voters will represent nearly a third of all voters by 2015, making them a larger proportion of the electorate and overtaking the seniors' bloc in size. Younger voters are becoming Democratic. In 2002, 37 percent identified as Democrats; 18 percent identified as Independents; and 39 percent identified as Republicans. In 2006, 43 percent identified as Democrats, 19 percent identified as Independents; and 31 percent identified as Republicans.[12]

HISPANIC VOTERS

Historically, Hispanic voters have been loyal to the Democratic Party. Over the past two decades, their support for Democratic presidential candidates has ranged from 61 to 72 percent.[13] Starting in 2000 and intensifying in 2002, 2004, and 2006, the Republican Party made a concerted effort to win a larger share of Hispanic voters. As the *Financial Times* noted, "Karl Rove, the President's top political strategist, has made reaching out to black and Hispanic voters central to building a permanent Republican majority."[14] In 2000, Al Gore won 62 percent of the Hispanic vote and George W. Bush nabbed 35 percent.[15] Bush improved his standing among Hispanic voters in his reelection campaign. In 2004, the Democratic nominee Kerry won a majority of Hispanic voters (54 percent), but 44 percent of Hispanics voted for Bush.[16] (Different exit polls in 2004 show different levels of support for Kerry and Bush, due in part to different sampling frames.) A major divide within the Hispanic community is defined by religious denomination. In the fall of 2004, Kerry was winning Catholic Latinos, with 66 percent of the vote, compared to 24 percent for Bush. Among non-Catholic Latinos, Bush led with 51 percent, and 38 percent were supporting Kerry.[17] Republicans also targeted the newer immigrant Hispanics. Latinos are a growing force in American politics and in ten to twenty years could turn "red" states such as Arizona and Texas a shade of blue.

In 2006 Democratic candidates for Congress fared better among Hispanic voters, who resembled base voters for the Democrats. In 2004 they were more likely to be swing voters. In 2006, 73 percent of Hispanic voters supported Democratic candidates for the House and 25 percent supported Republicans. Democratic candidates for the Senate also did well among Hispanics. Thirty-two percent voted for the Republican senatorial candidates and 60 percent voted for the Democrats.[18] Interestingly, Hispanic voters were more likely to be influenced by English-language television (28 percent) than they were by Spanish-language television (13 percent), Spanish-language radio (3 percent), or Spanish-language Internet sites (1 percent).[19] Once the general election was under way, Democrats commanded solid majorities among both Spanish- and English-speaking Hispanic voters. Among English-speaking Hispanic voters, Democrats led 59 percent to 20 percent. Among Spanish-speaking Hispanics, the vote was 70 percent Democratic and 16 percent Republican.[20]

In early 2007, the Democrats in Congress still maintained a strong image in the minds of Hispanic voters (68 percent favorable, 21 percent unfavorable), whereas Republicans had a weak image (32 percent favorable, 51 percent unfavorable). Bush remained a drag on his party, with job ratings at 21 percent approval and 76 percent disapproval.[21]

As the 2006 general election became fully engaged, Democrats held issue advantages over the Republicans. On the key issue of immigration, Hispanic voters preferred the Democrats in Congress (51 percent) to the Republicans (16 percent). On the war in Iraq, 49 percent preferred the Democrats and 21 percent preferred the Republicans. On economic issues facing families, 56 percent supported the Democrats and 18 percent supported the Republicans. On energy prices, 49 percent of Hispanic voters thought the Democrats would do a better job, compared to 17 percent for the Republicans. Even on their signature issue of terrorism and homeland security, Republicans trailed by a 10-point margin (38 percent to 28 percent).[22]

SECURITY MOMS

In the late 1990s political commentators and consultants discovered the power of the "Soccer Moms" vote. Broadly speaking, these voters were suburban married women with children. As prosperity increased and as the economy continued to grow at record levels, these women became more focused on the issue of education. In 1996, education was part of the famous M^2E^2 (Medicare, Medicaid, Education, Environment) strategy that President Bill Clinton successfully employed to win reelection. In that election, Soccer Moms split their votes between the two parties. They supported Clinton, but voted Republican in congressional races, helping Republicans retain control of the House. The gender gap remained a key factor in the 1998 midterm elections, and Democrats won when women favored them more strongly than men favored the Republicans.

Following the events of September 11, the political landscape of the twenty-first century saw the emergence of Security Moms, a vital part of the Republican political strategies for the 2002 and 2004 elections. In 2002 Republican candidates ran by emphasizing their support for President Bush, backing military action against Iraq, and inviting comparisons as to which party would do a better job of keeping Americans safe. Throughout the fall campaign, the president enjoyed very high job approval ratings. On average in the fall of 2002, more than 60 percent of voters approved of the job Bush was doing as president. Furthermore, Bush was most sharply defined as a strong leader who would stop at nothing to keep the country safe from another terrorist attack. Republicans held a strong, 32 percent advantage over the Democrats on the issue of anti-terrorism efforts.[23] In the presidential contests, Al Gore enjoyed an 11-point margin among women voters, but by 2004 Bush had narrowed the gender gap, with John Kerry beating Bush by only 3 points in the same demographic.[24]

Bush anchored his campaign on national security and terrorism, while hammering the perception that Kerry—a Vietnam veteran and the recipient of multiple Purple Heart awards—was not fully qualified to face the challenge of global terrorism. Women in particular were particularly concerned about terrorism and safety. Qualitative work done immediately after the election among swing women voters found that women felt they could count on Bush to do something about terrorism. They did not have a strong sense about Kerry and were unsure about his character and his leadership abilities. This helped make them wary about "changing horses" in the middle of armed conflict.

Swing women voters particularly remember the Progress for America Voter Fund's ad entitled "Ashley's Story." The ad, which aired in October 2004, told the story of a little girl who lost her mother in the September 11 attacks and how Bush comforted her on a visit to her hometown. Some swing women voters found the ad to be a little cheesy, but most liked the emotional strength and conviction it conveyed.[25] Another key event that contributed to heightened security concerns was the seizing of a school in Belan, Russia, by Chechen terrorists, who held the children hostage. On September 3, Russian security forces stormed the school, leaving more than 200 people dead. While the siege was occurring, the Republican Party was hosting its nominating convention, which emphasized the issue of terrorism. The day before the siege ended, Bush gave his acceptance speech, with its primary focus on security and protecting America.

President Bush's message strategy paid off. On Election Day, 75 percent of voters were worried about the threat of terrorism, and 58 percent felt that Kerry could not be trusted to handle terrorism. Just 40 percent thought that Kerry could be trusted. The results for Bush were the mirror opposite of Kerry's. Fifty-eight percent trusted Bush on the issue of terrorism and 40 percent did not trust him.[26] Women in particular were concerned about the threat of terrorism to the country and to their families.

Even more than voters overall, Security Moms went into the voting booth worried about the threat of another terrorist attack. Eighty-three percent were worried about terrorism, including 29 percent who said they were very worried. Security Moms were even less trusting of Kerry's ability to handle the terrorist threat. A mere 29 percent trusted Kerry to handle terrorism, compared to 48 percent who trusted Bush.[27]

Although Kerry won more women overall (51 percent to 48 percent), he lost the Security Moms (53 percent for Bush, 46 percent for Kerry). Fifty-seven percent of Security Moms approved of the job Bush was doing, compared to 53 percent approval ratings among the overall electorate. Fifty-one percent of women overall approved of the job Bush was doing as president. Thirty-four percent said that Iraq or terrorism was the most important issue in their decision for president.

Although Security Moms were not specifically asked in the 2004 exit polls whether or not they believed the war in Iraq was part of the war on terror, 57 percent of all women believed it was, and 43 percent believed it was not.[28]

The story regarding Security Moms was an altogether different tale in 2006. Overall, women voters supported Democrats 54 percent to 43 percent. In the midterm elections, Security Moms split their votes evenly between the two parties' candidates (49 percent apiece), and overall, Democratic candidates for Senate (50 percent) beat their Republican counterparts (46 percent). This result occurred despite the fact that 73 percent of Security Moms said that the threat of terrorism was an important factor in their vote for House candidates and in spite of Republican attempts to raise the national security issue should the Democrats regain the majority.[29]

In 2006 Security Moms were also negative in their assessment of the war in Iraq. Only 43 percent approved of the war, whereas 54 percent disapproved. Fifty-five percent did not believe the war had made the country more secure, but 41 percent believed that it had. Only 11 percent of Security Moms wanted to send more troops into Iraq, and 24 percent wanted to keep troop levels the same. Twenty-seven percent wanted to withdraw all of the troops, and 33 percent wanted to withdraw some of the troops from Iraq.[30]

Women voters, including Security Moms, will continue to play a vital role in determining who the next president will be. Swing women voters tend to be non–college-educated women who voted for President Bush in 2004, but flipped to the Democrats in 2006.

UNMARRIED VOTERS

One of the most important yet least discussed divides in American politics is the marital gap. In past elections most commentators have focused on suburban married women with children—the Soccer Moms of the late 1990s and the post-9/11 Security Moms. But there is another powerful force whose potential has not been fully tapped: unmarried America. Today, half of all households are headed by an unmarried person; unmarried households are the majority in twenty-three states and the District of Columbia.[31]

Unmarried voters have the ability to reshape American politics, but their participation rates lag behind those of married America. In 2004, 71 percent of registered married people voted, but only 55 percent of unmarried voters did so.[32] As societal trends have changed over the years, and with more people delaying the decision to get married, a larger proportion of the population is unmarried. However, unmarried voters are a growing portion of the electorate. In 2000, unmarried voters made up 35 percent of the electorate, but they edged up to 37 percent of the electorate in 2004.[33]

Currently, unmarried voters are strong supporters of Democrats, and unmarried women are even more supportive of Democrats than unmarried men. In 2004, 58 percent of unmarried voters went for Kerry and 40 percent went for Bush.[34] Among unmarried women, 62 percent voted for Kerry and 37 percent voted for Bush. Among unmarried men the gap is narrower, but still in double digits (57 percent for Kerry and 41 percent for Bush). Unmarried women self-identified as Democrats by a margin of 22 percentage points over married women in the 2004 presidential election. Unmarried men self-identified as Democrats by an18-point margin over married men.[35]

In 2006, unmarried voters were even stronger supporters of Democratic candidates in the midterms. Unmarried voters supported the Democratic candidates for Congress over the Republicans by a margin of 64 percent to 34 percent.[36] Support among unmarried women for the Democratic House candidates was 66 percent, compared to 32 percent for the Republicans. Unmarried men's support was slightly softer (62 percent Democratic to 35 percent Republican). In the midterms, unmarried women voted Democratic by a margin of 32 points and unmarried men did so by a 15-point margin. In 2006 the top issue of concern for both unmarried women (44 percent) and unmarried men (43 percent) was the war in Iraq.[37]

In 2004, the economy and jobs and the war in Iraq (29 percent for each) were the top issue concerns among unmarried women. The economy and jobs (35 percent) was the top concern among unmarried men.[38] This finding demonstrates how important the Iraq issue has become over the past two years. What characterizes unmarried America is its economic marginality. Among unmarried women who are most likely to turn out and vote, pocketbook issues dominate—especially salaries and wages that do not keep up with the cost of living (35 percent) and the rising cost of healthcare and prescription drugs (34 percent).[39]

Considering the historic nature of Hillary Clinton's candidacy, it is no surprise that unmarried women make up a crucial part of her base as she navigates the Democratic primary contests in 2008. Nationally, Hillary Clinton has 39 percent of the vote among all Democratic primary voters. The marriage gap is quite strong around the levels of her support in the primary. Although 39 percent of married women support Clinton's bid for president, almost half (49 percent) of unmarried women are currently supporting her candidacy.[40]

SENIORS

Traditionally, Democrats have counted on seniors. For some time, however, seniors have been a key swing bloc of voters at the presidential level. As far back as 1988, when the first President Bush was cruising to a 6-point win, he barely carried seniors nationally in his campaign against Michael Dukakis (50 percent to 49 percent). Four years later, Bill Clinton won seniors by a 12-point margin, but improved his party's total share (50 percent) of the seniors' vote by only a single percentage point. In 1996 Clinton's support dipped slightly (48 percent) among seniors.[41]

Democrats held onto seniors by a small margin in 2000, with Al Gore (51 percent) running against then-Governor Bush (47 percent).[42] Seniors flipped in 2002, however, despite a Democratic message strategy focused on providing a prescription drug benefit under Medicare and preventing the privatization of social security. Republicans won the senior vote (51 percent to the Democrats' 47 percent) in 2002 because they managed to mute differences between the two parties on seniors' issues. Seniors said the main reasons they voted for or considered voting for the Republicans that year were to get a prescription drug benefit for seniors (32 percent), to support President Bush (31 percent), to protect social security (30 percent), and to support the war on terrorism (30 percent).[43]

In the 2004 presidential contest between John Kerry and George Bush, among seniors the Republican Party bested the Democratic Party again, 52 percent to 47 percent.[44] The top reason for seniors to vote for Bush was the war on terrorism (35 percent).[45] Turnout was slightly higher among seniors in the 2004 presidential election. They made up 16 percent of the electorate that year, compared to 14 percent four years earlier.[46]

Democrats rebounded only slightly among seniors two years later. Democratic candidates for the House of Representatives tied with Republicans for the seniors' vote, with 49 percent apiece.[47] Democrats won increased support by seniors in 2006 despite the fact that seniors identify more with the Republican Party (39 percent) than they do with the Democrats (35 percent). Turnout among seniors was down from 2002. Nineteen percent of the electorate was made up of seniors in 2006. [48] In 2002, 22 percent of the overall electorate were 65 years of age or older. [49]

Seniors can make up a third of the 2008 electorate. How they vote will be a major factor in who wins. Seniors today resemble Reagan seniors more than Roosevelt/Kennedy seniors, in that they are tax- and security-conscious. They often view Democratic attacks on the Republicans' record on social security and Medicare with skepticism. The two parties will battle for the senior vote.

THIRD-PARTY SUPPORTERS

The American public has grown less enchanted with the two major political parties over the last seven years. In 2000 voters had positive impressions of both parties. Forty-six percent had a positive impression of the Republican Party, compared to 34 percent who had a negative impression. Forty-nine percent had a positive impression of the Democratic Party, and 32 percent had a negative one.[50] By 2006 voters were net negative in their assessment of both parties.

Thirty-eight percent held a favorable view of the Republican Party and 48 percent held a negative view. Thirty-nine percent of voters had a favorable view of the Democratic Party and 43 percent had an unfavorable one.[51]

Support has also grown for a third party. Just 45 percent of Americans believe the Democrats and Republicans do an adequate job of representing the American people. Forty-eight percent believe that both parties do such a poor job of representing the American people's interests that a third party is needed. In 2003, 56 percent of Americans believed that both parties were doing an adequate job of representing the peoples' interests, and only 40 percent felt that a third party was needed.[52]

Looking at third-party support as a bloc, those who support the idea tend to be male (52 percent) rather than female (45 percent). They also generally either have a four-year college degree (52 percent) or at least have been to college (51 percent). Seniors (40 percent) are less enthralled at the notion of an independent third party than are voters between the ages of 30 and 49 (51 percent) and voters between the ages of 50 and 64 (52 percent). Midwesterners (54 percent) are strong supporters of a third party, followed by Americans living out West (53 percent). In terms of partisanship, Independents (63 percent) and Democrats (50 percent) are more open to the idea of a third party than are Republicans (30 percent).

Ross Perot, the most recent credible third-party candidate, captured 19 percent of the vote in 1992. Perot voters have certain regional, partisan, and gender similarities with third-party supporters today. One major difference is that Perot voters tended to be less educated than third-party supporters overall. Men (21 percent) were more likely than women (17 percent) to vote for Perot. Perot voters tended to be younger (age 18 to 29, 22 percent; age 30 to 44, 21 percent), and voters who backed Perot tended not to be college educated (21 percent). Voters in the West (23 percent) and in the Midwest (21 percent) were Perot's strongest regional bases of support. Independents (30 percent) were more likely than Democratic (13 percent) or Republican (17 percent) partisans to vote for Perot.

There is some evidence that a third-party candidate could make a credible showing in the 2008 presidential election. Democracy Corps, a Democratic political organization, conducted a national survey earlier this year to test potential support for a third-party candidate. Using CNN anchorman Lou Dobbs and New York mayor Michael Bloomberg on the initial ballot, with Hillary Clinton as the Democratic nominee and John McCain as the Republican nominee, Lou Dobbs got 8 percent of the vote and Michael Bloomberg got 9 percent. In 1996, Ross Perot finished with 9 percent of the vote. When surveyors simulated the race by reading each candidate's message, support for both Dobbs and Bloomberg grew. For Dobbs, voters heard a message centered on cracking down on illegal immigration and attacking both parties for allowing lobbyists to run the government. Bloomberg's message focused on his being a successful can-do businessman and attacking the excessive partisanship in Washington, DC. With the addition of the messages, Dobbs's base of support grew to 15 percent, and Bloomberg's vote share also increased to 15 percent.[53]

CONCLUSION

Midterm elections are famously poor predictors of presidential elections. The political atmosphere is notoriously fickle and apt to change at any given moment. In 1986 the Democratic Party rebounded from its drubbing six years earlier to recapture the Senate. In 1988 the Republican Party kept the White House. In 1994 the Democrats lost the control of Congress that they had held for fifty-two years as the majority party. This fact led many commentators to conclude that President Bill Clinton was a sure-fire one-term president. Yet in 1996, as Election Day grew closer with each passing day, Clinton appeared to be a candidate who could not possibly lose reelection.

NOTES

1. Democracy Corps Poll, November 5–6, 2002 (1,763 likely voters).
2. *Investor's Business Daily/Christian Science Monitor* Poll, conducted by TIPP, October 7–13, 2002 (912 adults).
3. ABC News/*Washington Post* Poll, November 1–4, 2006 (1,205 adults).
4. Democracy Corps Poll, November 7–8, 2006 (1,011 likely voters).
5. 2000 VNS National Exit Poll.
6. 2004 Edison/Mitofsky National Exit Poll.
7. Democracy Corps Poll, November 2–3, 2004 (2,000 likely voters).
8. Lake Research Partners/Tarrance Group Poll, November 2–7, 2006 (500 likely voters).
9. Center for Information and Research on Civic Learning and Engagement's tabulation from the 2002 and 2006 November supplements of *Current Population Survey.*
10. Lake Research Partners/Tarrance Group Poll, November 2–7, 2006 (500 likely voters).
11. Lake Research Partners/Tarrance Group Poll, November 2–7, 2006 (500 likely voters).
12. Center for Information and Research on Civic Learning and Engagement's tabulation from the 2002 Madison/Mitofsky National Exit Poll.
13. *New York Times* exit polls, 1988–2000.
14. *Financial Times,* July 21, 2006.
15. VNS 2000 National Exit Poll.
16. Democracy Corps Poll, November 2–3, 2004 (2,000 likely voters).
17. *Washington Post*/Univision/TRPI National Survey of Latino Voters, October 15, 2004.
18. Democracy Corps Poll, November 7–8, 2006 (1,011 likely voters).

19. William C. Velasquez Institute 2006 Exit Poll (8 states; 1,320 Latino voters).

20. Latino Policy Coalition, conducted by Lake Research Partners, September 2006 (600 registered and likely Latino voters in twenty-two states and 1,200 registered, likely Latino voters in targeted congressional districts).

21. Latino Policy Coalition, conducted by Lake Research Partners, March 13–21 2007 (1,000 registered voters in twenty-three states).

22. Latino Policy Coalition, conducted by Lake Research Partners, September 2006 (600 registered and likely Latino voters in twenty-two states and 1,200 registered, likely Latino voters in targeted congressional districts).

23. 2002 Public Opinion Strategies Surveys.

24. VNS 2000 National Exit Poll; 2004 Edison/Mitofsky National Exit Poll.

25. Focus group research conducted by Lake Research Partners, November 2004.

26. 2002 Public Opinion Strategies Surveys.

27. 2002 Public Opinion Strategies Surveys.

28. 2004 Edison/Mitofsky National Exit Poll.

29. 2006 Edison/Mitofsky National Exit Poll.

30. 2006 Edison/Mitofsky National Exit Poll.

31. *Current Population Survey*, December 2006.

32. *Current Population Survey,* November 2004.

33. VNS 2000 National Exit Poll; 2004 Edison/Mitofsky National Exit Poll.

34. 2004 Edison/Mitofsky National Exit Poll.

35. Democracy Corps Poll, November 2–3, 2004 (2,000 likely voters).

36. 2006 Edison/Mitofsky National Exit Poll.

37. Democracy Corps Poll, November 7–8, 2006 (1,011 likely voters).

38. Democracy Corps Poll, November 2–3, 2004 (2,000 likely voters).

39. Greenberg Quinlan Rosner Research poll, January 28–30, 2007 (1,000 unmarried adults).

40. Democracy Corps Poll, March 20–25, 2007 (1,017 likely voters in long survey; 1,526 likely voters in short survey).

41. *New York Times* exit polls, 1988–2000.

42. *New York Times* exit polls, 1988–2000.

43. Democracy Corps Poll, November 5–6, 2002 (1,992 likely voters).

44. 2004 Edison/Mitofsky National Exit Poll.

45. Democracy Corps Poll, November 2–3, 2004 (2,000 likely voters).

46. VNS 2000 National Exit Poll; 2004 Edison/Mitofsky National Exit Poll.

47. The 2006 Election Night/Post-Election survey conducted by Democracy Corps has Democrats winning seniors by 2 percentage points (50 percent to 48 percent). The difference between this survey and the exit polls is due to question wording and sampling variation.

48. Democracy Corps Poll, November 7–8, 2006 (1,011 likely voters).

49. Democracy Corps Poll, November 5–6, 2002 (1,992 likely voters).

50. Democracy Corps Poll, November 2–3, 2004 (2,000 likely voters).

51. Democracy Corps Poll, November 7–8, 2006 (1,011 likely voters).

52. Gallup press release (September 14, 2006) from a Gallup survey of 1,002 adults, September 7–10, 2006.

53. Democracy Corps Poll, January 24–28, 2007 (1,002 likely voters).

About the Editor and Contributors

MORGAN E. FELCHNER is Deputy Assistant Managing Editor for Politics at *U.S. News & World Report*, Contributing Editor for PoliticsOnline, and a member of the National Press Club. She is a prominent on-air political analyst, regularly appearing on television shows on Fox News, CSPAN, CNN, CanadaTV, and local network affiliates. She serves on the Young Women Leaders Board at American University and on the Advisory Board for the University of Minnesota Institute for Law and Politics. She is the former editor of *Campaigns & Elections* magazine.

KAT BARR is the director of education at Rock the Vote (RTV). In this role, Barr oversees RTV's research on the youth vote, including opinion polling, field experiments, and demographic analyses, and RTV's work to disseminate this information to two key audiences: young voters and political leaders. Barr is one of the country's foremost experts on young voters, appears frequently in the press, and is the author of several publications, including most recently *Young Voter Mobilization Tactics II* and *Polling Young Voters.*

LISA GARCÍA BEDOLLA is associate professor of political science and Chicano/Latino studies at the University of California, Irvine. She is author of *Fluid Borders: Latino Power, Identity, and Politics in Los Angeles* (2005), which won the American Political Science Association's Ralph Bunche Award. Her articles have appeared in the *Journal of Politics, Politics and Gender, Latino Studies,* the *Harvard Journal of Hispanic Policy, State Politics and Policy Quarterly, Social Science Quarterly,* and in numerous edited volumes. Her research focuses on the political incorporation of Latinos and other racial/ethnic groups in the United States, with a particular emphasis on the intersection of race, class, and gender.

ROBERT W. BENNETT is the Nathaniel L. Nathanson Professor of Law at the Northwestern University School of Law, where he served as dean from 1985 to 1995. He has written extensively about constitutional law, constitutional interpretation, and democratic theory. His most recent book is *Taming the Electoral College* (2006).

KELLYANNE CONWAY is CEO and president of the polling company™, inc., a privately held, woman-owned corporation founded in 1995. The firm is headquartered in Washington, D.C., and maintains an office in New York City. She is one of the most quoted and noted pollsters on the national scene.

ALEC C. EWALD is an assistant professor of political science at the University of Vermont.

MARK FRANKLIN is the first holder of the Stein Rokkan Chair in comparative politics at the European University Institute, Florence, Italy. He is on leave from Trinity College in Connecticut, where he is the John R. Reitemeyer Professor of International Politics. He is the author of twelve books and more than a hundred book chapters and scholarly articles, and is a past or present member of five editorial boards. He is a past Guggenheim Fellow and Fulbright Scholar.

JAMES G. GIMPEL is a professor of government at the University of Maryland, College Park, where he has been on the faculty since 1992. He is the author of several books and numerous articles on elections, voting, and American politics.

DANIEL GOTOFF is a partner at Lake Research Partners. He has designed, conducted, and analyzed public opinion research for a wide range of candidates and issues. Gotoff also has led the firm's consulting in campaigns in Mexico and the Caribbean.

DONALD P. GREEN is A. Whitney Griswold Professor of Political Science at Yale University, where he has taught since 1989. He has written extensively on campaigns and elections, voter mobilization, and experimental research design. His recent books include *Get Out the Vote! How to Increase Voter Turnout* (second edition, 2008).

RICHARD L. HASEN is the William H. Hannon Distinguished Professor of Law. Hasen is a nationally recognized expert in election law and campaign finance regulation, and is co-author of a leading casebook on election law and co-editor of the quarterly peer-reviewed publication *Election Law Journal.*

MOSHE HASPEL is director of research and evaluation for the Office of University-Community Partnerships and adjunct assistant professor of political science at Emory University. He earned his B.A. in economics and political science from Yale University and his Ph.D. in political science from Emory University. His research interests include legislatures, political parties, elections, and political geography. His publications include articles in the *Journal of Politics*, *Social Science Quarterly*, *Journal of Legislative Studies*, and *Polity*.

CHRISTOPHER C. HULL teaches as an adjunct assistant professor at Georgetown University. Hull graduated magna cum laude from Harvard University in 1992 with a degree in government, and in 2005 he completed a doctoral program with distinction at Georgetown University's government department. Hull's research interests center on presidential nomination politics, campaign technology, and advertising strategy. His dissertation, "How Presidential Candidates Win State Nomination Contests: Explaining and Predicting the Iowa Caucus," was nominated for the E. E. Schattschneider Prize, the American Political Science Association's award for best dissertation of the year in American politics. In November 2007, he published his first book, *Grassroots Rules: How the Iowa Caucus Helps Elect American Presidents*.

KIMBERLY A. KARNES is a Ph.D. student in government at the University of Maryland, College Park. Her research focuses on political behavior, political participation, and urban/rural differences in American politics.

MARVIN P. KING, JR. is an assistant professor of political science and African American studies at the University of Mississippi. He received his Ph.D. from the University of North Texas. He teaches courses in American politics and government, Southern politics, and African American politics. His research interests include African American voting behavior and blacks and the American federal system.

H. GIBBS KNOTTS is associate professor of political science and public affairs at Western Carolina University. He holds a bachelor's degree in political science from the University of North Carolina at Chapel Hill and a doctorate from Emory University. His research interests include Southern politics, political behavior, and community development. His work has appeared in the *Journal of Politics*, *Public Administration Review*, *Social Science Quarterly*, and a variety of other journals and edited collections. He is also co-editing *The New Politics of North Carolina* (2008).

CELINDA LAKE is president of Lake Research Partners and is one of the Democratic Party's leading political strategists, serving as tactician and senior advisor to the national party committees, dozens of Democratic incumbents, and challengers at all levels of the electoral process. Lake and her firm are known for cutting-edge research on issues including the economy, healthcare, the environment, and education, and have worked for a number of institutions, including the Democratic National Committee (DNC), the Democratic Governors' Association (DGA), the White House Project, AFL-CIO, SEIU, CWA, IAFF,

Sierra Club, NARAL, Human Rights Campaign, EMILY's List, and the Kaiser Foundation. Her work also led her to advise fledgling democratic parties in several postwar Eastern European countries (including Bosnia) and South Africa.

DOTTY LEMIEUX runs the California campaign consulting firm Green Dog Campaigns, helping to elect progressive Democratic and nonpartisan candidates. She is also a land use and tree law attorney. She has two blogs: www.landusenews.blogspot.com, a site for news and information about legal issues relating to trees and property law, and the "Boomer Bytes" blog at www.sfgate/community/blogs.com, an eclectic mix of political satire and topical commentary.

MARK HUGO LOPEZ is research director at the Center for Information and Research on Civic Learning and Engagement (CIRCLE) and a research assistant professor at the University of Maryland's School of Public Policy. Lopez received his Ph.D. in economics from Princeton University in 1996. He specializes in labor economics, civic engagement, voting behavior, and the economics of education.

KARLO BARRIOS MARCELO serves as research associate at the Center for Information and Research on Civic Learning and Engagement (CIRCLE). He received his M.P.P. from the Gerald R. Ford School of Public Policy at the University of Michigan and his B.A. from the University of Maryland.

MELISSA R. MICHELSON is associate professor of political science at California State University, East Bay. Her research focuses on Latino political attitudes and behavior, including immigrant politicization and Latino voter turnout. She has recently published work in *Aztlan*, *PS: Political Science and Politics*, *Social Science Quarterly*, and the *Latino(a) Research Review*. She is also principal investigator of the evaluation of the James Irvine Foundation's California Votes Initiative, a multi-year effort to increase voting rates among infrequent voters—particularly those in low-income and ethnic communities—in California's San Joaquin Valley and targeted areas in Southern California.

ANDREW MYERS is president and CEO of Myers Research|Strategic Services, LLC. He has well over a decade of experience in politics and public opinion research, having worked on numerous elections from the local level to presidential campaigns, as well as assisting in message development for a broad array of institutional and corporate clients. Myers founded his firm in 2001 and since that time has helped elect more than 200 Democrats to offices throughout the nation at nearly every level of government. In addition, Myers has been recognized as one of the nation's leaders in state and local races, serving more candidates and winning more targeted races at the state and local levels than any other pollster in the country.

RICHARD K. SCHER is professor of political science at the University of Florida, Gainesville. Scher has published widely on Southern politics, Florida politics, campaigns and elections, and voting rights. He was a Visiting Fulbright Scholar in Hungary, serving as the John Marshall Distinguished Chair of American Government in that country, and is currently a Fulbright Senior Specialist. He has served as an expert witness in more than a half-dozen voting rights cases in federal court, always on the side of the angels. His current book project is *Trying to Vote in America: Disenfranchisement as Public Policy*, an examination of the hurdles potential voters in the United States face in attempting to cast ballots.

HEATHER SMITH is executive director of Rock the Vote, a national organization at the intersection of youth, politics, popular culture, and technology. Its mission is to increase the political clout and engagement of young people in order to achieve progressive change in our country. Under Smith's leadership, Rock the Vote is launching its most ambitious campaign ever in 2008: to register 2 million young people to vote, to educate them, and to turn them out to the polls. Prior to Rock the Vote, Smith founded and directed Young Voter Strategies, a nonpartisan effort supported by the Pew Charitable Trusts to re-energize our democracy through developing tools, data, and information to enable political campaigns and organizations to effectively run their own young-voter programs. In 2006 Heather was named one of *Campaign & Elections* magazine's Rising Stars, and in 2007 she was named "Best & Brightest" by *Esquire* magazine, all for her work with young voters.

PRISCILLA L. SOUTHWELL is a professor of political science at the University of Oregon. She received her Ph.D. from the University of North Carolina at Chapel Hill in 1983. She has served as associate dean for the social sciences since 2001. Her research centers on electoral politics in Europe and the United States, political behavior, and political parties. She is the author of over forty articles, most recently publishing in *Social Science Quarterly*, *Political Research Quarterly*, and the *Social Science Journal*.

PHILLIP STUTTS has worked on four presidential campaigns and John Thune's U.S. Senate race, and he managed Governor Bobby Jindal's Louisiana campaign in 2003. He also served as the national 72-Hour/GOTV director during the 2004 Bush-Cheney reelection campaign. Currently, Stutts serves as the vice president for grassroots development for the public affairs firm The Herald Group.

SHELLEY WEST is project director for the polling company™, inc./WomanTrend. She joined the firm in October 2004 as a research associate.

KRISTINA WILFORE is one of the country's leading experts on state policy and politics—having spent ten years working in approximately thirty-five state capitals and on dozens of ballot initiatives across the country. As executive director of the Ballot Initiative Strategy Center, she works with state and national progressive organizations to reinvigorate the initiative process by providing guidance on strategy and message to key initiative campaigns, coordinating ballot language research and drafting efforts, polling, training activists and placing them on targeted initiatives nationwide, and directing funds to critical campaigns.

THADDEUS WINDT is a senior analyst at Lake Research Partners. He has designed and analyzed survey and focus group research for candidates at all levels of the electoral process, including presidential, senatorial, gubernatorial, congressional, and mayoral candidates, as well as working with a wide range of issues, including media reform, healthcare reform, and the environment. He has a B.A. from George Mason University and and an M.A. from the George Washington School of Political Management.

CAPTAIN SAMUEL F. WRIGHT, JAGC, USN (Ret.), retired from the Navy Reserve in 2007 with thirty-seven years of active and reserve service, mostly as a judge advocate (lawyer). His military decorations include two Meritorious Service Medals, a Joint Service Commendation Medal, and two Navy Commendation Medals. For more than thirty years he has been involved in a nationwide effort to reform absentee voting laws and procedures, for the benefit of military and overseas citizens. He earned his law degree from the University of Houston in 1976 and an advanced law degree in labor law from Georgetown University in 1980. He is a member of the bar of the District of Columbia.

Index

The letter *f* following a page number indicates a figure; *t* indicates a table.